Population Policy:

Research Priorities in the Developing World

Prepared by Carmen A. Miró and Joseph E. Potter

Report of the International Review Group of Social Science Research on Population and Development

Bernard Berelson, John C. Caldwell, P.B. Desai, Jose Encarnacion, Akin L. Mabogunje, Riad B. Tabbarah, Raul Urzua

St. Martin's Press
New York

All rights reserved. For information, write:
St. Martin's Press, Inc., 175 Fifth Avenue, New York, New York 10010
Printed in the U.S.A.
First published in the United States of America in 1980
ISBN 0-312-63158-8

Library of Congress Cataloging in Publication Data
Miro, Carmen A
    Population Policy.
    Includes bibliographies.
    1. Underdeveloped areas – population policy.
    2. Underdeveloped areas – population   I. Title
HB884.M57   1980   304.6'6'091724
ISBN 0-312-63158-8   80-18671

In Memory of Bernard Berelson

When this report was about to go to press, IRG's secretariat received the sad news of Bernard Berelson's death. Without claiming that Barney, as his friends called him, shared all the points of view and recommendations contained in the report, there is no doubt that from the inception of the Group he had a major influence on the manner in which IRG's work was organized and contributed significantly to its various activities. The report "Social Science Research for Population Policy", published as Appendix 1 is but a small reflection of the important contribution made by Barney to the Group's work.

It is with great regret that we faced the brutal fact that we would not have the benefit of Barney's criticism of this final version of IRG's report. To the extent that the report will contribute to guide future efforts to solve the many population-related problems to which Bernard Berelson untiringly devoted so many years of his life, the group would like to offer it as a tribute to his memory.

CONTENTS

APPENDICES TO THE FINAL REPORT

Copies may be obtained from *Books on Demand*, University Microfilms International, 300 North Zeeb Road, Ann Arbor, Michigan 48106.

PREFACE

The International Review Group of Social Science Research on Population and Development (IRG) was constituted in 1976 and entrusted with the task of making recommendations for future research that would contribute to the formulation and improvement of population policies in the developing countries. The establishment of IRG had its origin in discussions between representatives of donor agencies and scholars from Africa, Asia, and Latin America which came to the conclusion that although several surveys of the state of knowledge on aspects of the population-development link were available, there was a need for a broader perspective that only a systematic interdisciplinary evaluation could provide.

The IRG received financial support over a period of approximately two years from a group of nine govermental, inter-governmental, and nongovernmental organizations composed of the Ford Foundation, the International Development Research Centre, the Norwegian Agency for International Development, the Population Council, the Rockefeller Foundation, the Swedish International Development Authority, the United Kingdom Ministry of Overseas Development, the United Nations Fund for Population Activities, and the World Bank.

Organized as an *ad hoc* body, the Group's members were: Bernard Berelson of the Population Council, John Caldwell of the Australia National University, P. B. Desai of the Institute of Economic Growth (Delhi), José Encarnación of the University of the Philippines, Akin Mabogunje of the University of Ibadan, Riad Tabbarah of the U.N. Economic Commission for Western Asia, and Raúl Urzúa of the Latin American Demographic Centre. Carmen Miró served as IRG's President and Joseph Potter as her Associate in the project's Secretariat, located at El Colegio de México.

During the course of the project, the President convened four meetings of the Group. The first two (México City, 4–6 October 1976; Princeton, New Jersey, 25–27 January 1977) served to delineate the primary area of concern — those issues perceived by policymakers as population-related problems, particularly in areas amenable to modification through policy intervention within a ten-year period — and the nature of the regional reviews and other documents to be prepared by the members and consultants. Preliminary versions of these papers were presented and discussed at the Group's third meeting (México City, 1–4 August 1977) while the final meeting (New York, 4–8 December 1978) was devoted to the revision of this Report.

The basic background papers for the project were the regional reviews of the state of knowledge on population and development, major gaps therein and possible ways of filling such gaps prepared for Middle South Asia (Desai), East and South-East Asia (Jones), Arab countries (Tabbarah, Mamish and Gemayel), Sub-Saharan Africa (Mabogunje and Arowolo, and Ware), Latin America (Urzúa), and the developing world in general (Berelson). In addition, papers referring to the population policies and the institutional research and training capacity of most of the regions were produced. These 13 documents appear as separate appendices to this Report.

During 1978, the IRG organized three regional Workshops on Research Priorities for Population Policy (Colombo, Sri Lanka, 26–28 April; México City, 28–30 June; Nairobi, Kenya, 6–8 September). These were co-sponsored, respectively, by the Marga Institute, El Colegio de México and CELADE, and the Population Studies and Research Institute of the University of Nairobi. The Workshops were intended as a forum in which government officials responsible for policy decisions bearing on population problems, well-known scholars in the population field, and personnel from donor agencies could exchange views as to the gaps in knowledge relevant to policy design. For discussion at the Workshops, the Group either prepared or commissioned a series of position papers on research needs on mortality, fertility, family planning, internal and international migration, the titles of which are included in the list of selected documents appearing at the end of this volume.

In preparing the final Report for the project, the IRG Secretariat's primary concern was to distill what had been learned from the Workshops and from the regional reviews and other documents prepared for the project. The Report reflects the views of the members as expressed in the Group's Meetings and in their comments on a draft version of the Report, but the members cannot be held individually responsible for all of the conclusions and recommendations expressed herein.

A task such as that carried out by IRG is made possible thanks to the collaboration of many institutions and persons. Included at the end of the Report, is a list of persons that participated in the activities organized by the Group and who contributed ideas, suggestions and recommendations useful in the preparation of this Report.

Special mention should be made of El Colegio de México. The facilities and support provided by El Colegio made it possible for the Secretariat to work in a pleasant and rewarding atmosphere and contributed greatly to the success of two of the Group's Meetings and the Latin American regional Workshop. El Colegio's President, Victor Urquidi, was always sympathetic to our needs and followed with interest the development of IRG's activities.

Gavin Jones, of the Australia National University, who prepared the review of the status of knowledge and research for South-East and East Asia (appendix 3) and who collaborated for a period with the Group's Secretariat in México City also deserves recognition.

The Secretariat staff, though small, was dedicated and conscientious. Rose María González, Laura Holland, Gail Mummert, and Teresa Ulloa merit a special note of thanks from the Group. This is particularly true in the case of Linda Lumley, our editor, who handled the arduous task of introducing clarity into texts which, in many cases, were written by persons for whom English was a second language.

INTRODUCTION

Public and governmental concern for fertility, mortality, migration, and the characteristics of a population that they in turn determine — its rate of growth, age structure, and spatial distribution — are usually prompted by a variety of factors. It seems clear that demographic outcomes can do much to either promote or frustrate a country's uppermost development objectives, whether these be in the realm of eliminating poverty, achieving economic growth, maintaining internal security, or securing freedom from foreign domination. But, on the other hand, often at issue are such basic human prerogatives as the rights to a long and healthy life, to move from one place to another without interference, and to have the number of children one desires. Reproduction and migration are central to the strategies that families and individuals adopt for survival and, when possible, the enjoyment of life; and the attainment of longevity and the forestallment of death has always been one of mankind's primary goals.

Population policies may either impinge on or promote the basic freedoms just mentioned. Those that work by way of limiting such freedoms are clearly of extreme consequence and can only be justified by convincing evidence that such interventions will yield tangible benefits for the society as a whole. In addition to promoting or curtailing liberty, population policies are likely to have immediate effects on the welfare of individuals, families, groups, and organizations, while constituting direct financial costs and administrative burdens for the state. To cite just a few examples: the provision of free health and family planning services, or the establishment of location incentives for industry, resettlement benefits for migrants, or repatriation benefits for nationals living abroad all entail quickly felt consequences of these sorts.

At present there is a readily apparent movement towards activism in population policy in the Third World. In recent years, not only have a large number of developing countries adopted initial policies to accomplish such objectives as the reduction of fertility, the lessening of rural-to-urban migration, and the elimination of mortality differentials, but in many parts of the world measures are now being considered or adopted that are considerably more forceful than those that were being contemplated a decade ago. Some of the most well-known examples are the mobilization of powerful administrative mechanisms to reduce fertility in China, the 'ujamaa' programme of villagization in Tanzania, the arrangements for controlling international migration and restricting the rights of foreign, as compared to native, workers in countries such as Kuwait and Singapore, and the wide variety of primary health care schemes that are being advocated by the WHO and international forums such as the Alma Ata Conference. In these circumstances there is an obvious and urgent need for information and knowledge that will enable governments to design and implement policies in such a way that they attain their ultimate objectives. Ideally, the knowledge base should help policy-makers to distinguish the range of options that are available to them, and also to understand what concomitant changes in economic and social structure may be required to ensure that the policies adopted will be both effective and conducive to a true and lasting increase in welfare.

At the present time, the findings of social science research are sometimes but not always utilized in the design and formulation of the wide variety of population policies being implemented in the developing world. This situation could be improved by a shift in the orientation of research toward questions that have a greater bearing on policy, by assembling and organizing existing knowledge in such a way that it is accessible to policy-makers, and by doing research that facilitates population policy-making within a relatively short time. On the other hand, for social science research on population and development to advance to the point where evaluation and prediction can be carried out with a reasonable degree of certitude, considerable progress needs to be made in theory building and the verification of causal mechanisms.

In the past 20 years, considerable progress has been achieved in discovering the nature of the relations between population and development. Perhaps most noteworthy are the number of major misconceptions that have been disproved. The present state of knowledge on the determinants and consequences of demographic behaviour is, however, somewhat uneven: Important areas remain where no central paradigm has emerged and where several different views or schools of thought compete with one another. Disagreement on questions such as the determinants of fertility decline or the consequences of rapid urbanization persist not so much for lack of attention, but rather because the issues are complex and resist simplification.

In order to increase the usefulness of social science research on population and development, and to ensure progress on the critical questions that remain before the field, work must proceed at an increased pace on several fronts:

1. *Descriptive research that will provide information on levels, trends, and differentials in fertility, mortality, and migration.* Besides the importance of descriptive knowledge of demographic behaviour as a foundation for much of the research mentioned below, it is also of direct use to policy-makers.

2. *Evaluative research that will attempt to measure the demographic impact of development projects and policies.* The need for more and better

evaluation extends from those programmes and projects with immediate demographic objectives, such as family planning programmes and specific public-health measures, to those thought to be strongly linked to population but without specific demographic objectives such as education, nutrition, and rural development programmes.

3. *The development of sound theoretical frameworks for the analysis of determinants and consequences of demographic behaviour.* At the heart of most controversies over population and development issues are some of the most difficult questions facing the social sciences. There appear to be promising ways of tackling most of them, but the effort required is a sustained one whose contribution to improved policy may lie several years in the future.

4. *Analysis of the political processes through which population policies are arrived at.* Better knowledge of the politics of population policy-making would provide criteria for determining (*a*) the kinds of research findings most likely to have an effect on policy adoption, (*b*) the interest groups and sectors of government most likely to utilize research, and (*c*) the government organizations best able to take on the responsibility for both developing and advocating policy options.

5. *Research on the relations between development style, population processes, and population policies.* It is often asserted that the larger developmental context − and the political structure and policy options behind it − places severe limits on the kinds of population policies that may be successfully implemented, but the questions of just where these limits lie and what are the forces determining them in individual countries have received relatively little attention in the past and should constitute a priority topic for future research.

While researchers in developed countries and in international organizations may make important contributions towards fulfilling this research agenda, the bulk of the work can and should be done by social scientists in the individual developing countries. For this goal to be realized, however, significant and focused efforts will have to be dedicated to training the additional researchers and policy analysts that the task requires, and to developing and sustaining the institutions in which the work is to be done.

These are among the principal conclusions of the evaluation of the current state of social science research on issues perceived as population-related problems in the developing world conducted by the International Review Group of Social Science Research on Population and Development (IRG). Established in 1975 with the financial support of nine private, governmental, and non-governmental international organizations, the IRG undertook the task of reviewing social science knowledge on population and development and formulating recommendations to guide research and the over-all allocation of research resources over the next ten years by means of staff meetings, the commissioning of over sixty regionally based documents, and three regional workshops which brought scholars, policy-makers, and donors together to decide on research priorities for population policy. The main conclusions reached by the IRG in the course of its two and one-half year review and evaluation are presented in this Report. In addition, thirteen documents prepared by IRG members and consultants have been selected for publication as appendices to this Report and appear as separate volumes.

Some Particular Characteristics of the IRG Review

There are several distinctive characteristics of the task that the IRG set for itself that made its mission somewhat different from that of other review efforts that have been completed recently on the subject of population and development.[1]

The first of these is the intention to speak directly to policy considerations. The 'final goal' of the project, as defined at the first meeting of the Group, is 'to recommend directions for research and for resource allocation to research that will contribute to the formulation and to the improvement of population policies in the developing countries'. Population policies, as understood by the IRG, are those measures aimed at affecting demographic variables directly, as well as changes in the direction of broader development policy that are taken for the purpose of modifying population trends. The policy relevance of research on a particular issue is usually determined by the degree to which it helps to answer whether, in fact, there exists a problem that warrants governmental intervention, and if so, what can or should be done about it. The IRG's task involved both identifying the issues and, ultimately selecting, from among all the different topics that could be researched in the future, those that would be particularly likely to facilitate better policies. The time horizon adopted was approximately 10 years. Thus, the Group's attention was not confined to applied research that could have an effect within a year or two, but extended to more fundamental work that could be expected to have an impact on policy within a decade.

The second distinctive feature of the IRG's review is that it was approached on a regional basis: issues were identified as they were perceived in the several regions and subregions of the developing world, and the state of knowledge of population and development was assessed on a region-by-region basis. This approach is exemplified by both the six regional reviews of social-science research on population and development prepared for the IRG and the regional workshops undertaken by the Group.

The third characteristic particular to the IRG's effort is that the scope

[1] See, for example, Birdsall, 1977; Bilsborrow, 1976; Cassen, 1976; and Ridker, 1976.

of its review extended to such matters as the role that political processes and institutional arrangements play in the adoption and implementation of population policy, the utilization of research findings in policy-making, possible mechanisms to increase research input to policy design, and especially, the institutional and human resource capacities existing in the different regions.

Content of the Report

In the course of its work the IRG took into consideration regional patterns and trends in demographic dynamics and the social and economic framework within which these have been operating, the main population issues that have been defined in the countries of the different regions, the positions of governments on these issues, and the policies that have been adopted to affect demographic processes. Background information on these topics is provided, in a highly condensed manner, in Part I of the Report, organized according to the five regions and subregions with which the IRG has dealt: Africa South of the Sahara, the Arab countries, Middle South Asia, Latin America, and East and South-East Asia. Also included in the chapters on each region is a broad overview of the status of population research in the regions, the coverage and reliability of the data base, and the availability of institutional and human resources that could be mobilized to undertake demographic and related social-science research.

In nearly all phases of the project, the Group devoted considerable attention to assessing the state of knowledge on each of the demographic variables — mortality, fertility, internal migration, and international migration. Evaluating the state of this knowledge for each of the regions and subregions was one of the objectives of the regional reviews prepared for the IRG. Also, the Group had at its disposal, and considered, a number of reviews of the literature on the demographic variables that have been published in recent years. The three regional workshops took up the implications for policy of the results of both previous and prospective research on population and development. The first four chapters of Part II present a summary evaluation of the state of knowledge of each of the primary demographic variables, examine the policy relevance of this knowledge, and set forth some concrete recommendations for the 'variable specific' research that the Group feels would be most likely to facilitate and influence policy formulation and implementation in the next decade. The last chapter in Part II dispenses with the preceding variable-specific format to discuss six general types of analysis that apply to all, or nearly all, of the demographic processes and that the IRG feels are worthy of emphasis in future research.

Part III of the Report addresses the important issue of improving institutional and human resource capacities for social-science research on population and development in the developing countries. Drawing on the summary review of research capacity for each of the regions contained in Part I, it begins with an overview of the present situation and an assessment of the most pressing needs for training and institutional development. A brief analysis of the factors that have determined the size and structure of the current pool of resources is taken up next. There follows a discussion of what the IRG considers to be major issues concerning the amount and direction of future support for both research and training in population and development. Considered are such questions as project v. institutional grant mechanisms, the kinds of institutions best suited to undertake policy-relevant research, the role of local v. foreign resources, and which countries deserve the greatest priority. Part III concludes with four general guidelines for future support of the field.

The concluding chapter of the Report sets out what the Group believes are the procedural implications of its report for each of the three audiences to which it is addressed: (1) the social-science community throughout the world, (2) policy-makers in the developing countries, and (3) the donor community.

References

Bilsborrow, Richard E. 1976. *Population in Development Planning: Background & Bibliography.* Chapel Hill: The University of North Carolina.

Birdsall, Nancy. 1977. 'Analytical Approaches to the Relationship of Population Growth and Development.' *Population and Development Review*, 3 (1 and 2), 63–102.

Cassen, Robert H. 1976. 'Population and Development: A Survey.' *World Development*, 4 (10/11), 785–830.

Ridker, Ronald G. 1976. *Population and Development: The Search for Selective Interventions.* Baltimore and London: The Johns Hopkins University Press.

PART I   THE REGIONS: BACKGROUND FOR THE DEFINITION OF RESEARCH PRIORITIES

Introduction

The three workshops conducted by the IRG in fulfilment of its task served, among other things, to underscore the soundness of the decision — taken at the Group's inception — to undertake the review of the state of social science knowledge on the relation of population and development by regions of the developing world.

While a rather comprehensive outline of recommended research in that extensive field could probably be laid down in a general manner for the developing world as a whole, any attempt to define research priorities more attuned to the situation of the different groups of countries should be preceded by a consideration, even if in a broad manner, of their demographic dynamics and the social and economic setting in which these have been operating, the main population issues that have been identified in these countries, and the position of their governments regarding the adoption of policies to affect demographic variables. It is also indispensable to have a broad overview of the current status of population research, of the coverage and reliability of the data base, and of the availability of institutional and human resources that could be mobilized to undertake demographic and related social research. This is attempted in the following five chapters, albeit in a very succinct manner, for the five developing regions with which the IRG has dealt.

Inputs to prepare this section were drawn from the six regional reviews and other papers contributed by the Group's members as well as from other sources. The statistical information cited here does not always represent the latest estimates; nor are the data equally valid. For the sake of preserving a certain degree of comparability among regions, for certain types of data the same source has been used throughout, even when more recent estimates (as in the case of demographic data) were available for certain regions or countries.

The Group recognizes that when defining research intended to be of direct policy relevance to a specific country, the conditions of that country must help determine what knowledge is required. For the type of broad recommendations that the IRG necessarily has to make, an examination of the regions' main characteristics should provide an adequate basis. It should be borne in mind, however, that the characterizations that follow may — and in some cases do indeed — ignore some of the subtleties of certain specific situations.

1 AFRICA SOUTH OF THE SAHARA

Africa South of the Sahara comprises forty-eight countries and territories, of which one (South Africa) is customarily included among the industrialized countries, although its economic development has brought high living standards to only a small part of its population. As in the other regions, these countries present a great diversity — in terms of magnitude of population, territorial size, average population density, colonial background, current political system, natural resource endowment, basis of economic structure, and pace of economic growth and level achieved, to mention only a few. They nevertheless share important characteristics that set them apart from countries in other developing regions, particularly those related to kinship and family organization and the social systems into which they fit.

Basic Socioeconomic and Demographic Characteristics

Together, the countries of Sub-Saharan Africa had an estimated population in 1975 of close to 280 million (UN, 1974, as assessed in 1973), with 15 countries and territories having fewer than one million inhabitants. Almost 75 per cent of the population of the region (207 million) are concentrated in only 13 countries with populations of over 5 million. These 13 countries are located in 3 of the subcontinent's 4 subregions as follows: 7 countries totalling 90 million in East Africa; 3 countries totalling 37 million in Central Africa; and 3 countries totalling 80 million in West Africa. (Some estimates report the population of these last 3 countries — Nigeria, Ghana, and Ivory Coast — as approaching 90 million in 1975.)

In contrast to countries such as Zaïre, with an area of almost 2.5 million square kilometres and an average density of 11 persons per square kilometre, there are others, such as Rwanda and Burundi, with territories of less than 30,000 square kilometres and average densities of 162 and 136, respectively.

Rates of population growth vary widely among the countries of this region. Recent estimates (UN, 1974, as assessed in 1973) report some of the lowest growth rates in the developing world (under 2.0 per cent) for several of the Sub-Saharan African islands (e.g. Mauritius, Reunion), where fertility has declined rapidly in recent years, and in some of the countries most affected by infertility and subfecundity (Equatorial Guinea, Gabon, Guinea-Bissau); while some of the highest growth rates in the world (3.6 and 3.4) are found in Zimbabwe and Kenya, respectively.

The structure of production also varies greatly among the countries and territories of the region.[1] On the one hand, there are countries such as Burundi and Uganda, where agriculture contributed 64 and 55 per cent, respectively, to the gross domestic product in 1976; and, on the other hand, there are countries such as Zambia and Congo, where this proportion was only 14 and 15 per cent, respectively. In the case of Nigeria, because of activities related to the exploitation of oil deposits, industrial production represented 50 per cent of the GDP (World Bank, 1978, Table 13).

In general, the countries of the region are poor and undeveloped. Of the thirty-two countries examined, with only one exception (Ivory Coast), all had average annual per capita gross national products (GNP) below US $600 in 1976. Per capita GNP ranged from US $100 in Ethiopia and Mali to US $610 in Ivory Coast, with the thirty two countries distributed as follows:

GNP per capita (in US $)	Number of Countries
Below 150	10
150–249	10
250–399	6
400–549	3
550 and over	3
Total	32

The preceding averages, low as they are, hide the true magnitude of the prevailing poverty, since a considerable proportion of the population participates in the GNP with much smaller shares. It has been estimated that severe poverty affects at least one-third of the population of most countries of the region and that in some East African nations this proportion is over one-half (World Bank, 1978).

In Africa South of the Sahara, more than in any other developing region, per capita food production suffered some severe setbacks in the last decade. These have been attributed mainly to poor performance in agriculture caused by the drought that affected the region, particularly the Sahel countries. Only in one-quarter of the thirty-two countries was food production around 1975 higher than it had been ten years before, but in no case did the increase exceed 25 per cent. In some of the countries hardest hit by the drought, the reduction in per capita food production ranged between 15 and 40 per cent.

[1] The figures cited in the following paragraphs are taken from World Bank, *World Development Report*, 1978, and refer to the thirty-two countries with a population of over one million.

Poverty is accompanied not only by malnutrition but also by illiteracy. Around 1974 only one country (Tanzania) had a level of adult (15 years and over) literacy (63 per cent) comparable to prevailing averages in most of Latin America. In seventeen countries, only 30 per cent of adults knew how to read and write. More recently, governments appear to be paying considerable attention to public education, judging from the increase in the percentages of children aged 6–12 enrolled in primary school in most countries in 1975 as compared with 1960. In fact, eight countries claim universal or near universal enrolment rates (World Bank, 1978, Table 18).

To further complicate the economic and social situation of these countries, they not only are very poor, but they also — with very few exceptions — seem to be trapped in economic stagnation, showing very little evidence of moving ahead from the early stage of development in which they find themselves. In six countries of the region, average per capita GNP decreased during the period 1960–76, and in fifteen countries the increase was below 2.5 per cent per year. During those years no country achieved an average annual per capita growth greater than 6 per cent, the target set for the UN Second Development Decade. Only one of the smallest countries (Lesotho) came close to this mark, with an average annual increment of 4.6 per cent. Not even the mineral-rich countries of the region were able to do better.

An added impediment to development that the Sub-Saharan African countries face is that resulting from the prevailing organization of international trade. Being mainly suppliers of primary products, they are very vulnerable to fluctuations in the international prices of these commodities. The problem is even more acute in those countries in which exports consist of only one or a very few products. The poor performance in the agricultural sector, coupled with the fluctuating international prices of some of the products of this sector and of some minerals, probably explains why average annual rates of growth of exports during the period 1970–6 were in general not only rather small but negative in twelve of the countries of the subregion, thus adding balance-of-payment problems to the other development constraints affecting them.

Besides being a region of great diversity, Africa South of Sahara is also one of extremes and contradictions, especially in terms of population dynamics. Compared to other regions in the world, it is in the very early stages of the demographic transition. Although mortality has declined everywhere and markedly in some countries, levels are still among the highest in the world.[2] 'Except in a few islands, infant mortality rates in all of tropical Africa are high. Official figures, which certainly underestimate the level, show that for the area as a whole at least 120 out

[2] The expectations of life at birth for the thirty-two countries in 1960 and 1970 were estimated as follows (although it should be noted that these estimates of change are based in some cases on assumptions of continuing change):

of every 1,000 live-born children die before reaching age one' (Ware, 1978, p. 33). There are still many districts within the region where one-third of all children die before reaching school age (Adegbola, 1977). In terms of reproductive behaviour, it is at the same time the world's most fertile region and the area apparently with the highest incidence of infertility and subfecundity. In general, the level of fertility appears to have remained practically unchanged in the last 15 years. It has been estimated that in 1960 all countries of the region except one had crude birth rates of 43 or more per 1,000. In 1975 the number of exceptions had increased to two and the majority of the countries continued to show levels of fertility of 49 or more (16 nations in 1960 and 14 in 1975). Yet, as Ware points out (1978, p. 60), 'it is probable that more Africans are troubled by problems of subfertility than by the perception of excess fertility. Lux (1976) estimates that during the period of the 1930s through the early 1960s, one-tenth of the population of tropical Africa was affected by subfertility of some kind. In the same period, there were still areas of Zaïre where 30 per cent of all women had never given birth prior to menopause (Romaniuk, 1967). Since then, there has been little firm evidence of large-scale major improvements.'

Sub-Saharan Africa is overwhelmingly rural and the least urbanized region of the world. At the same time, one of the major demographic problems in the subcontinent is the rapid rate of urbanization and the inability of the urban place to play a sufficiently dynamic role in the process of development (Mabogunje and Arowolo, 1978, p. 11).

Against the background of very high fertility that generally prevails in the region, one finds that at the same time 'rates of female work force participation are among the highest in the world' (Ware, 1978, p. 77). This is closely linked to the role played by women both in the family and in the larger kinship groups.

The potential for demographic growth is perhaps one of the highest in the world. Several factors are or will be responsible for this: (*a*) one of the highest rates of population growth caused by a level of fertility that far exceeds a still very high mortality level, generating, in turn, a population with a very young age structure, and (*b*) an expected increase in the already high growth rate due to the combined influence of the mortality declines that are likely to occur, and increases in fertility arising from a reduction of the incidence of infertility and subfecundity.

(*cont.*)		*Number of countries*	
	e_o^o	*1960*	*1970*
	37 and under	26	0
	38–40	3	9
	41–4	3	17
	45 and over	0	6

Source: World Bank, 1978, Table 17, p. 108.

Of course, the evolution of the population dynamics of the subregion will not be independent of the path and pace of future socioeconomic development. In spite of the evident constraints that these countries have been facing, progress seems to have been accomplished in important areas, such as education and health. Some figures have already been cited in connection with the former. The advances in the latter can be appreciated by reference to the improvements in the still very low expectations of life at birth (e_0^0), improvements that, although in most cases modest, are by no means negligible (see footnote 2). If, on the other hand, as has been repeatedly said, the proportion of the population severely affected by poverty has increased in recent years, the expansion of educational and health services probably reached a rather small percentage of the poor population of these countries.

The prospects for fertility declines in this region do not appear very promising in light of the probable path of social development and economic growth, particularly in so far as such declines might depend, on the one hand, on modifications of the present social organization, and, on the other, on innovative approaches to expand social services.

Population Issues and Government Policies on Population

In a subcontinent where thirty-four countries out of forty-seven have populations of less than 5 million inhabitants occupying (with very few exceptions[3]) rather vast territories, it is not surprising that rapid demographic growth is not considered a problem by most of these countries. As Mabogunje and Arowolo (1978, p. 44) claim, the attitude 'has tended to be to watch the annual increase with some degree of quiet satisfaction'. There are pockets where the pressure of population on land has been recognized, but the solutions put forward have involved moving population from certain areas to others and not precisely efforts to reduce the rate of demographic growth. The policy suggestions have dealt more with non-demographic measures, such as agricultural settlement schemes, deliberate 'ruralization' of industries or industrialization of rural-based crafts and production processes (Mabogunje and Arowolo, 1978, p. 12).

The best evidence of the little importance attributed by governments of this subregion to the need for a policy to curtail population growth is the very small number of them that have adopted such a policy. The first Sub-Saharan African government to commit itself to a programme of fertility reduction was that of the small island of Mauritius. This case has been amply discussed in the pertinent literature as one of the 'success

[3] The exceptions are a few small islands in the Indian and Atlantic Oceans with very high densities (for example; more than 400 in Mauritius) and some countries with very small territories (Lesotho, Sierra Leone, Togo, Rwanda, and Burundi) with average population densities higher than the larger countries.

stories' of family planning programmes, having been credited with an important contribution to the achievement of a 29 per cent reduction in the birth rate of the island in ten years (Mauldin and Berelson, 1978, p. 110). Four other countries have adopted policies aimed at reducing population growth. Two of them set quantitative targets as early as 1966 (Kenya) and 1969 (Ghana). The third one was Botswana in 1970, with Senegal being the latest addition in 1976 (Nortman and Hofstatter, 1978, Table 6, pp. 19–21). The fact that the birth-rates of the first three countries cited continue to be high and almost stable could be taken to indicate that in spite of the measures formally adopted, there have not been significant changes in the services put at the disposal of the population or that people are not interested in availing themselves of these services. As regards the fourth case, it is perhaps too early to pass judgement.

The authorization given by the governments of another twelve countries for the delivery of family planning services either by government health departments or by private institutions might be interpreted as implying that the provision of these services is not necessarily frowned upon when they are justified by health and welfare measures. African countries seem to attach so much importance to guarding the health of mothers that, going far beyond any other developing region, the post-Bucharest consultation attended by official representatives adopted a resolution urging their governments to 'pass legislation permitting qualified medical practitioners to perform abortion on request on grounds of the health, welfare and survival either of mother and child or both of them' (Economic Commission for Africa, 1975, paras. 10 and 11). Again, the fact that five of the programmes referred to above were authorized in 1970 or before and do not seem as yet to have had any impact on the level of fertility in the countries where they are being implemented raises the question of how much demand for family limitation exists.

While neither African policy-makers nor scholars seem to attach great importance to measuring or avoiding the effects of high fertility (and concomitant high demographic growth rates) on national income, they appear to be very much interested in their impact on education, health, housing, and nutrition in relation to specific goals set by the different countries. Equally important to them is an understanding of the relation between fertility and income distribution (IRG, 1978, p. 10).

As opposed to issues related to population increase, those associated with population distribution have been an obvious concern of most Sub-Saharan African governments. In answer to the UN Third Inquiry among Governments on Population Policy conducted during 1976, twenty-six governments of the region stated that they were implementing policies to 'slow down the flow' of internal migration (UN, 1976, Table 1, pp. 16–17). In fact, several types of policies are said to have been implemented in an effort to redirect rural outmigration, to discourage it in order to prevent further urban concentration, and to foster deconcentration of already crowded cities. Policies have also been enacted in an effort to settle nomadic populations. While these policies have generally not attempted to impose a direct regulation on the movement of people, one can find examples of 'induced colonization programmes' (Cantrelle, n.d., p. 140). Most commonly, the desired outcome has been sought through adoption of economic and social policies presumed to facilitate the achievement of the desired objective. Many examples of spontaneous and some of the induced colonization and resettlement schemes can be cited in Sub-Saharan countries (e.g. the resettlement and colonization programme in Upper Volta, the Mande farmers in Ivory Coast, the Yoruba farmers in the cocoa belt of Nigeria, the Gezira scheme in the Sudan, and the resettlement programmes associated with the construction of the Volta Dam in Ghana and the Kainji in Nigeria).

While it has been claimed that in general these schemes have not met with success, no systematic evaluation of their results appears to have been conducted. The 'Autorité de l'Aménagement des Vallées des Volta', responsible for the Upper Volta programme, has undertaken 'an intensive multidisciplinary evaluation' of that programme, which may provide an example for attempts to evaluate similar projects in other countries (IRG, 1978, p. 7).

Policies to discourage rural out-migration have taken various forms, usually seeking to promote rural development by investments in the agricultural sector directed either at protecting cultivators of small holdings (Ivory Coast and Kenya) or at implementing large capital-intensive schemes (Ghana and Sudan) (World Bank, 1978, p. 49). Perhaps the most striking example of a programme addressed at retaining population in rural areas is that being implemented in Tanzania under the so-called 'villagization' programme. As one Tanzanian participant in the IRG Nairobi Workshop put it, a debatable aspect of the programme is 'how successful it has been in reducing migration to Dar es Salaam and other principal cities' (IRG, 1978, p. 7).

Although the countries of this region have very low levels of urbanization, the growth of the urban population of almost all Sub-Saharan African countries has proceeded at a very fast pace in the last two decades. Because this growth has been concentrated in a few large cities, creating the problems associated with urban congestion, urban de-concentration programmes have been advocated, but their implementation has not proceeded in a successful manner. Mabogunje and Arowolo (1978, p. 41) argue that 'apart from lack of funds to prosecute such a plan, it seems that from the economic standpoint agglomeration of industrial and commercial activities in a few centers is a sure way to ensure maximum economic benefits under conditions of economic take-off'.

In summary, while spatial redistribution of the population appears to be a very important issue, both in terms of its effect on development strategies and of its demographic consequences, few specific policies have been implemented with a recognized degree of success in achieving the stated goals.

Africa has one of the world's highest rates of population movement — both of an intra-continental nature and toward the developed countries of Europe and America — and international migration has become an issue of major policy concern to most Sub-Saharan African governments (IRG, 1978, p. 7). With the advent of independence, many governments enacted legislation to regulate movements across the borders of their countries and, in some cases, to limit the number of resident foreigners. These measures have been predicated on the assumed benefits accruing to the natives, but 'doubts now exist as to whether such policies produced the beneficial effects for the national population that were once claimed for them' (IRG, 1978, p. 9). A rather recent concern among certain Sub-Saharan African countries, probably sparked by the Sahelian drought, is the role played by population pressure in the potential aggravation of distress in a situation of scarce natural resources. In terms of its relevance for policy, such a situation brings the need for physical and environmental planning, including measures to correct population distribution, to the forefront (IRG, 1978, p. 3).

A general conclusion can be drawn at this point. Sub-Saharan African governments appear to be generally interested in certain population issues but most do not seem to have recognized the need for designing a population policy to deal either with a selected demographic variable or with a combination of them (Ghana is perhaps the clearest exception). Nine of these governments reported to the UN Inquiry cited above the existence of an institution responsible for population policy formulation. It is, nevertheless, difficult to find information on the role actually played by these institutions in the population field. In all probability they remain more as formal legislative or administrative units than as operative mechanisms.

Status of Population Research, Data Base, and Institutional and Human Resources for Research

No attempt will be made here to offer, even in a general manner, a description of the state of knowledge on population and related development issues. This is left to the Mabogunje and Arowolo and Ware reviews, included as Appendices to this Report. Furthermore, other comprehensive bibliographies on various aspects of the demography of this region are cited in those reviews. The comments that follow are intended to give a very broad indication of (*a*) the direction taken in the recent past by population research in this area of the world, including some of its limitations, and (*b*) some of the factors assumed to have influenced the direction taken, including a brief discussion of the data base and a succinct examination of the institutional and human resource capabilities in the field.

Recent Research Directions

Tabbarah *et al.* (1978, pp. 4 and 5) have suggested that population research follows, in a sense, chronological steps associated with the degree of 'maturity' achieved in relation to the formulation and implementation of population policies. These 'steps' are identified as follows:

1. Collection of data, their analysis to ascertain and improve their quality, make the appropriate estimates, and determine the various population trends;

2. Identification of consequences of population trends for economic and social development;

3. If trends are considered detrimental and have to be modified, investigation of their determinants and their interrelations with the various aspects of development to devise policies for modifying them;

4. If policies are formulated and implemented, periodic evaluation to improve their effectiveness and obtain feedback with regard to both the determinants and consequences of population trends and the new data that may be required to study them.

Demographic research in the Sub-Saharan African countries seems to have moved in step with the stage of maturity as regards population policy formulation and implementation in which most of the countries of the subregion find themselves. Some specific characteristics are worth pointing out:

1. Demographic research is a relatively recent newcomer to scientific activities in the region. In fact, Mabogunje and Arowolo (1978, p. 2) place the initiation of 'serious research into population issues . . . from after 1966'.

2. Before that, and until very recently, research in this field was mainly concerned with measurement and identification of levels and trends. Outstanding examples of this are the large-scale sample surveys for measuring vital rates that were undertaken by the Institut National de la Statistique et des Études Économiques (INSEE) in all francophone countries as early as 1955.

3. Initial attempts to study the relations between certain population parameters and other aspects of development were at the intuitive level and were often extrapolations to the African situation of supposed relationships from some other cultural or historical setting.

4. In the beginning, as in other developing regions, research on family planning, intended as a means of learning about the determinants of fertility, dominated the scene — especially that based on KAP-type surveys. Unfortunately, these surveys contributed little to the understanding of fertility behaviour. Since they did not have a measurement objective, they did not help to estimate national levels of fertility, not to mention more disaggregated data. This situation has improved with the availability of new estimation techniques and the modest expansion of the data base,

soon to be amplified by recent population censuses and the national studies that are part of the World Fertility Survey programme. In addition, more attention is now being given to causes of current fertility levels. Francophone researchers tend to pay more attention to biological determinants of fertility (lactation, nutrition, disease, etc.), while anglophones appear to lay more emphasis upon socioeconomic factors. The operation of these factors at the family level is receiving considerable research attention.

5. Second in importance in the region are studies of internal migration, a subject that has received attention all along. From the beginning these studies have attempted to go beyond measurement in search of explanations linking population movements to aspects of economic and social development.

6. There has been a relative neglect of mortality. Of 600 recorded studies published between 1969 and 1975, only seventeen referred exclusively to mortality (Mabogunje and Arowolo, 1978, p. 7). The development of new techniques for estimating mortality as well as some specific surveys conducted primarily in francophone countries have given some impetus to the analysis of mortality. Studies of the relations between health, population, and development are still to be emphasized.

7. The concentration of research has been not only thematic but also geographic. Most research activities have tended to be concentrated in a few countries. Of 64 projects under way in 1970–1, more than half (36) were being conducted in only four countries of the region, with Nigeria accounting for nearly one-third (19 projects). It is interesting that of the 64 projects, only 14 were being developed in francophone countries (Mabogunje and Arowolo, 1978, Table 1).

8. Research has had an urban bias, and until very recently very few studies have been concerned with the rural sector. Yet, in spite of the efforts made in conducting urban studies, it cannot be said that the study of urbanization as a process has received sufficient attention (Mabogunje and Arowolo, 1978, p. 5).

9. One of the latest additions to population research in the region is that relating to population and development. The 1969 Nairobi Conference and the 1971 African Regional Population Conference perhaps marked the initiation of more ample discussion on the topic. More recently, some of the articles contained in the first issue of *Jimlar Mutane*, the Review of the Population Association of Africa first published in 1976, attest to the growing interest in the study of these relationships, at least among anglophone demographers.

Factors Influencing the Direction of Research

Several factors have been identified as contributing to the status of population and related research summarized above. The most frequently mentioned, and probably the most important, factors are outlined below.

1. Where universities are rather young, as they generally are in the region, research initially receives little attention and is less developed than it would be in a setting with a long-standing tradition of scientific inquiry. In Africa, demography and the social sciences applied to the study of population were to some extent exceptions, and anglophone Sub-Saharan Africa became during the 1960s and 1970s perhaps the only developing region where the majority of universities had some kind of demography programme. However, these two fields of study, particularly the latter, are still in the process of defining scope, constructing theories, and refining analytical tools, a situation that makes their introduction in a new environment more difficult. In addition, in order to attract the interest of the local intellectual community, demographic research has to overcome the frequent accusation that it constitutes a vehicle for the transmission of foreign ideas contrary to the national interest.

2. The size and nature of foreign assistance to population research has introduced certain biases. It has been claimed that in the past population assistance attached undue importance to the field of family planning, in spite of the recognized fact that researchers had not even been able to determine the level of fertility that family planning programmes were supposed to regulate. Other constraints imposed by population assistance are cited as inhibiting the kind of free hand needed by scholars to achieve a 'balanced' population research agenda — namely, 'lack of continuity, too rigid criteria governing how aid must be spent, delays in approval and receipt of assistance, and local currency shortages' (Mabogunje and Arowolo, 1978, p. 8).

3. Governments of the region generally attach very little importance to population growth as an issue of direct relevance to development efforts. The controversial nature of the topic of population and development and the widespread feeling that high population growth rates do not hinder development might explain the general lack of interest in policies aimed at demographic change. As late as 1971, as attested by discussions taking place at the African Regional Population Conference, the subject evoked strong ideological allegiances.

4. The differences among countries in their perception of and attitudes toward the problems posed by population growth has helped to create differences in levels of research activities and capacities.

5. The style of development characterizing the majority of these countries has led to the location of a large percentage of economic activities in urban centres. This has also promoted the concentration of social facilities (including universities and other research centres) in those cities.

Mabogunje and Arowolo (1978, p. 6) venture that there is also a 'general apathy of research scholars towards the countryside'.

6. The data base for research is rarely adequate in either coverage or quality.

7. There is a shortage of institutions interested in and capable of undertaking demographic research and staffed with enough personnel with the required qualifications (a topic that will be examined below in somewhat more detail).

The Data Base

Although periodic enumerations of the population and special demographic surveys exist for certain African countries or parts of them from the nineteenth century onwards, the quality of most of these data is generally regarded as poor. It was not until very recently that a considerable number of countries in the region undertook modern population censuses. Vital registration data on births, deaths, and marriages are far from satisfactory. The situation is one of limited coverage and under-registration, plus defective quality of the data registered. Estimates of mortality have had to rely on data obtained through single-round retrospective surveys, and those of fertility have been based on indirect and fragmentary evidence provided by combining census and sample survey results.

The availability of data has been improving and expectations are that it will be considerably improved in the very near future. With UNFPA support, many countries of the region either have taken recently, or plan to take, a population census or a large sample population survey. Although the results of most of these censuses are yet to be analysed, the UNFPA is continuing its support for the analysis phase.[4] In addition, as of January 1978, seven countries were participating or had confirmed their participation in the World Fertility Survey programme. Furthermore, many specialized surveys are under way or being planned.[5] As the mass of new demographic data continues to increase gradually, the panorama of demographic

[4] The 1977 Report of the Executive Director of the United Nations Fund for Population Activities cites twenty-nine Sub-Saharan African countries as having received support for census operations in that year.

[5] The *Bulletin de Liaison*, published three times a year by the French Group of African Demography, and recently joined by its English-language counterpart (*RIPS Newsletter*), often contains long lists of surveys planned or in progress. Two projects are worth mentioning in view of the previously mentioned contention that mortality has been a neglected subject: the comparative study of mortality levels, trends, differentials, and socioeconomic implications being promoted by the Population Division of the UN Economic Commission for Africa in Zambia, Tanzania, Kenya, and Uganda; and the survey on infant and juvenile mortality to be undertaken in the urban areas of Cameroon, Benin, Congo, Upper Volta, Chad, and Togo with the collaboration of the Regional Demographic Training and Research Institute at Yaounde.

research will change radically, provided the collection of data is accompanied by equally important efforts to ensure easy and opportune access to the data by those interested in using them. The existence of this barrier was mentioned at the IRG Nairobi Workshop (IRG, 1978, p. 4) as a factor forcing researchers to 'collect their own' data.

Institutional and Human Resources

Four distinct features become evident when examining the institutional and human resource capabilities for population research in Sub-Saharan Africa. First, anglophone and francophone countries differ in level of development in terms of numbers of both institutions and professionals with adequate training and experience. Secondly, there is a trend towards locating research and teaching activities within university settings in anglophone countries and, at least until very recently, primarily within institutions outside the normal university framework in francophone countries. Thirdly, capacities are highly concentrated in a very few countries of the region, both among francophone and anglophone nations. Fourthly, the role of foreign scholars in African demographic research has been considerable, both by those working in countries of the region and by teaching and research institutions abroad, paying particular attention to African population issues.

There is no recognized standard by which to gauge the needed supply of demographers and social scientists specializing in population. Demand can be expected to change with time, but it does seem that demand would bear some relation, among other things, to population size, extent and nature of population-related problems, degree of importance attached by scholars and policy-makers to the need to study population dynamics and their relation to development, the existence of a national population policy, and the interest shown by students in choosing a career in which demography and population studies constitute the core or an important part of the curriculum. Considering at least some of the preceding factors, there is clear evidence that Sub-Saharan Africa, like much of the Third World, faces a shortage of institutions and scholars devoted to teaching and research in population. No accurate estimate of the number of nationals of the region trained in population has come to the IRG's attention, but it is generally accepted that considerable strides have been made in recent years. According to a directory published in 1978 by the UN Economic Commission of Africa (ECA), when the data for this directory were compiled (1975) there were 172 nationals of Sub-Saharan countries working as 'demographers' within that same group of countries. An important percentage of these professionals have specialized training in demography and many hold postgraduate degrees from European and American universities. As expected, a significant portion of these scholars are trained in disciplines closely related to population studies, for example, sociology, geography, statistics, medical demography, economics, and computer science. In addition, there were forty-two non-Africans working in the population field in these countries in 1975. While the listing in the directory should only be taken as a crude approximation of the real situation, and while numbers do not necessarily imply capabilities, it gives a general idea of how human resources in population are distributed in the region and in which countries more intensive activity seems to be taking place. The country with the highest number of professionals is Nigeria (45), followed by Ghana and Zaïre (both with 15). The third country is Cameroon, where, as in Ghana, a UN subregional demographic training and research centre operates. All the other countries show very small numbers of population professionals.

The picture suggested by the ECA directory must have changed in the last three years because of the increase in the number of research and training institutions, both at the national and at the subregional level. The two UN demographic centres in Accra and Yaounde have now been operating for about six years and the number of their students has been continually increasing.[6] In addition, both have now instituted research programmes that contribute to improving the level of training. French-speaking Africans also have access to the UN centre operating in Romania, and of course they continue to receive support from the French Overseas Office of Scientific and Technical Research (ORSTOM), which operates local branches in several francophone countries. Another important contribution is being made by the reinforced Population Division of the UNECA, which has been actively involved in the African Census Programme and gives technical assistance in many aspects of demographic analysis to countries requiring it. An active publication programme on population subjects is also being developed by the ECA. There are at least two university programmes offering postgraduate degrees in demography (Ghana and Tanzania), and several universities in Nigeria (Ibadan, Ife, Lagos, and Nsukka) and one in Kenya have majors in demography within related departments. The departments of sociology, economics, and geography of at least twenty-five universities in the region have courses in population subjects. In several French-speaking countries (Ivory Coast, Niger, and Togo) centres responsible for scientific research in general are paying particular attention to demographic studies. The National University of Zaïre (Kinshasa) offers a two year licence in demography since 1973, the only one in Francophone Africa. Many government departments and agencies are promoting population research, and in some instances they have been directly engaged in training (e.g. Manpower Board in Ghana, Agency for the Development of the Volta Valley in Upper Volta). The most recent addition to research capacity in the area is the Socioeconomic and Demographic Unit at the Sahel Institute in Mali.

[6] In its first five years of existence (1971-6), the Regional Institute for Population Studies located in Ghana granted 73 diplomas, 8 master's degrees, and had 9 M.A. theses under assessment (UN, 1977, p. 42).

An indication of the importance of the contribution to the understanding of population phenomena in Sub-Saharan African countries made through the training and research activities undertaken abroad by interested institutions[7] is the significant number of non-African scholars that are recorded in the ECA directory as presently engaged in African demographic studies. Forty-seven professionals are identified, of which the largest groups are located in French, American, and British institutions.

In summary, although there are not enough demographers (particularly in East Africa) to undertake all the necessary studies, and the situation will be even more critical when the new census and survey data become available, present capacities, both in terms of institutions and researchers, can go a long way towards meeting the needs of the Sub-Saharan countries, provided efforts are adequately co-ordinated, sufficient official support is forthcoming, and appropriate funding is available.

References

Adegbola, O. 1977. 'New Estimates of Fertility and Child Mortality in Africa South of the Sahara.' *Population Studies*, 31 (3), 467-86.

Cantrelle, Pierre *et al.*, ed. No date. *Population in African Development*, Vol. 2. International Union for the Scientific Study of Population. Dolhain, Belgium: Ordina Editions.

International Review Group (IRG). 1978. 'Draft Summary Report of the Third IRG Workshop on Research Priorities for Population Policy.' Nairobi, Kenya. 6-8 September. IRG/95.

Lux, André. 1976. 'Le Problème de la Stérilité en Afrique et ses Implications de Politique Démographique à propos de deux Ouvrages Récents.' *Canadian Journal of African Studies*, 10 (1), 143-55; see also *Population*, 31 (4-5); 970-4.

Mabogunje, Akin L., and Arowolo, O. 1978. 'Social Science Research on Population and Development in Africa South of the Sahara.' Appendix 7 to the Final Report. El Colegio de Mexico: IRG.

Mauldin, W. Parker, and Bernard Berelson. 1978. 'Conditions of Fertility Decline in Developing Countries, 1965-75.' *Studies in Family Planning*, 9 (5); 90-147.

Nortman, Dorothy, and Hofstatter, Ellen. 1976. 'Population and Family Planning Programs: A Factbook.' *Reports on Population/Family Planning*, No. 2 (8th edn.). New York: The Population Council.

Romaniuk, Anatole. 1967. *La Fécondité des Populations Congolaises*. Paris: Mouton.

---

[7] Some of these institutions are: Australian National University, Canberra; Centre for West Africa Studies, University of Birmingham, Eng.; International Labour Office, Geneva; Inter-University Demographic Programme, Brussels; Michigan State University, Lansing; Organization for Economic Co-operation and Development (OECD), Paris; Office of Population Research, Princeton; University of Durham; University of Liverpool; University of London (London School of Economics and the Centre for Overseas Population Studies); University of Montreal; University of Paris, Institute of Demography; and University of Pennsylvania.

Tabbarah, Riad, Mamish, M. and Gemayel, Y. 1978. 'Social Science Research on Population and Development in the Arab Countries.' Appendix 9 to the Final Report. El Colegio de México: IRG.

United Nations Department of Economic and Social Affairs. 1974. *World Population Prospects as Assessed in 1973.* Population Studies, No. 60. ST/ESA/SER.A/60.

United Nations Economic Commission for Africa. 1975. *Regional Post World Population Conference Consultation.* 11 March. E/CN. 14/POP/135.

United Nations Population Commission. 1976. Preliminary Report on the Third Population Inquiry among Governments: Population Policies in the Context of Development in 1976. E/CN.9/XIX/CRP.6.

— 1977. Report on the Progress of Work (1975-1976) E/CN.9/XIX/CRP.4.

Ware, Helen. 1978. 'Population and Development in Africa South of the Sahara: A Review of the Literature, 1970-1978.' Appendix 7A to the Final Report. El Colegio de Mexico: IRG.

World Bank. 1978. *World Development Report, 1978.* Washington, D.C.: World Bank.

2 THE ARAB COUNTRIES[8]

The nineteen Arab countries,[9] located in two distinct geographical areas of the world (North Africa and South West Asia), have characteristics that in many respects distinguish them from their neighbours. The most important of these is that they are well endowed with one of today's most precious non-renewable resources: petroleum. And while they present significant differences in demographic and socioeconomic indicators, there is greater cultural homogeneity among the majority of these countries than in other developing regions.

Basic Socioeconomic and Demographic Characteristics

The total population of the two subregions exceeded 142 million in 1975 (UN, 1974, as assessed in 1973) but the Arab population of North Africa (98 million) was more than twice as large as that of South West Asia (44 million).

The North African Arab countries had an estimated average annual rate of population growth in the 1970–5 period of 2.74 per cent, higher than that of all other African subregions. This can be explained by a faster and more significant decline in mortality in the former countries. With the exception of Sudan, the North African countries had life expectancies at birth exceeding fifty-two years in 1975 (World Bank, 1978, Table 17). In Egypt and Tunisia (which contain 44 per cent of the subregion's population) fertility has shown a downward trend, with estimated average annual crude birth rates of 37.8 and 40 per 1,000, respectively, in the 1970–5 period. None of the other North African Arab countries has shown any significant changes in fertility levels in the twenty-five-year period 1950–5 to 1970–5, and CBRs have remained at levels above 45 per 1,000 (UN, 1974, as assessed in 1973).

Estimates for the Asian Arab countries place their average annual rate of population growth (over 3 per cent) above that of the North African Arab countries, and well above that of the other Asian subregions. With

---

[8] This chapter has been prepared on the basis of IRG Appendix 9 by Tabbarah, Mamish, and Gemayel. Certain portions of that paper have been quoted verbatim.

[9] Mauritania and Somalia also belong to the Arab League, but since they are located in West and East Africa, respectively, they have not been included in this region.

the exception of Kuwait, the declines in mortality have not been as significant as in Arab North Africa. Three countries of the subregion (Saudi Arabia and the two Yemens, comprising almost 40 per cent of the subregion's population in 1975) had life expectancies of 45 years in that year. In addition, almost all countries (except Lebanon) continued to present rather high and stable levels of fertility. The two largest countries of this subregion — Iraq and Saudi Arabia — had average annual crude birth rates exceeding 48 per 1,000 in 1970–5. While the high growth rates in several of the Asian Arab countries are the result of heavy international immigration, it is evident that the contribution to population growth of fertility and mortality is very different in the two groups of Arab countries.

Most of the Arab countries are highly urbanized. In eight of the nineteen countries, the percentage of population living in cities in 1975 was estimated at over 45 per cent, and in one extreme case (Kuwait) at 89 per cent. The levels achieved are a reflection of the fast pace of urban growth. In the period 1970–5, ten of these countries registered average annual urban growth rates of 5 per cent and over. In some cases international immigration played a very important role in speeding up the pace of urban concentration.

In other socioeconomic indicators, the Arab countries show great disparities among themselves. For example, while the infant mortality rate in 1975 was estimated to be 160 per 1,000 live-born children in the Yemen Arab Republic, it was about 22 in Jordan. Equally broad differences have been documented for adult literacy: 68 per cent in Lebanon in 1974 and 15 per cent in Saudia Arabia (World Bank, 1978, Tables 17 and 18).

Evidently, for some oil-exporting Arab countries, indicators such as average per capita gross national product (GNP) turn out to be even less meaningful than they are in other developing countries in reflecting the access of the less privileged classes of society to the benefits arising from the extraordinary oil revenues flowing into their countries. For example, while Saudi Arabia had an annual average per capita GNP of US $4,480 in 1976 (World Bank, 1978, Table 1, p. 77), the life expectancy of its population around the same year was estimated to be only 45 years, the percentage of population literate was incredibly low (15 per cent of adults aged 15 and over), and the percentage of urban population was 21. On the other hand, a country like Egypt with a per capita GNP of only US $280 had a life expectancy of 52 years, a 40 per cent literacy rate, and a percentage of urban population of 48. Other circumstances that could explain the lack of coherence between the level of GNP and certain indicators of social development include style of development, pattern of income distribution, and degree of popular political participation.

In spite of these contradictions the Arab countries in general have done better economically than most of the Sub-Saharan Africa countries and many Asian countries. In the period 1970–6, with perhaps two exceptions, all countries experienced modest annual increases in per capita GNP, although the increase was significant only in Saudi Arabia (7 per cent) and Libya (10 per cent).

These figures should not hide the fact that there are some very poor countries in the two subregions: Yemen Arab Republic and the People's Democratic Republic of Yemen, in Asia; and Sudan and Egypt, in North Africa, where considerable progress is yet to be achieved in educational and health services for the population.[10] Unlike the petroleum-exporting countries of the area, the future socioeconomic growth of these countries depends on their possibilities for industrial and agricultural development, which have generally been rather meagre in the last 15 years.

Population Issues and Government Positions on Population

Population growth rates, although relatively high in most of the Asian Arab countries, have not generally been considered by the governments of these countries as a barrier to their development, and in some instances have been judged necessary for their future development. In some countries of the region, the rate of growth is affected more by immigration than by natural increase, and in such circumstances a reduction of the rate of demographic growth may be achieved initially by means of restriction on immigration rather than on fertility. Of the nine Asian Arab countries that replied to the UN Third Inquiry on Population and Development (1976), four indicated that their rate of population growth was satisfactory, one (Jordan) that it was too high, and four expressed no view. Of the three countries that did not reply (Lebanon, Kuwait, and the United Arab Emirates), at least the latter two had previously shown no concern for their population growth rates, as evidenced by a pro-immigration policy. This has started to change: Kuwait, for example, recently decided to restrict immigration, and the importance of immigration in the population growth of the United Arab Emirates is beginning to decline.

Some concern has been expressed with regard to high fertility rates, mostly with respect to certain socioeconomic groups and in relation to their effects on health, welfare, and the status of women. Four of the twelve Asian Arab countries (Lebanon, Syria, Jordan, and the People's Democratic Republic of Yemen) are particularly interested in this aspect of population policy. Kuwait and the Yemen Arab Republic seem to be moving in this direction. Iraq allows a private institution established in

[10] In fact, the four countries are included by the UN in the list of the forty-five countries 'most seriously affected' by adverse economic conditions.

1971 to utilize government facilities to provide family planning services. Two North African countries (Egypt and Tunisia) have affirmative policies to diminish fertility and have set quantitative targets to either reduce it or decrease over all growth. A third country, Morocco, contemplated in its 1973–7 Five-Year Plan, 'activities to inform, educate and motivate the population to practise voluntary family planning' (Nortman and Hofstatter, 1978, Table 6).

The UN/UNFPA Post-World Population Conference Consultation for the ECWA region, attended by high-level government representatives from twelve Arab countries, recognized that 'despite progress made by the region in the fields of health care, mortality rates are still high' and recommended that 'special importance' be given to 'the reduction of mortality rates, especially among infants and children' (ECWA, 1975, pp. 10–11). Another major concern that has appeared in various regional conferences and in national statements is with differential mortality, particularly mortality among certain socioeconomic groups and in certain least-developed areas.

One of the main population issues of concern to practically all Asian Arab countries is that of internal migration, particularly rural-to-urban migration and the rapid growth of primate cities of these countries. In Lebanon, for example, more than 75 per cent of total non-agricultural employment is concentrated in Beirut and its suburbs, while in Jordan more than 90 per cent of non-agricultural employment is concentrated in the Amman/Zarka area. Furthermore, in all of these countries the primacy of the capital city is rapidly increasing. Many of the capitals are experiencing increasing shortages in housing and in certain public services such as water and electricity. At the same time, in some of these countries, many rural areas, villages, and small cities are being depleted of their working populations and the potential for agricultural production is becoming increasingly under-exploited.

Some Asian Arab countries, as well as some African Arab countries, have expressed strong interest in obtaining demographic and socioeconomic information on their Bedouin populations and in formulating policies to improve their conditions. While most of these countries are interested and actively involved in formulating policies for the settlement of these nomadic populations, some have expressed the view that, at least in the short run, policies must be devised to take the necessary social services and amenities to the Bedouins rather than vice versa. It should be noted that some Bedouin movements are across national boundaries, making the problem one of international rather than internal migration and necessitating action by more than one government.

Another main area of concern for Asian Arab countries, and, in fact, for practically all Arab countries, is that of international migration, particularly the migration of workers and of qualified personnel. Most of the migration of Arab workers, except that taking place from the

Maghreb countries (Algeria, Morocco, and Tunisia) to Europe, is among Arab countries — mainly from Egypt, Lebanon, Syria, Jordan, the two Yemens, and Oman towards the oil-exporting Arab countries. The questions posed by this migration differ somewhat from those posed by the migration of workers to Europe. Many Arabian Gulf countries, for example, have experienced such high rates of immigration relative to their populations that the majority of their population is actually non-native, composed of nationals of Arab labour-exporting countries. If such a situation were to develop in other regions of the world, it would be socially and politically unacceptable, at least to the receiving country. However, in most intergovernmental conferences in the Arab region, intra-regional migration has been considered a separate issue from extra-regional migration and, on balance, a positive contribution to Arab development and integration as opposed to international migration. Nevertheless, it has been deemed both necessary and urgent to obtain more information on the extent and nature of these population movements and to devise ways of harmonizing the relevant policies among the sending and receiving countries so as to maximize the benefits of these movements to the countries concerned and to reduce the hardships for the migrants and their families.

The emigration of highly qualified personnel from the Arab countries towards Western Europe and the Americas is also considered a major problem by most of the Arab countries. The extremely rapid development of these countries, sparked mainly by the increased oil revenues, has created considerable demand for highly qualified personnel in almost all fields of development, and shortages of various skills are considered a major bottleneck to future development. Accordingly, a number of Arab countries (such as Iraq and Libya) have initiated various policies to attract Arab talent. These policies have not been totally successful, however, particularly because of the lack of a suitable data base on Arab talent abroad and the insufficient research (and thinking) on the subject.

Status of Population Research, Data Base, and Institutional and Human Resources for Research

Recent Research Directions

The preceding discussion of the main population issues of concern to the Arab countries provides an adequate background for examining the recent trends in research activities in this group of countries in order to determine how well these concerns are being reflected in the research undertaken.

The first striking fact one encounters when surveying what has and is being done in population research in Arab countries is the predominance of the North African countries in research activities. A systematic review of both published and unpublished materials conducted by Tabbarah, Mamish, and Gemayel reveals the following distribution of population research conducted in this region in the period 1960–76:[11]

Area	Number of Documents
Arab Asia	156
Arab North Africa	488
Egypt	(225)
Maghreb	(228)
Other North Africa	(35)

With regard to the Asian Arab countries, a number of observations may be made. First, recent research on methods of data collection has focused mainly on comprehensive censuses and multi-purpose surveys and has not yet been concerned with specialized surveys, for example, on fertility and mortality, internal migration, and international migration. While some fertility and mortality surveys have recently been completed, publication of the methodologies is just beginning.

Secondly, 30 per cent of all collected research on Arab West Asia deals with questions of population growth and fertility. In fact, more than half of the research on population and development (that is, consequences, determinants, and interrelationships) deals with the consequences of population growth; and virtually all the research on population policies deals specifically with family planning — that is, with the two areas that were explicitly given low priority in the various recommendations adopted by the countries of this subregion in recent conferences. This bias has been attributed by some Arab scholars (Tabbarah, Mamish, and Gemayel, 1978) to the relative availability of international funds for activities in these areas and the relative dearth of such funds for activities in the areas of internal and international migration.

Thirdly, research on fertility and population growth in the Asian Arab countries deals principally with demographic analysis and consequences of population trends and, to some extent, with family planning policies, with very little work having been done on the socioeconomic determinants of fertility. Such research has recently begun to appear, particularly in relation to the contribution of education and the status of women to fertility decline.

Fourthly, with regard to internal and international migration, the two areas in which governments of all Arab countries are most interested,

[11] Tables presenting a detailed distribution of research by the four subgroups of countries and by population variables are included in Tabbarah, Mamish, and Gemayel, 1978, IRG Appendix 9.

research is still at an early stage of development (and, in the case of international migration, extremely scanty) in that it still concentrates largely on demographic analysis and only marginally on identifying determinants and consequences of migratory movements or on the formulation, implementation, and evaluation of migration policies.

Finally, it is also clear that the study of the interrelationships between population and development is as yet almost totally absent in the Asian Arab countries.

The conclusions reached with regard to Asian Arab countries also apply to the North African countries of Libya and Sudan, as well as to Egypt and the Maghreb countries, although to a much lesser degree. Egypt, for example, seems to have a broad base of research covering most national population concerns. The primary emphasis is on fertility and population growth — two factors that the government considers major barriers to development. Furthermore, Egypt has a good deal of comprehensive research, that is, in-depth studies of the population situation in the country in relation to social and economic development. Nevertheless, little attention seems to have been paid to the issue of international migration and particularly the migration of professionals and skilled technicians, which in a sender country such as Egypt is of great concern.

Population research in the Maghreb countries appears to have made considerable advances in the past 10 years, particularly with the creation of the Association Maghrébine pour les Études de Population. Since 1969 these countries have organized three colloquia and plan to hold a fourth in 1980. The last colloquium covered a variety of topics: demographic phenomena, internal and international migration, urbanization, role and status of women, and population policies (see *Démographie Africaine*, 1978, no. 27, p. 55).

An important feature of population research in the Arab countries is that it is in large part 'solicited' research, that is, not due to the personal initiative of the individual researcher. Thus, 80 per cent of the research identified in Tabbarah, Mamish, and Gemayel (1978) consists of either theses written in fulfilment of the requirements for a degree in demography (particularly from the Cairo Demographic Centre) or papers written for conferences and seminars sponsored or funded mostly by international agencies.

It is difficult to identify schools of thought or major debates from the population literature concerned with the Arab countries. There are several reasons for this. First, as was already noted, a major part of the research is concerned with data collection and analysis and is therefore descriptive. While this research has, in many instances, reached fairly sophisticated levels — particularly in relation to the application or adaptation of demographic research and analytical techniques to Arab conditions and data — it does not lend itself to the development of controversial ideas and theories, as is the case with research on population and development or population policies. Secondly, research on population and development and population policies is scarce except in a few countries (Egypt and the Maghreb countries), which have conditions that are not always similar to those found in other Arab countries. Finally, the majority of elementary research, 'particularly that in the form of master's- or bachelor's-level theses, seldom contains deep or original thought or is the subject of controversies and heated debates. Nevertheless, some interesting lines of thinking have already emerged with regard to issues on which research has been concentrated, particularly the consequences of population growth, the determinants of fertility and fertility policies and, to a much lesser extent, certain aspects of migration' (Tabbarah, Mamish, and Gemayel, 1978, p. 20).[12]

The Data Base

There has been a tendency to attribute the rather low level of development of demographic research in the Arab countries to what is considered a very poor population data base. While it is true that continuous registration of births and deaths in many countries of the region is still below the minimum level needed for the proper measurement of present conditions and estimation of future trends, other demographic information (although far from adequate) is available for a larger percentage of the population than in other developing subregions of the world, has a broader subject coverage, and in some instances has been gathered within shorter intervals. Data have been gathered not only through population censuses but also, more recently, by means of multi-round and multi-purpose surveys. Taking 1960 as a point of departure, at least one census each has been undertaken in countries that together comprise 54 per cent of the Arab population. Iraq, Jordan, Syria, Egypt, and Algeria, for example, conducted sample surveys as recently as 1976. Three countries (Tunisia, Syria, and Yemen Arab Republic) are participating in the World Fertility Survey, and it is expected that Egypt will also join the programme.

The problem does not seem to be one of lack of data-gathering. The difficulty seems to lie in the restricted access to data that most researchers encounter. This is either because the data have not been properly processed or because administrative limitations are imposed on their use. In other instances, available data have not been subjected to analysis. Of course, the shortage of personnel with the proper training contributes to the latter situation.

[12] Several examples of interesting research are cited in Tabbarah, Mamish, and Gemayel (1978, pp. 21–8).

Institutional and Human Resources

Arab countries have expressed concern for the shortage of qualified population researchers. They are too few and too thinly spread, often working in isolation from each other (Hill, 1978, p. 2). To an outsider to the region, the lack of human resources capable of undertaking population research in the Arab countries comes as a surprise, considering that a UN-sponsored centre has been operating in Cairo as a regional institution to serve the Arab countries since 1963. According to a document published by the UN Population Division (UN, 1975, vol. 1 Table 1, pp. 397–8), in the 10-year period from 1963 to 1972 the Cairo Demographic Centre trained 296 students in the General Diploma Course, 35 in the Special Diploma Course, and 11 in the Research Course. Assuming a similar average output during the following 5 years, more than 500 professionals would have received some form of demographic training at the centre. Because of its location, Egypt has benefited the most from this training facility. Almost 30 per cent of the students graduating from the centre in 1963–72 were Egyptians. Sudan and Syria sent an average of three to four students to the centre every year during the same period, while Iraq and Libya trained thirteen and twelve demographers, respectively. While the junior professional level training at the Cairo Demographic Centre should prepare its graduates to contribute effectively to the analysis of the data referred to above, it seems that the majority of these are not working in the field.

Furthermore, professionals with higher training capable of analysing and interpreting the relations between demographic phenomena and the process of socioeconomic development are also lacking. Perhaps this explains why so much of the research has remained at the purely descriptive level. Unfortunately, some of the older and more reputable institutions of the region, such as the American Universities in Cairo and Beirut, have not been successful in organizing proper programmes. A number of Arab universities (Aleppo, Jordan, Baghdad, and Lebanon) have recently included demographic training in their curricula, but the shortage of qualified personnel, particularly Arab-speaking instructors, has been a major bottleneck in the initiation of programmes. More importantly, there is a severe shortage of training materials in Arabic, which has necessitated the translation of foreign language textbooks for this purpose. However, because of the time lag required for a textbook to be identified, translated, and published, much of the demographic training in Arabic utilizes dated material, a particularly serious defect in a field where techniques are developing and changing very rapidly.

Hill (1978) has identified the following reasons for the apparent lack of interest of Arab professionals in the population field: (1) the relatively weak demand for research and evaluation; (2) the difficulty of obtaining funds to support research in population; (3) the lack of encouragement professionals receive from their colleagues and their employers to investigate controversial issues; and (4) the poor salaries paid in the public sector, including the universities.

Some recent developments in the area lend hope for an improvement in the situation described above, both in terms of institutions and of human resources. First, the Population Division of the UN Economic Commission for Western Asia, located in Beirut, has been strengthened in recent years. Most of the research sponsored by the ECWA is in conjunction with regional conferences and seminars that are organized at the request of governments of the region. Since the main governmental concern so far has been in the areas of data collection and analysis, research of this sort constitutes more than 65 per cent of ECWA-sponsored output. About 24 per cent deals with population and development, and some 10 per cent with population policy. However, the population work programme of the ECWA for 1978-9, while still emphasizing demographic analysis because of the recent outpouring of population data as a result of the sample surveys and WFS participation mentioned earlier, also focuses on issues of population and development and, to some extent, questions relating to population policies. With regard to categories of variables, the ECWA has so far paid almost equal attention to all categories except that of international migration. However, since 1976, it has been conducting a modest programme in the latter field, the research output of which is only now beginning to appear in published form.

In the second place, the annual Middle East Awards (MEAWARDS) programme recently created by the Population Council and the Ford Foundation represents another institutional mechanism that is expected to strengthen and encourage population research in the region.

References

Hill, Allan G. 1978. 'Population Research and Training Institutions in the Arab World.' Appendix 10 to the Final Report. El Colegio de México: IRG.

Nortman, Dorothy, and Hofstatter, Ellen. 1976. 'Population and Family Planning Programs: A Factbook.' *Reports on Population/Family Planning*, no. 2 (8th edn.). New York: The Population Council.

Tabbarah, Riad, Mamish, M. and Gemayel, Y. 1978. 'Social Science Research on Population and Development in the Arab Countires.' Appendix 9 to the Final Report. El Colegio de México: IRG.

United Nations Department of Economic and Social Affairs. 1974. *World Population Prospects as Assessed in 1973*. Population Studies, no. 60. ST/ESA/SER. A/60.

— 1975. *The Population Debate: Dimensions and Perspectives*. Population Studies, no. 57. ST/ESA/SER.A/57, vol. 1, pp. 397-8.

United Nations Economic Commission for Western Asia. 1975. *Final Report of the UN/UNFPA Post-World Population Conference Consultation for the ECWA Region*.

United Nations Population Commission. 1976. Preliminary Report on the Third Population Inquiry among Governments: Population Policies in the Context of Development in 1976. E/CN.9/XIX/CRP.6.

World Bank. 1978. *World Development Report, 1978*. Washington, D.C.: World Bank.

3 MIDDLE SOUTH ASIA

Middle South Asia — one of the most populous subregions into which Asia is customarily divided — contains nine countries, one of which (India) has the second largest population in the world. This group of countries shares a rich common cultural history extending back over several millenia that has contributed to shaping the customs, norms, values, and beliefs to which most social classes rigidly adhered until very recently. This characteristic has been identified as one of the factors that has influenced the slowness with which changes have been introduced in these countries. Traditionally the social structure allowed very little mobility, but this situation appears to be loosening up somewhat in recent times. In fact, the caste system is said to have been undergoing modification since early this century.

Basic Socioeconomic and Demographic Characteristics

The total population of Middle South Asia was estimated to be more than 837 million in 1975 (UN Assessment of 1973), of which more than 90 per cent was concentrated in India, Bangladesh, and Pakistan. This does not mean that the remaining six countries are small in terms of population size. This is true only of Bhutan and the Maldives; the population of the other four countries taken together was 79 million in 1975.

One striking characteristic of several countries of this region is their high population density. This is particularly crucial since, unlike many countries in developing regions of the world, they have no agricultural frontier for expansion and thus must depend on increases in yields for badly needed increases in agricultural production. Bangladesh, with an average of more than 558 inhabitants per square kilometre, has one of the highest population densities in the world. India and Sri Lanka have average densities approaching or exceeding 200. Besides occupying territories that are small relative to their populations, these countries are experiencing rather high average annual rates of demographic growth. Although generally lower than the averages for Africa and Latin America, growth rates are still of a magnitude that implies a potential doubling of the population in 30 years or less in most countries of the subregion. It should be further emphasized that, with the exception of Sri Lanka and to a lesser extent India, these intermediate-level rates of growth are not due to decreases in fertility but rather to continuing high mortality. In Afghanistan, the estimated life expectancy at birth in 1975 was only 35 years. Bangladesh, Bhutan, and Nepal had life expectancies at birth below 45 years in 1975, while the value for India, Iran, and Pakistan was around 50. The only country having a life expectancy similar to that registered in several Latin American countries and in some Eastern European countries was Sri Lanka at 68 years (World Bank, 1978, Table 17).

Together with Indonesia in South-East Asia, three countries of this subregion (India, Bangladesh, and Pakistan) contain two-thirds of the world's absolute poor (World Bank, 1978, p. 38). This is in part revealed by the level of per capita gross national product (GNP), which was US $110 in Bangladesh, US $150 in India, and US $170 in Pakistan in 1976. The only country of the subregion having a per capita GNP exceeding US $200 was oil-exporting Iran, with a value approaching US $2000. Of course, one should not overinterpret the significance of this indicator. As pointed out in the preceding chapter, it does not adequately reflect how the national product is actually distributed or the availability of social services among the different sectors of society. This has been evident when comparing certain social indicators for Iran and Sri Lanka. Although Iran had a per capita GNP almost ten times higher than Sri Lanka, adult literacy was 50 per cent in 1974 as compared to 78 per cent in Sri Lanka. Also, Sri Lanka had a life expectancy at birth in 1975 seventeen years higher than that in Iran. In addition, its average annual crude birth rate was less than 29 per 1,000 in the period 1970–5, while the same index for Iran remained above 45 per 1,000 during this period. The level of Sri Lanka's fertility reflects the social changes that have taken place among its population and is not related to a high percentage of urbanization (a relatively low 24 per cent in 1975 as compared with 44 per cent in Iran in the same year). These differences are still more striking if one considers that, during the 1960–76 period, GNP increased annually at an average rate of 2 per cent in Sri Lanka and at 8 per cent in Iran.

During the first half of the 1970s the other countries of the subregion, with the exception of Pakistan (with an average annual growth in GNP of 3.1 per cent), were economically near stagnation, principally due to the very slow growth of the agricultural sector, upon which the majority of the population depends in these predominantly rural countries. All the other countries of the subregion except Iran have a very low percentage of urban population. In Bangladesh, Bhutan, and Nepal, for example, this percentage was below 10 in 1975. Even in India, with eleven cities of 1 million and over, the percentage of urban population was only about 22 per cent in 1975 (World Bank, 1978, Table 14). It is clear that in Middle South Asia, more than in any other Third World region, development efforts need to be concentrated in the rural areas.

Population Issues and Government Positions on Population

In 1952 India became the first country of the world to adopt an official policy aimed at reducing fertility. This decision was preceded by many years of public debate on the significance of population growth and its impact on development possibilities (Desai, 1978, pp. 16–18). Since that date, the Indian average annual crude birth-rate seems to have dropped from a level of 42.3 in the period 1950–5 to 39.9 in 1970–5. Many explanations have been advanced for the modest results of the activities addressed at achieving a reduction of fertility in India: lack of effective official implementation of the programme, poor administration at the service level, cultural barriers, low level of social development. There have been, however, examples of success in reducing birth rates in certain parts of India. The most frequently cited case is the state of Kerala, where fertility started to decline in the early 1960s. Kerala has been described as having the highest population density (549 per square kilometre), the highest rate of female literacy (54 per cent), the largest average village size, and one of the lowest urban and rural infant and general mortality rates (Dandekar, 1977, p. 360). All of these favourable indicators, together with a higher average age at marriage, have contributed to produce a birth-rate that in 1974 was around 26 in both urban and rural areas. Kerala has also been singled out as a state with a dynamic and progressive political leadership over a long period of years – a factor that has contributed to its present advanced level of social development. This has been cited in support of the argument that 'low levels of fertility result from public policies which effectively increase levels of social justice and economic equity throughout society' (Ratcliffe, 1978, p. 16).

Other countries of Middle South Asia that have official policies addressed at curtailing the level of fertility are – in the order of date of adoption – Pakistan (1960), Sri Lanka (1965), Nepal (1966), and Bangladesh (1971). All of them have set quantitative targets. The government of Iran entrusted the Ministry of Health in 1970 with the development of a family planning programme. The only country that can claim an important degree of success is Sri Lanka, where a 25 per cent decrease in the birth rate has been accomplished in a 20-year period. This has occurred partly as a result of a shift towards a pattern of marriage at later ages. As pointed out above, Sri Lanka also presents some very favourable social indicators.

It is worth noting that in the cases of Bangladesh and Nepal, the population policy adopted has set targets for the reduction of general mortality in the first country and of infant mortality in the second. Furthermore, in Nepal the policy has the following additional objectives: (*a*) to check immigration into Nepal; (*b*) to control existing patterns of migration from rural to urban areas; (*c*) to increase the density of population in agricultural areas; and (*d*) to develop small towns in selected areas. This places Nepal in the category of countries that have a rather comprehensive population policy (Desai, 1978, pp. 21–2).

With the rather low level of urbanization, very high average density, and scarcity of agricultural land found in several of the countries of this region, internal migration policies would appear to be very important. According to the UN Population Commission's (1976) report on 'Measures Undertaken at the National, Regional and International Levels to Implement the World Population Plan of Action', India, Iran, and the Maldives, Pakistan, Nepal, and Sri Lanka are implementing policies intended to decrease the flow of internal migration, while Bhutan appears to be attempting to accelerate it and Bangladesh to reverse it.

It is also understandable that, faced with conditions such as those described above, international migration is not a primary concern in these countries. The exception, of course, is the government sponsored 'export' from many countries of this region of skilled and semi-skilled workers to the oil-producing countries of the Middle East. (Keely, 1980).

In summary, the recognition of population growth as representing one kind of a problem or another is quite general in the countries of Middle South Asia. This is also true to some extent of Afghanistan, whose 1972–7 economic plan takes note of such issues as high mortality, unemployment, and population distribution. Bangladesh, India, and Pakistan have experimented with incentive schemes to lower fertility, and the first two plus Iran have included delayed marriage as part of their population policy. Concern about the interrelation between socioeconomic development and fertility decline is reflected in the policies of Bangladesh (Desai, 1978, pp. 20–5).

Status of Population Research, Data Base, and Institutional and Human Resources for Research

Recent Research Directions

Population research in Middle South Asia has a longer history than that in any other developing region, with Indian scholars having taken the lead. An examination of the population studies conducted in the sub-region in the recent past reveals the overwhelming participation of Indian professionals (Desai, 1978). Desai's survey shows that in the six-year period 1971–6, more than 1,600 pieces of literature on demographic topics were prepared in India. In contrast, the other six large countries of Middle South Asia together produced only a little over 1,000 titles, even when the search is extended as far back as 1950. Among these, the largest contribution was that of Pakistan, followed by Bangladesh and Sri Lanka. While numbers tell nothing about the quality of the work performed,[13]

[13] Desai's review (IRG Appendix 2) discusses the substantive content of many of the research pieces referred to.

they serve as a rough indication of the importance of population studies in the different countries, and to some extent of the level of human resources available to undertake such studies.

In India, as in many other developing countries, family planning as a topic initially received the most research attention: for the period through 1970, 30 per cent of all published research on population was devoted to family planning. While the predominance of family planning as a research topic appears to have declined somewhat (27 per cent of all population literature, including unpublished materials, during the period 1971–6), nuptiality – an important variable in the determination of fertility levels – remains a neglected subject, accounting for only 2 per cent of writings since 1970. Internal migration (20 per cent) has been the second most frequent subject of study for population specialists in India. The bulk of the writings under this heading refer to urbanization and are concerned with examining the urban situation rather than with analysing the process of urbanization. Population growth – including trends, projections, and general policy prescriptions – accounted for 14 per cent of all literature on population during 1971–6, while 12 per cent referred to fertility and 10 per cent to structure and composition of the population. Mortality and morbidity studies were very few (7 per cent), and international migration was almost entirely neglected during the period.

Nearly one-half (47 per cent) of the total stock of Indian population literature identified by Desai consisted of methodological exercises related to data collection, evaluation, processing and analysis, or general discussions of trends and status. Such studies fall precisely into the first two 'steps' in the evolution of population research referred to earlier (see Chapter 1, p. 16). They provide the basis for creating an awareness concerning the consequences of population trends for economic and social development. Materials concerned with the interaction between population and development variables (grouped by Desai under the three categories of consequences of population trends, their determinants, and interrelations between demographic and other socioeconomic factors) together accounted for less than one-third of the total volume with the bulk of the writings on determinants relating to fertility and family planning.

If the above classification of demographic research undertaken in India during the early 1970s is valid, we can conclude that population research has remained at a rather low level of development, with very little, if any, theoretical sophistication. Considering that India has had a well-defined population policy since 1952 and that basic data have been more plentiful than in other developing nations, research has lagged well behind the demands posed to population scholars by social, economic, and political events.

The classification of literature for the rest of Middle South Asia (again, including 'processed' as well as published materials, but here covering the period roughly 1950–76) yields a broadly similar picture. Here, too, family planning claims first place in descending order of importance, with 30 per cent of the total. Internal migration, including urbanization, has received considerably less attention (5 per cent), while population growth (including trends, projections, and general policy prescriptions) and general writings account for a much larger share of the total; together they form over 31 per cent of the literature as compared to the corresponding figure of 21 per cent for India. It may also be noted that international migration has received, comparatively speaking, more attention in the case of the rest of Middle South Asia, though still very little (3 per cent). Descriptive and methodological writings claim an even larger bulk of the total (60 per cent) than in India. Studies of consequences, determinants, and interrelations — represent only 21 per cent of the population literature of these six countries (Desai, 1978, Tables B1–B17).

The Data Base

The availability of basic demographic data in this subregion varies among the countries. Nevertheless, considering the overwhelming numerical preponderance of India's population, it can be argued that demographic data are available for most of the population of the subregion, unlike other developing regions. India possesses a sizeable data base, together with an infrastructure of institutions, centres, and official establishments that generate all manner of data on population. The basic sources of demographic data are: the decennial census, which has a 100-year history; the vital registration system, initiated in some parts at about the same time as the census; the National Sample Survey, established along with the introduction of planning; the Sample Registration Scheme, launched in the mid-sixties to provide an alternative source of estimates of vital rates to the vital registration system, which had always been grossly inadequate; and a great number of sample surveys on population variables, with an emphasis on fertility and family planning. A staggering quantity of raw statistics has accumulated and continues to do so at a rapid pace. Yet, for the purpose of research, it has been necessary for individual scholars to use all possible ingenuity to evaluate and process the data according to their own needs (Desai, 1978, pp. 34–5).

In Nepal a data base has been created by conducting three successive censuses (1952–4, 1961, and 1971). Analysis of the census data does not, however, seem to be well developed. In addition, a demographic sample survey was conducted in 1974–5.

Bangladesh and Pakistan share with India a common history of population census-taking and vital registration up to the time of independence in 1947. Between 1947 and 1971, in addition to census and vital registration data, efforts to produce up-to-date data on mortality and fertility in

Bangladesh and Pakistan included the Population Growth Estimation Project in the early 1960s, the National Impact Survey conducted during 1968-9, and the Population Growth Survey, begun about the same time. In 1974 Bangladesh conducted both a census and a Retrospective Survey of Fertility and Mortality.

To add to the significant wealth of data on the subregion, Nepal, Pakistan, and Sri Lanka have already published a first report within the World Fertility Survey programme and Bangladesh will be issuing one soon.

In addition to the data that can be considered of a traditional nature, Middle South Asia abounds in examples of non-traditional sources of data useful for population studies, such as village-level studies conducted by anthropologists, demographers, economists, and other social scientists. As in other developing regions, there is also a valuable fund of knowledge on population phenomena that has been generated by other kinds of studies, for example, in the field of regional development and urban planning.

To conclude, it appears as if Middle South Asia is one of the subregions of the developing world where a more ample data base exists.

Institutional and Human Resources

Considering the presence of Indian institutions and scholars, this subregion can perhaps be assessed as having a reasonably adequate capacity for demographic and related social science research. If this capacity is placed against the size of the subregion's population, however, then the emerging picture is of a deficient capacity. A survey undertaken on the occasion of the Second Asia Population Conference (UN, 1975, p. 401) reported that there were fifty-six institutions undertaking research and teaching in the population field in India. Of these institutions, ten had population and demography as their major field of interest. The largest group listed economics as their main area of emphasis, followed by social sciences, and two indicated the subject of family planning as their special concern. Many of these institutions offer training at the postgraduate level. Another training facility that has contributed significantly to the increased availability of personnel trained in population is the International Institute for Population Studies (IIPS), the first centre for demographic training and research established by the United Nations in 1957. Sponsored by the Indian government, the IIPS provides training at both the national and regional levels to prepare personnel capable of designing and carrying out scientific and didactic activities in the field of population. IIPS offers a one-year 'certificate' and a two-year 'diploma' course. Doctoral degrees awarded by the University of Bombay, with which IIPS is affiliated, can also be obtained in demography under the guidance of the institute. During the period 1957-71, almost

400 students graduated from IIPS, 79 per cent from the 'certificate' course. Only five students worked towards a Ph.D. degree in demography at IIPS during this period. The national distribution of graduates shows a very strong representation of Indian students (64 per cent). Less than 9 per cent of graduates were from Afghanistan, Iran, Nepal, Pakistan, and Sri Lanka, and the remainder came from other Asian countries.

The other countries that reported the existence of population research and training institutions to the UN survey were Pakistan (12),[14] Iran (6), and Sri Lanka (6), but only in Iran were some of these institutions primarily concerned with population and demography.

The UN Economic and Social Commission for Asia and the Pacific (ESCAP) also makes an important contribution to the training of personnel capable of carrying out different activities in the field of population. The Commission has regularly organized seminars and working groups in which valuable exchange of knowledge and experiences, particularly in the field of family planning programmes, has taken place. It has also convened numerous expert groups to examine specific fields of activity. These groups evaluate the situation in a specific field, recommending guidelines for its future development. One of the groups convened in 1977 examined the field of population and development planning.

Another important contribution of ESCAP, because of its value in maintaining liaison and communication between scholars of the region, is the publication of a *Directory of Key Personnel and Periodicals in the Field of Population* for the entire region and the quarterly *Asian and Pacific Population Programme News.* Another useful guide is the *Directory of Institutions Engaged in Research, Teaching and Training in Demography*, first published in 1972 and twice up-dated.

The preceding succinct examination of the institutional capacities for population teaching and research in Middle South Asian countries suggests that they are insufficient, with India enjoying a slight advantage over the others. While most of these governments seem to be seeking to implement population policies, our brief examination of the type of population studies undertaken in the recent past suggests that research remains at a rather incipient level of development. There is no doubt that descriptive and methodological research has been useful in identifying and quantifying the basic characteristics of specific demographic situations and their expected future evolution. In most circumstances, it has been the only basis for policy decisions. Policy-makers, however, require a better understanding of how demographic dynamics interact with social, economic, and political phenomena, which are precisely the areas to which public policies are generally addressed.

India, with a recognized tradition of research in the general social-science

[14] The data seem to refer to the period prior to the separation of Bangladesh and Pakistan.

area,[15] could probably play an important role in helping to support, expand, and strengthen the move already under way in the population field towards emphasizing theory construction and testing as a means of studying causation. There are already examples in India of the important contributions that scholars in disciplines other than demography, notably economics, can make. Top academic economists have not only contributed to the development of good scientific research, but have also played a significant role in policy-making. The task is one of going beyond the traditionally restricted definition of 'demographic' research.

References

Dandekar, Kumudini. 1977. 'Relationship between acceptance of contraception and socio-economic factors: comparative studies of Kerala and Uttar Pradesh.' In *International Population Conference, Mexico,* 2:357–74. Liège, Belgium: IUSSP.

Desai, P. B. 1978. 'Social Science Research on Population and Development in Middle South Asia.' Appendix 2 to the Final Report. El Colegio de México: IRG.

Keeley, Charles B. 1980. 'Asian Worker Migration to the Middle East.' Center for Policy Studies, Working Papers. New York: The Population Council.

Ratcliffe, John. 1978. 'Kerala: Testbed for Transition Theory.' *Populi,* 5 (2), 11–16.

United Nations Department of Economic and Social Affairs. 1974. *World Population Prospects as Assessed in 1973.* Population Studies, no. 60. ST/ESA/SER.A/60.

United Nations. 1975. The Population Debate: Dimensions and Perspectives. Population Studies, No. 57. ST/ESA/SER.A/57, Vol. 1, p. 401.

United Nations Population Commission. 1976. Preliminary Report on the Third Population Inquiry among Governments: Population Policies in the Context of Development in 1976. E/CN.9/XIX/CRP.6.

— 1976. 'Measures Undertaken at the National, Regional and International Levels to Implement the World Population Plan of Action.' E/CN.9/XIX/325.

World Bank. 1978. *World Development Report, 1978.* Washington, D.C.: World Bank.

[15] This is well documented by the series of surveys of research in the different social science fields published by the Indian Council of Social Science Research during the first half of the 1970s.

4 LATIN AMERICA[16]

Although Latin America is undoubtedly part of the underdeveloped world, the relatively advanced status it has when compared with other developing regions has led many to classify it as occupying an intermediate position in the international stratification. Demographic indicators also put the region in an intermediate position.

Basic Socioeconomic and Demographic Characteristics

The total fertility rate for Latin America as a whole has fallen steadily since 1955–60 and has recently been estimated to be 5.3. This is lower than the rates found in Africa and most of Asia. Life expectancy at birth (62 years) is also higher than in the other developing regions, but it is still 10 years less than in the already developed countries.

This combination of fertility and mortality rates has brought about one of the highest rates of natural growth in the developing world. Projections (medium variant) carried out by the Latin American Demographic Centre (CELADE) assume that the rate of growth will decline to 2.6 per cent by the year 2000. According to these projections, the total fertility rate is likely to fall from its present level of 5.3 to 3.97 in the period 1975–2000, a rather conservative decline considering the downward trend of fertility experienced by several countries of the region. At the same time, it is anticipated that life expectancy at birth will increase to 70 years in the same period.

On the basis of the above projections, CELADE has estimated that the population of economically active age (15–64 years) will increase from 54 to 58 per cent of the total by the end of the century. This increase at an average rate of 2.9 per cent per year — faster than the growth of the total population — from now to the year 2000 depends mainly on the current age structure of the population and a decline in the rate of mortality, and to a lesser extent on the decline in fertility that is projected to occur. The pace at which the population of economically active age is expected to grow indicates that the required rate of employment generation in Latin America during the next 15 to 20 years will be greater than in other developing regions.

[16] Most of the material for this chapter has been extracted from Urzúa, 1978b, IRG Appendix 11.

Latin America has experienced massive population redistributions. The proportion of the total population residing in urban areas[17] increased from approximately 26 per cent in 1950 to 45 per cent in 1975, and urban areas absorbed 65 per cent of the total population growth of the region during the same period. City primacy is also high: in fourteen countries more than 50 per cent of the urban population was residing in one city in 1975. On the other hand, the average annual rate of growth of the rural population (1.6 per cent between 1950 and 1975) shows a clear tendency towards decline, and in a few countries (Argentina, Chile, Uruguay, and Venzuela) the rural population has even declined in absolute numbers.

In sharp contrast with the high concentration of the urban population, the rural population is widely dispersed. For example, population census figures show that in six countries of the region the proportion living in places with 500 or fewer inhabitants ranged between 19 per cent in Argentina and more than 44 per cent in Ecuador.

A very tentative approximation of what the urban situation might be in the next 25 years has recently been made by the UN Economic Commission for Latin America (ECLA). Using national census definitions of urban (usually 2,000 inhabitants) and assuming the continuation of past trends, it is estimated that the urban population will increase from 194 million in 1975 to more than 460 million in the year 2000, an increase of more than 237 per cent. On the other hand, according to the same estimates, the rural population would increase only 25 per cent.

The above figures are all regional averages and hide wide inter-country differences. The recognition that various countries are going through different stages in the process of demographic change has led to attempts to classify the countries of the region into more homogeneous categories. A UN study adopted fertility and mortality rates as classification criteria and distinguished three main categories. The four countries (Argentina, Cuba, Chile, and Uruguay) placed in the first category account for 15 per cent of the region's population and have already reached fertility and mortality levels leading to moderate growth rates. The proportion of the population under age 15 has been declining in recent years, and will continue to do so in the future, while that of persons of economically active age will remain at present high levels or will increase. In 1975 over 65 per cent of their populations were living in localities of 20,000 or more inhabitants. Urbanization is expected to continue but at a slower pace than previously. Finally, with the exception of Cuba, the absolute size of the rural population of these countries will decline.

The second category is comprised of five countries (Brazil, Colombia, Costa Rica, Panamá, and Venezuela) with natural growth rates as high as the Latin American average, but where fertility has begun to fall, in some

[17] 'Urban' is here defined as places with populations of 20,000 or more.

cases significantly, in recent years.[18] Average life expectancy at birth is already over 60 years. In all of these countries, the proportion of the population under age 15 will decline sharply while that of economically active age will grow steadily from now to the end of the century. Urbanization in these countries is more recent than in the countries of the first group, but it has been particularly intensive in the last 25 years. Their rural population is still growing, but at the relatively low rate of 1.5 per cent or less annually.

The third group includes all the other Latin American countries and is characterized by having shown until very recently no clear indication of fertility decline. Three different subgroups are distinguished within it, according to their present mortality levels. Although it may be reasonably expected that the rate of natural population growth will decline more rapidly in the countries where mortality is presently lower, it has been estimated that the countries in this group will have population growth rates of around 2.5 per cent annually by the year 2000. Urbanization is still at relatively low levels, but it has accelerated over the last 25 years.

Intra-country differences with respect to both mortality and fertility must be added to those existing between countries. Almost all empirical evidence shows that rural fertility is higher than urban, the magnitude of the difference being related apparently to the level of fertility in the country as a whole. In a number of countries regional fertility differences are at least as large as rural–urban differences. At the same time, there are sharp regional differentials in mortality.

A word should be said about the countries of the Caribbean. Data collected by the UN in 1975 for the latest available year show a wide range of variation in fertility, mortality, and rates of natural increase. All of these countries have population densities higher than the rest of the region, but birth, death, and natural growth rates are lower than the Latin American average. Although there are differences between countries as to the intensity of the change, they have been experiencing a downward trend in crude birth rates since around 1965-6. Because of high emigration, the annual rates of population increase (about 2 per cent annually between 1950 and 1970) have been much lower than natural growth rates.

Along with high population growth rates and massive population redistributions, the region as a whole has been experiencing rather high rates of economic growth, whether measured from an historical or a comparative perspective. According to the most recent data available, the average annual growth rate of gross national product (GNP) rose from around 5 per cent during the 1950s to about 5.5 per cent in the 1960s, and to 6.3 per cent in the first half of the 1970s. The average growth of 5.5 per cent for the 1950–75 period implies a quadrupling of the Latin American product in the same period.

[18] The Dominican Republic and México should now be added to this category.

Because of high rates of population growth, per capita average growth of GNP between 1950 and 1975 was only 2.6. When shorter periods are considered, however, it is found that between 1967 and 1973 per capita growth averaged 3.7 for the region as a whole, and that Costa Rica, Panamá, the Dominican Republic, and Brazil had much higher per capita rates of growth.

Rapid economic growth in the region has radically changed the structure of production. Manufacturing industry contributed 18 per cent to the gross domestic product (GDP) in 1950 and 25 per cent in 1975, while the contribution of the agricultural sector declined even more than could have been expected because of the displacement of demand that usually accompanies higher income levels.

The proportion of the labour force employed in agriculture decreased in all countries, but employment in manufacturing industries experienced a much smaller growth than their share in the GDP, while it considerably increased in commerce, building and construction, and services. These trends in sectoral employment are closely related to the inability of recent and past economic growth to erradicate or significantly decrease wide differences in productivity between as well as within sectors of economic activity. The magnitude of these differences and the complexities of interchanges, dominance, and dependence between technologically 'modern', 'intermediate', and 'traditional' activities within national economic structures have led many to speak of the 'structural heterogeneity' of Latin America, as opposed to 'dualistic' economies in which two economic structures are assumed to co-exist almost independently.

Although the boundaries between 'modern', 'intermediate', and 'traditional' activities are sometimes difficult to define, recent estimates show that around 1970, for the region as a whole, the modern sector (mainly based in manufacturing industries and mining, and to a lesser extent agriculture) absorbed only 12 per cent of the labour force while accounting for 50 per cent of the production of goods; while the 'traditional' sector, heavily agricultural, absorbed one-third of employment and contributed only 5 per cent to GNP.

The most accepted view of this characteristic of contemporary economic change in Latin America is that modern, relatively high-productivity activities will continue to expand at a faster rate than other less technologically advanced activities, but that they will fail to absorb the greatest part of the labour force, which now subsists outside of them.

Structural heterogeneity goes together with a high concentration of modern economic activities in a small number of metropolitan areas. Thus, a recent study on the subject has estimated that the provinces (or states) of Buenos Aires and Santa Fé in Argentina; Guanabara, Rio, and São Paulo in Brazil; and the Federal District and the states of México and Nuevo León in México, produce 57.1 per cent of the total value of Latin American industrial output. The same pattern is repeated within all the countries for which information is available. Metropolitan areas concentrate not only a high proportion of the industrial product, but also those technical services and commercial and financial activities that complement the manufacturing sector. In addition, they are usually the seat of the main political and administrative authorities, as well as of the most important communication networks.

Although modern methods of production are still not very common in the Latin America agricultural sector, some important changes are also occurring in it. The increased demand for agricultural products, and particularly for foodstuff, of a growing population can be solved through expanding the agricultural frontier and/or improving the productivity of the land already under cultivation. Some countries — notably Brazil, México, Colombia, and Paraguay — have made efforts in the first direction, but in other countries the agricultural frontier is already almost exhausted, and in most of them the needed capital investment has made this strategy unfeasible. As a consequence, the area under cultivation has grown at a slow and declining rate, falling from 2.6 per cent between 1960 and 1965 to 0.5 per cent between 1970 and 1973 for Latin America as a whole.

The emergence of modern farms and plantations has not altered the old latifundio–minifundio complex nor the high degree of concentration of agricultural property. To change this situation, and at the same time increase productivity, a number of Latin American governments have approved more or less radical agrarian reform programmes, some of which have been implemented. Recent political changes as well as the high cost of these programmes, problems encountered in their implementation, weak political organization of the rural working classes, and other factors have gradually diminished their importance. Agricultural extension, the creation of rural social organizations, and community development programmes are seen as complementary measures to agricultural modernization along capitalistic lines.

The various ways in which agricultural production has been reorganized have deeply altered labour relations. A rural proletariat is now found in connection with plantations and agricultural farms, while old 'peon' relationships on latifundia have to different degrees been replaced by at least partial cash payment. In addition, co-operative forms of labour relations are found in many countries, while independent minifundia owners have shown no sign of disappearing or even decreasing. These changes have increased the 'structural heterogeneity' of the sector: archaic latifundia, modern plantations and commercial farms, minifundia of different types, Indian communal lands, and agrarian reform settlements can all be found in a single country, many times linked by a number of mutually sustaining relations.

Some rough estimates of the impact the trends in economic change and development described above have had on income distribution are available. Information for Argentina, Brazil, Chile, Colombia, México, Paraguay,

Honduras, and Venezuela has been used by ECLA to estimate per capita income in 1960 dollars as well as changes in the share of the various socioeconomic strata in the total income of the region. The share of the 50 per cent poorest strata remained practically unchanged in the following ten-year period, but among them, the relative position of the 20 per cent poorest worsened somewhat, while the gains of the following 30 per cent amounted to 15.4 per cent of the total income increase experienced in the decade. At the other end, the share of the 10 and the 5 per cent highest strata decreased, while the following 20 per cent experienced a substantial increase. In other words, inequality within the 50 per cent lowest strata has increased, but concentration at the top has decreased somewhat, with the middle income groups having obtained the lion's share of income increases in the decade.

These changes correspond to those shown by the occupational statistics for the same period, namely, the rise in the relative importance of the urban middle and upper strata, a trend common to all countries for which information is available, except Uruguay. Both trends combined are expected to give a reasonable degree of political stability to the prevailing style of development because the groups that have gained something greatly outnumber those that have not, and the highest gains are naturally found among the better-educated and better-organized upper–middle groups, whose support should be particularly essential.

Summarizing the major recent trends in economic and social development of the region, Latin America has been experiencing high rates of total and per capita economic growth, which have brought about important changes in the productive structure and in the sectoral and regional distribution of employment. At the same time, sharp contrasts between technologically advanced and traditional activities have remained or have been accentuated both in rural and urban areas; income distribution remains highly unequal, but there has been a tendency for middle–income groups to increase their share, and the middle occupational strata have considerably expanded.

Population Issues and Government Positions on Population

Imbalances between labour force supply and demand, widespread poverty and malnutrition, and housing, health, and educational deficits are among the problems that Latin American governments are trying to solve in different ways and on which population trends are considered to have some influence.

It is generally recognized that the characteristics of Latin American economic development and the demographic trends related to them are at the basis of the pervasive employment problems being faced by Latin American countries. Total labour underutilization in the region was an estimated 27 per cent of the economically active population in 1970. Only 20 per cent of that underutilization has been attributed to open unemployment, the other 80 per cent being different forms of under-employment, more or less equally divided between rural and urban areas. Open unemployment is estimated to be no more than 2 per cent of the agricultural labour force, but it is considerably higher in urban areas. On the other hand, massive underemployment in rural areas brings total underutilization of the rural labour force to 29 per cent, as against 25 per cent in towns. Nevertheless, roughly 60 per cent of total under-utilization − unemployment and underemployment included − of the labour force is concentrated in cities and towns.

Students of the subject tend to agree that, perhaps with a few short-lived exceptions, no matter how fast the modern sector might grow, its absolute size is too small to accommodate an ever-increasing labour force created by the combined influences of high rates of urban natural growth and rural–urban migration. This conclusion clearly poses the problem of finding a style of development that can combine rapid growth and high labour force absorption, with policies aimed at provoking a sustained decline in fertility so as to reduce the dependency burden of those of working age and to, eventually, slow the growth of their absolute numbers. A failure to find such a combination will make even worse a situation that has already reached dramatic dimensions.

While recent trends in economic development are leading to high income concentration, at the other end of the scale are large numbers of individuals living under conditions of extreme poverty throughout Latin America. Recent estimates based on a minimum balanced diet according to national nutritional patterns show that about 35 per cent of the population in nine Latin American countries have income below the cost of that diet.

Malnutrition among children under 5 years of age is one of the most serious problems. Sample surveys conducted in thirteen Latin American countries and three English-speaking Caribbean countries between 1965 and 1970 found percentages of undernourished children ranging between 37 and 80. Second-degree undernourishment (weight 25 per cent below normal) affected 20 per cent or more of the sample in five countries, with the highest rates found in Central America and the Caribbean. Rightly so, poverty and malnutrition are two closely related problems the govern-ments of the region are concerned about.

Housing is a third problem very much discussed in recent years, particu-larly with respect to its deficiencies in the larger urban centres. It has been estimated that in 1970 the urban housing deficit in Latin America was 8.9 million units while the usually forgotten rural deficit reached 9.9 million units. The urban housing problem is further compounded by the presence of rapidly growing shanty towns, which are ecologically isolated from the rest of the urban environment and have almost no physical infrastructure.

Pressures to expand formal education are another consequence of demographic and socioeconomic changes. Primary school enrolment has grown steadily in most countries, and the proportion of the population receiving no schooling is now relatively small. Despite that progress, however, the population with no formal schooling has increased in absolute numbers for the region as a whole, and national proportions still vary between 20 and 40 per cent of the population of primary school age, except in Argentina, Costa Rica, Cuba, Chile, and Uruguay, where the proportion is lower.

Employment problems, poverty and malnutrition, housing deficits, and shortages of basic health and education services (in general and for specific areas and social groups) are some of the primary problems that have been identified as derived from prevailing demographic and economic trends. The need to solve these problems and the belief that they are influenced by the patterns of population growth and distribution are the main reasons why interest in formulating population policies is growing in Latin America.

About the beginning of the 1960s there was little or no awareness in the region of the way demographic factors relate to employment, income distribution, poverty, malnutrition, housing, health, or education, and are relevant for the success or failure of socioeconomic policies aimed at solving problems in those areas. The situation is quite different now. After a period of heated arguments for and against population policies and, more specifically, fertility-regulating policies, the debate now centres around determining how, when, and for what purposes population variables can be introduced into social and economic planning.

There seems to be agreement now that if population policies are not identical with development policies, neither are they solely aimed at reducing fertility. On the contrary, deliberate actions to influence any of the demographic variables are defined as population policy actions. Thus, family planning programmes are considered a part of fertility-reducing policies but by no means identical to population policies. Thus defined, policies are formally orientated by a value framework strongly rejecting foreign intervention and pressures in the decision-making process as well as the use of coercive means to achieve desired goals. The consensus reached on a broad definition of population policies as well as on the value framework orientating them has been further strengthened by agreement on the need to make population policies an integral part of development policies.

With respect to the sensitive issues of fertility-reducing policies, besides the previously mentioned value framework and the insistence on relating them to development, a number of governments make a distinction between birth control and family planning, acknowledging support of the latter but not the former. Birth control, according to this distinction, corresponds to a fertility-reducing policy, while family planning is a family welfare policy orientated towards reducing induced abortion and maternal and infant morbidity and mortality caused by highparity and closely spaced births.

Despite the collectively agreed upon precautions and guidelines for action given above, Latin American governments have been reluctant to make public statements regarding the measures they are taking in the area of fertility. In fact, the process of policy adoption and implementation in this field has been in general very gradual, starting with private family planning programmes and slowly moving towards government supported programmes and formal policy statements.

At the beginning of 1978 the positions of Latin American and Caribbean governments on fertility-reducing and family planning policies were as follows:

1. Eight countries (Barbados, Colombia, Dominican Republic, El Salvador, Guatemala, Jamaica, México, and Trinidad-Tobago) have adopted policies to reduce fertility as a means of decreasing over-all population growth. Some of the countries have set quantitative targets and most of them have declared that the policy is intended to achieve a better balance among resources, possibilities of development, and demographic growth. All have implemented a government-sponsored family planning programme.

2. Twelve countries (Brazil, Chile, Costa Rica, Cuba, Ecuador, Haiti, Honduras, Nicaragua, Panamá, Paraguay, Perú, and Venezuela) have either included the delivery of family planning services within their official health programmes or have allowed private institutions to use government installations for that purpose. In all these cases it has been declared that the policy is not directly concerned with population growth, but was adopted in recognition of the duty of the State to provide these services to improve maternal and child health.

3. In three countries (Argentina, Bolivia, and Uruguay), only private programmes are allowed to operate.

While the development plans of the majority of Latin American governments include population redistribution as a problem to be solved, relatively few have implemented specific policies related to population distribution. Brazil, Colombia, Venezuela, and México have explicit and specific policies, and Argentina, Cuba, and Chile have regional development policies and some public measures orientated towards adjusting the pattern of population distribution to development objectives. Bolivia, Ecuador, Panamá, Costa Rica, Nicaragua, Honduras, El Salvador, Haiti, and the Dominican Republic formally regard population redistribution as a problem, but have no explicit policy to solve it. And Guatemala, Paraguay and Uruguay do not consider population redistribution in their development plans at all.

Most Caribbean countries have at least an implicit policy of trying to slow down the rate of growth of the principal urban centre, mainly through rural development measures and redirecting the allocation of industries.

As for policies with respect to international migration, a negative evaluation of the impact of immigration of unskilled workers has led some countries to establish legal restrictions on it. This notwithstanding, a number of bilateral and multilateral agreements attempting to protect migrants in this category have been signed by Latin American governments.

The policies of many Latin American governments towards selective immigration of professional, administrative, and highly trained workers are, on the other hand, positive and designed to encourage it. For instance, three Latin American countries — Bolivia (1976), Honduras (1971), and Paraguay (1974) — have modified their migration laws with the specific purpose of making immigration more attractive to this type of worker. Furthermore, Argentina, Bolivia, Brazil, Chile, Colombia, Costa Rica, Ecuador, El Salvador, Honduras, México, Nicaragua, Panamá, Paraguay, Perú, Dominican Republic, Uruguay, and Venezuela are participating in the programme of selective migration to Latin America organized by the Inter-Governmental Committee for European Migrations. Most Caribbean countries and territories, however, require work permits, which are in theory given only if no nationals are available to fill the specific post, for skilled workers and professionals to be accepted as legal migrants.

Although emigration of unskilled workers has been included as one of the critical situations on which action was recommended at the Second Latin American Meeting on Population (1975), only Colombia and Mexico have specific policies designed to solve some of the problems faced by migrants of this type, and none has a policy aimed directly at reducing it. Haiti, the Dominican Republic, and the English-speaking Caribbean countries encourage this type of migration as one way of solving unemployment problems and of reducing population growth.

Finally, a number of governments have attempted to reverse the trend towards the emigration of professionals and skilled workers by waiving the payment of customs duties and making other legal exceptions for those returning home.

All the above developments are clear demonstrations that Latin American governments are ready and willing to integrate population policies into regional and sectoral policies, and more generally, into development plans. In addition, the number of national population councils already organized to that purpose provide the institutional arrangements for formulating and implementing such policies.

Status of Population Research, Data Base, and Institutional and Human Resources for Research

Recent Research Directions

Population research in Latin America has moved along a continuum from basic demographic analysis of available data to the construction of elaborate theoretical frames attempting to explain the relation of demographic behaviour to structural aspects, such as the over-all style of development, the organization of the labour market, political processes, and the power structure.

A systematic and concerted effort — guided primarily by the Latin American Demographic Centre (CELADE) — to exploit analytically the available data, including the application of methods of indirect measurement, provided most Latin American countries and the region as a whole early in the 1960s with a reasonably accurate picture of their demographic situation and future population perspectives. The monitoring of demographic trends in the region has been instituted as a permanent exercise. This type of research, mainly descriptive, greatly contributed to increasing the awareness of population problems in general as well as their specific nature.

Because of their importance in shaping the demographic trends prevalent in most countries of the region, the study of fertility and migration also received early attention in the region. By the mid-1960s, several Latin American countries had undertaken studies of urban fertility based on comparative surveys. These were later complemented by studies of small cities and rural areas. While not very elaborate theoretically, these studies mark the beginning of important research on fertility that was conducted in the years following their execution.

The same can be said of internal migration studies, which were also undertaken in several cities in the early 1960s. These studies provided the first indications of the magnitude and characteristics of the rural-urban migration flow and offered a basis for the planning of more elaborate investigations, some of which concentrated on the analysis of determinants of migration, including structural ones. More recently some studies have been carried out that attempt to broaden the consideration of consequences of migration beyond the individual level (Urzúa, 1978b, pp. 108–12).

Despite the above contributions, research on population continued for many years to be primarily concerned with measurement on a rather aggregated scale. Little effort was made in these initial stages in the direction of theory construction to explain the relation of demographic phenomena with other socioeconomic factors. Efforts with this objective in mind started to appear in the region in the latter part of the 1960s and early 1970s. Both national institutions and the Latin American Faculty of Social Sciences (FLACSO) and CELADE began to examine the relation of employment, urbanization, rural development, and class structure to population growth and distribution.

The Commission on Population and Development of the Latin American Council of Social Sciences (CLACSO), through its working groups on internal migration, processes of reproduction of the population,[19] and

---

[19] This working group's area of study includes both biological processes and reproduction of the population and social processes of reproduction of the labour force.

systems of integrated sociodemographic information, has contributed in a significant manner to laying the ground for further theoretical work on some of the above-mentioned topics.

As a fourth working group of that Commission, a regional programme of social research on population and development (PISPAL) was launched in 1973 in which thirteen Latin American research centres are currently participating. This programme has helped to attract to the population research field professionals of several disciplines (sociology, economics, political science, social history, anthropology, and urban planning), which has led to a wide diversification in the topics of research and to serious efforts to fill the gap in knowledge of the relationships between population processes and the processes of economic and social development. Through its programme of research grants, PISPAL has fostered research exploring the mutual interaction of population processes with agrarian structures, urban development, colonization schemes, social institutional arrangements, political participation, salary policies, and employment policies and strategies.

Some attention has also been paid in the region to research related to the measurement of the impact of family planning programmes. Progress along this line of research has been modest, however, for two reasons. First, until very recently, data emanating from the programmes were not adequate for this purpose. Secondly, the methods of analysis used have not succeeded in disentangling the effects of the programmes from other non-programmatic factors.

In summary, demographic research in Latin America seems to have achieved a certain degree of maturity. The constant monitoring of demographic trends seems to be assured and the broadening of the field to encompass the study of the relations between population and development seems to be well under way.[20]

The Data Base

In general, the Latin American countries have a certain tradition of census-taking, particularly in the population field. During the latter part of 1940 plans were laid down for taking the 1950 population censuses on a comparative basis in terms of concepts included in the questionnaires and their definition. This approach was also taken for the 1960 and 1970 round of censuses and it is planned for the 1980 censuses. The Inter-American Statistical Institute (IASI) has been the co-ordinating agency of these concerted programmes, which have allowed Latin America to achieve an extraordinary record of census-taking for a developing region, with

---

[20] The review prepared by Raúl Urzúa for the IRG (Appendix 11) describes in detail the specific lines being followed in this type of research in the region. In addition, PISPAL published in 1975 and 1976 inventories of population research undertaken during different periods in Argentina, Brazil, Colombia, Chile, and México.

between twenty-two and twenty-four censuses taken during each of the 10-year periods since 1946. These figures indicate that most countries of the region have had regular decennial censuses in the last three decades. In many cases the record of decennial censuses goes back to the beginning of this century and in some cases even earlier.

Contrary to the development achieved in census-taking, many countries of the region have poor vital registration systems, which makes the estimation of current fertility and mortality levels difficult. To remedy this lack, several countries of the region have taken sample surveys to obtain measures of fertility and mortality. These surveys have been of two types: the following of a selected population over a period of time by means of repeated interviews, and single interview surveys to gather retrospective data. In the last few years eleven countries of the region have undertaken fertility surveys as part of the World Fertility Survey programme.

An almost untapped source of basic demographic data is that collected by the social security systems. In several countries of the region these systems cover significant proportions of the population about which they gather information that could be used for research purposes.

Another development worth mentioning regarding the data base for population research is the effort being made by a group of Latin American social scientists to define the type of data that should be collected to improve sociodemographic research.

Finally, an important shortcoming in the Latin American data base is the highly aggregated manner in which statistics are customarily made available both in geographical terms and in terms of the different social groups. This, in turn, is reflected in the lack of detail with which demographic trends and related factors are treated in research. Also, as compared to Africa and Asia, there have been fewer studies of villages or other rural communities.

Institutional and Human Resources[21]

The institution that has contributed the most to the training of demographers in the Latin American region is CELADE. The teaching and training activities of the Centre have taken many forms: (i) intramural first- and second-year courses on demographic analysis; (ii) a programme of specialization lasting three years; (iii) in-service training for research fellows; (iv) a master's course in economics with specialization in demography; (v) different types of short seminars to train professionals in specific subjects (i.e. techniques of evaluation of family-planning programmes, use of computers in demographic analysis); and (vi) a series of national intensive courses in demography given in fifteen countries of the region. Recently, CELADE has added a master's degree programme in

[21] For a more detailed country-by-country review of population research and training institutions in Latin America, see Urzúa, 1978a, IRG Appendix 12.

Social Sciences in Population, which is being conducted in collaboration with FLACSO. More than 1,000 students have benefited from these different courses. Undoubtedly, during the first years, the most important contribution was the training of demographic analysts, many of whom are at present working in government departments and universities of the region. During the years 1958–77, CELADE trained close to 400 professionals from twenty Latin American countries and Puerto Rico at different levels of proficiency in demographic analysis. In general, it can be said that in each country of the region there is now at least a critical minimum number of persons who can undertake demographic analysis. (This is not to say, however, that all of these persons are actually working in the field of demography.)

CELADE's contribution to the development of demography is not limited to the training of personnel. Since the mid-1960s the Centre has had an active research programme that began by paying preferential attention to formal demographic analysis, moving later into the field of the relations between population and development, and entering in the early 1970s the population policy research area. CELADE has also developed a very extensive programme of specialized publications that includes a quarterly, *Notas de Población*, and a bi-annual, *Boletín Demográfico*.

When the capabilities for teaching and research in the region are examined, special mention should be made of the Centre for Economic and Demographic Studies (CEED) located at El Colegio de México. Founded in 1964, CEED offers a master's degree in demography and has contributed to the training of a significant number of Mexican scholars as well as students from other parts of Latin America. Its research programme reflects some of the interests of the Mexican government, and several of its contributions are associated with the stance recently taken by the government regarding the national population policy. The Centre publishes the quarterly, *Demografía y Economía*.

There are two other institutions in the region that both offer postgraduate degrees and conduct research in population. These are the Centre for Regional Planning and Development (CEDEPLAR) of the Minas Gerais Federal University of Brazil and the Centre for Demographic Studies (CEDEM) of the University of Havana, Cuba. The Catholic University in Perú offers a master's degree in sociology with a major in demography. In addition to the teaching activities referred to above, an undergraduate programme in statistics and demography has recently been started at the University of Nuevo León in Monterrey, México. The institutions embarked solely on research are much more numerous. A national institution deserving particular mention, especially because of its contribution to research, is the population centre functioning within the Brazilian Institute of Statistics and Geography (IBGE). This centre was founded in early 1940, and during its early years contributed significantly to the development of population research in general and to the study of the Brazilian population in particular. Unfortunately, during a long period the centre was largely inactive, but recently, with an upsurge of interest in population studies in Brazil, primarily promoted by an awards competition initiated some years ago by the Ford Foundation, the IBGE centre has begun to increase its activities and is now publishing a quarterly bulletin.

The Institute of Social Research of the Mexican National Autonomous University (ISUNAM) has been a pioneer in promoting social science research in population in Latin America. It has been joined in the last decade by several important centres, both official and private. Some of them are: the Population Studies Centre (CENEP) in Argentina; the Brazilian Centre for Analysis and Planning (CEBRAP); the Regional Population Centre (CCRP) in Colombia; and the Institute of Social and Population Studies (IDESPO) in Costa Rica. With the exception of the last, all of these institutions plus another group of ten centres collaborate in the Programme of Social Science Research on Population and Development in Latin America (PISPAL). While they are perhaps the leading social science research centres in the region, they in no way exhaust the list of those working in this field. With the exception of two international centres working at the regional level and the Mexican ISUNAM, the rest of those belonging to PISPAL are private institutions not directly attached to any university programme. This imposes certain limitations on their contribution to the field. The first relates to the utilization of their research findings. Governments might not pay the same degree of attention to their research findings as they would if these centres were official institutions. Secondly, not being university institutions, their potential as a place to train young social scientists is not fully realized.

Because many of the graduates from CELADE returned to work in government departments, particularly national offices of statistics, in several countries of the region (Argentina, Bolivia, Costa Rica, Cuba, Chile, Ecuador, Panamá, and Perú) these offices have established population units that contribute to basic demographic analysis. Perhaps the most significant recent development in the area of government involvement in population-orientated research is the organization (either within the planning ministry or the body with executive responsibility for population policy) of a small corp of professionals from various disciplines entrusted with the task of preparing studies to help the decision-making processes. Examples of this can be found in Bolivia, Colombia, Costa Rica, México, Panamá, Paraguay, and the Dominican Republic.

Finally, as in other developing regions, there is the contribution to research of international organizations. FLACSO is not only collaborating with CELADE in an interdisciplinary postgraduate programme on population and playing an active part in the development of the PISPAL programme, but has several social scientists permanently engaged in population research at its headquarters in Buenos Aires, Quito, and Santiago. The UN Economic Commission for Latin America (ECLA) also contributes to research in this area, primarily through its Social Development Division. The Regional Employment Programme for Latin America and the Caribbean (PREALC) completes the network of regional institutions more actively engaged in population and related research of direct relevance to policy formation.

In summary, while the institutional and human resource capacities for population research in Latin America are not equally distributed among the different countries, they are not insignificant. Capabilities should be strengthened in some countries, and certain specific kinds of training, such as that related to the inclusion of population policies in development planning, need to be developed. What appears to be the most urgent need is to establish an adequate link between policy-makers and research institutions and scholars in order to ensure that greater utilization of research findings is made by the former and more attention is paid by the latter to the potential use that policy-makers can make of research results.

References

United Nations. 1976. *Demographic Yearbook, 1975.* New York: United Nations.
Urzúa, Raúl. 1978a. 'Population Research and Training Institutions in Latin America.' Appendix 12 to the Final Report. El Colegio de México: IRG.
— 1978b. 'Social Science Research on Population and Development in Latin America.' Appendix 11 to the Final Report. El Colegio de México: IRG.

5   SOUTH-EAST AND EAST ASIA[22]

Basic Socioeconomic and Demographic Characteristics

South-East and East Asia encompasses an area with perhaps 1,280 to 1,430 million inhabitants in 1975[23] — a figure representing 30 per cent of the world's population and over 40 per cent of that of the developing world. As the scene of marked declines in both mortality and fertility and of widespread implementation of fertility control policies of a type and with a degree of success found only occasionally elsewhere, the region has attracted considerable attention among demographers in recent years.

Yet, as in the case of the other developing regions reviewed above, South-East and East Asia comprises a very varied group of countries, both in terms of demographic characteristics and of socioeconomic and political organization. In fact, the region can be conveniently divided into three segments, or groups of countries, for analytical purposes. Segment 1 includes China, an enormous state with at least two-thirds of the region's total population, singled out due to its distinctive political system and uncertain demographic situation. The members of the Association of South-East Asian Nations (Indonesia, Malaysia, Philippines, Singapore, and Thailand) plus South Korea, Taiwan, and Hong Kong comprise Segment 2. With a population of just over 300 million, these eight countries are characterized by economies patterned along the Western model and Western influence in other spheres as well. Finally, Segment 3 includes the three nations of Indochina (Vietnam, Kampuchea, and Laos) plus Burma and North Korea, with roughly 130 million inhabitants. The most heterogeneous of the three segments, this group of political entities has maintained a degree of isolation from Western contact and has a socialist political organization.

The paucity of data available on China's population size and growth rate, let alone for more sophisticated indexes, makes it a demographic enigma. However, estimates place its total population at approximately 836 million (World Bank, 1978, Table 1). The crude birth- and death-rates for 1975 have been estimated at 26 and 9 per 1,000, respectively, producing the rather low rate of natural increase of 1.7 per cent

[22] This chapter draws on Jones (1978) and Caldwell and Caldwell (1978), IRG Appendices 3 and 4 respectively.

[23] The range is due to differing estimates of China's population.

per year and an expectation of life at birth of 62 years (World Bank, 1978). These figures constitute evidence of a marked decline in mortality over the last few decades and a much more precipitous and recent fall in fertility. Certainly, concerted attempts to increase the availability of medical services, to change attitudes towards marriage, to exert pressure for smaller families through economic planning targets, to uproot Confucian principles, and to change the system of pay for women workers have combined to produce a significant impact on vital rates in China (Goodstadt, 1978). But, as Aird (1978) has pointed out, data are incomplete, sometimes visibly defective, and mostly from atypical units and should therefore be viewed critically. In terms of GNP per capita, the amount of $410 in 1975 was considerably lower than that for most Segment 2 countries. The level of urbanization (around 20 per cent) and rate of urban growth from 1970 to 1975 (3.3 per cent) were likewise lower than comparable figures for nations grouped in Segment 2.

In contrast with the Chinese case, the dramatic economic and demographic changes experienced — perhaps more rapidly than in any other region of the world — by most Segment 2 countries in recent years have been well documented. In fact, these countries have been viewed as a type of laboratory for the examination of change. Every country has experienced some fertility decline. Such decline has been spectacular in Singapore (where replacement-level fertility was achieved in 1975 with a fall in the birth-rate from 28.3 to 17.8 in a ten-year period) and Hong Kong, considerable in Korea, Taiwan, Thailand, and parts of Indonesia, and moderate in Malaysia. Similarly, mortality levels in 1975 ranged from a low of 5 per 1,000 in Singapore, Hong Kong, and Taiwan to 10 in Thailand and the Philippines and 17 in Indonesia. Indeed, the life expectancies of the first three nations are only a few years lower than the average reported for the industrialized world (World Bank, 1978, Tables 15 and 17).

Selected indicators of socioeconomic development tend to further document the 'success stories' of a number of Segment 2 countries. Annual growth in GNP per capita in the 1960–76 period generally exceeded the levels achieved by other developing regions, reaching 7.5 and 7.3 per cent in the case of Singapore and South Korea. Per capita GNP exceeds $1,000 in Taiwan ($1,070), Hong Kong ($2,110), and Singapore ($2,700); lies between $500 and $1,000 in Korea ($670) and Malaysia ($860); and is under $500 only in Indonesia, Thailand, and the Philippines. Industrial growth from 1970 to 1976 was also quite high, ranging from 7 or 8 per cent per year in Hong Kong, Thailand, and the Philippines to an impressive 14 and 17 per cent in Taiwan and South Korea, respectively. Adult literacy in 1974 exceeded 80 per cent in all countries except Malaysia (60), Indonesia (62), and Singapore (75), and in the cases of Hong Kong and South Korea surpassed the 90 per cent mark.

In contrast with the performance of the majority of the countries classified in Segment 2, the situation in Indo-China, Burma, and North Korea is rather bleak. Although data are not readily available for Indo-China — a region plagued by military conflict — crude birth rates are reported to exceed 40 per 1,000 and the expectation of life at birth is only 40 in Laos and 45 in Kampuchea and Vietnam. Birth rates are slighly lower and life expectancies slightly higher for Burma and to a greater degree, for North Korea. In terms of per capita GNP, one again finds these countries at the lower end of the scale, with values ranging from $70 to $160. Only North Korea ($470) has a figure comparable to those of Segment 2 countries.

Population Issues and Government Positions on Population

Perhaps the foremost policy concern in the South-East and East Asian region as a whole is population growth. But, once again, governments have adopted different — and sometimes diametrically opposed — stances regarding this and other population issues. Therefore, it is important to maintain the tripartite grouping of countries outlined above in the discussion that follows.

Segment 2 countries are probably the only group of near contiguous nations that explicitly accept the thesis that their economic growth would be accelerated if their rate of population growth were reduced. The economic plans of Korea, Thailand, the Philippines, Indonesia, and Malaysia all point out the negative effects of rapid population growth, specifically mentioning employment, education, and housing problems. China has also firmly committed itself to the reduction of population growth and — along with the Segment 2 countries of South Korea, Malaysia, Taiwan, and Thailand — has established a quantitative target for the rate of natural increase. Segment 3 nations, on the other hand, do not generally accept this premise. Burma and Laos have expressed satisfaction with their present growth rate. Vietnam is the exception in so far as it has adopted growth targets that suggest that it views a lower rate of population growth as beneficial.

Policies designed to reduce fertility were adopted in the region throughout the 1960s and 1970s: China (1962), Singapore (1965), Malaysia (1966), Indonesia (1968), the Philippines and Thailand (1970), Korea (1971), Hong Kong (1973), and Vietnam (1977). All these countries operate vigorous government-sponsored family planning programmes geared to fertility control (Hong Kong is the exception, with private programmes), although the goals of improving maternal and child health and the status of women are also acknowledged. The programmes do, however, differ greatly in their costs (ranging from half of the health budget in South Korea to less than 1 per cent of it in Thailand) and strategies (post-partum programmes in South Korea and Singapore, use of co-operative organizations in the Philippines, and mobile teams in Malaysia, to mention just a few examples). Singapore's family planning programme is by far the most aggressive of Segment 2 countries; the government is concentrating all efforts towards the goal of the two-child family as the social norm. There is evidence of increasing pressure for young women to have only two births in China as well (Aird, 1978).

Government policies regarding fertility control in South-East and East Asia have indeed contained a certain degree of coercion, particularly in terms of incentives and disincentives, and this has become a source of controversy in the region. Incentives for family planning such as compensation payments have been tried in South Korea. Disincentives — first employed in Singapore later in South Korea, Taiwan, and the Philippines — include reduced maternity leave and reduced pay while on leave, loss of priority for public housing, and cancellation of tax exemptions and allowances for more than two or three children.

Policies in the health field that might have an impact on mortality levels in the region do not generally identify specific goals. Nearly every development plan does, however, express the broad intention to improve health facilities and services, that is, in terms of measurable indices such as number of physicians and proportion of population having access to piped and treated water and to sanitary toilet facilities. In addition, nearly every Segment 2 country is committed to some kind of rural health service; China has also devoted considerable efforts to expanding medical services to rural areas. Clearly, Hong Kong and Singapore have already attained the health levels of the industrialized world, while most other Segment 2 nations and North Korea anticipate doing so by the end of the century. For the remaining Segment 3 countries, that target appears to be further off.

With an average annual growth of its urban population on the order of 4 to 5 per cent during the first five years of this decade (World Bank, 1978, Table 13), there is generalized concern in the region over the effects of rapid urbanization. Governments are particularly apprehensive of the growth of primate cities, especially in Indonesia, Thailand (where Bangkok is roughly forty-five times bigger than Chiang Mai, the second largest city), and the Philippines. The debate over the role of the primate city and the appropriateness of a medium-city development strategy is as yet unresolved, but problems of employment as well as in the provision of adequate housing, education, and health services are becoming more acute. According to an ESCAP estimate, between 20 and 25 per cent of the urban population of Vietnam and the Philippines live in slums and squatter settlements.

In view of this situation, most Segment 2 countries have adopted policies ranging from alternative urban growth centres to integrated rural development schemes and, in some cases, resettlement programmes.

Indonesia has the most conspicuous internal migration policy. Extreme population pressure on the islands of Java and Bali and the availability of unused land on the outer islands led the Indonesian government to implement a transmigration programme aimed at accelerating the economic development of the resettled areas as well as alleviating population pressure on overcrowded Java and Bali. Rural–urban migration was further checked in this nation when the Jakarta governor announced a 'closed city' policy in 1970. In addition to this so-called 'sponsored' redistribution of population, significant spontaneous movements to virgin or underutilized land have also occurred in Thailand, the Philippines, and Malaysia. In Segment 1 and 3 countries there is much greater control over both urbanization and internal movements. Both Kampuchea and Vietnam (where the government has announced an ambitious regional development plan designed to substantially reduce the number of inhabitants of Ho Chi Minh City, formerly Saigon) have recently moved urban populations into rural areas, while China has a considerable history of doing so.

International migration has not generally been considered a population issue in the region, but recently some governments have expressed concern over the movement of substantial numbers of political refugees, particularly from former Indochina to Thailand, Malaysia, Singapore, Indonesia, and Australia. Hong Kong and Taiwan have also accepted persons from China. Although the acceptor countries have not acted in a concerted manner to cope with this problem, some are becoming less inclined to admit any more refugees and all make permanent immigration nearly impossible. Thus, the refugee problem will probably remain a controversial topic. In addition, some nations such as Thailand and the Philippines lose a considerable number of medical personnel through migration to the Western developed countries. However, the migration of highly skilled manpower does not appear to be as acute or as generalized as in other developing regions.

Status of Population Research, Data Base, and Institutional and Human Resources for Research

Recent Research Directions

Demographic research in South-East and East Asia has been mainly concerned with measuring levels, patterns, and trends in fertility and internal population distribution and − to a lesser degree − mortality. International migration has not been a subject of study in this region, although the political refugee problem has aroused concern recently. Research on socio-economic and demographic interrelationships has been receiving increased attention, but has thus far concentrated on the analysis of fertility differentials, migration selectivity and the factors account for such differentials. Before outlining the major trends in research activities by demographic variable, it should be mentioned that the vast majority of demographic studies referred to here are concentrated in Segment 2 countries. This is because the IRG did not have access to sufficient information on the status of population research in Segment 1 and 3 nations. However, judging from the paucity of demographic data on China (Aird, 1978) and the countries grouped together in Segment 3, it would appear that relatively few studies have been conducted.

Fertility studies in the region are the most numerous and have examined the rather substantial declines in birth-rates registered in many Segment 2 nations, notably in Thailand, Indonesia, the Philippines, Singapore, and West Malaysia in South-East Asia and Taiwan and Korea in East Asia. In addition to attempting to understand the influence of factors such as place of residence, husband's occupation, and wife's labour force participation and education, research has revealed the important role that rising age at marriage has played in lowering fertility throughout the region. China is perhaps the most extreme example, with minimum ages of 24 years for females and 26 for males and even higher ages for Party members being strongly urged.

Considerable research into the impact of family-planning programmes on fertility has also been undertaken. In fact, of the five developing regions that fall within the IRG's purview, South-East and East Asia undoubtedly have the largest number of studies designed to test ways of improving programmes through altering the emphasis placed on different methods or on reaching different groups, the methods of communication used, the content of the messages, the supply and management systems adopted, and so forth. Taiwan, for example, has been the focus of a tremendous variety of research projects built into a series of national KAP and acceptor follow-up surveys. Studies of this kind have been conducted in most other countries with family planning programmes, but unfortunately − unlike the case of Taiwan − they have tended to be of an *ad hoc* and arbitrary nature. The need for a goal-orientated and carefully designed research programme to guide the development and reform of family planning programmes can hardly be overemphasized (Jones, 1978, p. 45).

One related regional current of research, based on the testing of a conceptual framework for childbearing motivation and family size limitation, is the Value of Children Project, begun in 1972. The first phase of the study was conducted in six countries: Japan, Korea, the Philippines, Taiwan, Thailand, and the USA (Hawaii). The second phase of the project, now under way, includes all of these countries (except Japan) as well as Indonesia, Singapore, Turkey, and the continental United States.

Nuptiality and possible ways to influence it are among the most neglected areas in social-science research related to population in this as well as other regions of the developing world. Although a few studies examining the   complex relationships between patterns of marriage and marital dissolution, on the one hand, and fertility, on the other, have been conducted, knowledge of the cultural determinants of marriage in the highly varied cultural settings existing in the region is lacking. One key question, as yet unresolved, is the likely effect of the trend away from parent-arranged marriages. Attempts have been made to identify those aspects of socioeconomic development that have an important effect on age at marriage and, consequently, on fertility. One recent study (Smith, 1976) postulates that trends in three modernization processes − urbanization, educational development, and expansion of non-agricultural employment − are likely to encourage continued delays in marriage over the coming decades.

Internal migration, although a neglected topic in the past, is becoming a more important focus for social-science research. A number of comparative studies examining available data on migration from rural areas challenge the conventional wisdom about migrants' characteristics and motivations (such as the notion of male dominance in migration flows, and the assumption that rural–urban migration is a response to and cure for rural inequality). Nevertheless, many more village-based micro-studies are needed to investigate motivation to migrate, actual patterns of movement, income transfers, and the net effect of mobility on the village economy and society. Such studies are relatively scarce in Thailand, Malaysia, the Philippines, and Indonesia (Jones 1978, p. 67). Unfortunately, the majority of the growing literature on internal migration in the region compares and contrasts migrants' characteristics and patterns of movement without dealing with their causes and consequences; that is, it tends to fall into a conventional mould. Research has not yet considered certain factors peculiar to the Asian situation such as: the effect of family structure and marital patterns and arrangements on migration patterns and vice versa (such as the tradition of males migrating for extended periods of trading observed among matrilineal ethnic groups in Indonesia); the apparent increase in autonomous female migration; and the impact of the worsening land-tenure situation and technological change in agriculture on migration.

Research documenting recent mortality levels and trends has been conducted in most South-East and East Asian nations, revealing wide intercountry differentials. However, knowledge of mortality differentials by social class is scandalously lacking. Studies are available only for Indonesia and the Philippines. Research into adult mortality levels and differentials is also needed, since most of what is known about mortality in the region refers to infant and childhood mortality. Finally, in terms of policy oriented research, much remains to be done. Jones (1978, pp. 53–8), for example, cites the need to identify the links between nutrition, sanitation, and general living levels on the one hand, and provision of public health facilities on the other hand in reducing the incidence and/or severity of particular health problems.

The Data Base

The coverage and quality of demographic data in South-East and East Asia vary widely. Here again, Segment 2 countries are in a more favourable position than most Segment 1 and 3 nations. Those Chinese vital statistics that are made available for analysis are believed to suffer from problems of differential under-registration and to be drawn from small administrative units unrepresentative of the over-all demographic situation (Aird, 1978, pp. 232-3). Data collection in Indo-China has been disrupted by military conflict. Decennial census-taking (in the case of Taiwan, every 5 years) and vital registration systems are relatively well established in Segment 2 countries. Specialized surveys and village-level studies add to the wealth of information produced in the region.

Data on fertility are probably the most voluminous. Hong Kong, Indonesia, South Korea, the Philippines, and Thailand have participated in the World Fertility Survey and are in the process of analysing the information collected on fertility levels and differentials, nuptiality, preferences for number and sex of children, and contraceptive practice. Research instruments in the field of family planning evaluation have included the KAP survey, the acceptor follow-up survey, and surveys designed to test different delivery approaches, among others.

Mortality data, particularly that needed to produce estimates of mortality differentials by socioeconomic class for countries as a whole and for regions within them, is inadequate. But, as Jones (1978, pp. 57-8) notes, a number of factors lend considerable hope to the situation: attempts to upgrade the quality of the data are being made, and in Malaysia, Singapore, and Taiwan the data are already good enough for such analysis; Brass mortality estimates by socioeconomic group could be derived from special tabulations from a number of censuses in the region, and the same should be true of the 1980 round of censuses; and a number of surveys have also collected detailed mortality data. Nevertheless, prospective surveys should be emphasized, since they are probably the best source of accurate data on cause of death.

Migration surveys are scarce and, as such, research has been limited to analyses of broad census data. In most countries of the region the 1970 round of censuses contained a number of questions related to migration (normally, place of residence 5 years before), and tabulations were produced that provided a good basis for studies of the general patterns of movement. Access to census tapes was needed for further analysis, because migration data by their very nature are bulky and not amenable to exhaustive presentation in published census reports. In addition, the published reports sometimes overlooked key tables, such as place of birth by place of previous residence in the case of the Indonesian census. Thus, while it is clear that census data have proved to be valuable in the analysis of regional migration flows, they do suffer from a number of shortcomings.

Based necessarily on arbitrary administrative divisions and arbitrary time boundaries to define the migration process, they impose a strait-jacket on the kind of analysis that can be undertaken. In a sense, they 'cover up' the intricate patterns of movement that actually take place: the commuting patterns, circular movements, seasonal movements, etc. Studies based on field research would be able to throw more light on these movements.

Institutional and Human Resources[24]

In a region as diverse as South-East and East Asia, it is not surprising that capacity for social-science research on population and development varies considerably among countries. Unfortunately, information was not available for Segment 1 and 3 countries, but a recent appraisal of institutions and human resources in selected Segment 2 nations (Indonesia, Malaysia, the Philippines, Singapore, South Korea, Taiwan, and Thailand) gives a general idea of the situation prevailing in the region as a whole. Although a substantial capacity for undertaking such research exists, resources are quite weak in some countries, present capacity is underutilized, and additional capacity needs to be developed for the future.

Of the seven nations included in the evaluation effort of the East–West Population Institute, the Philippines, South Korea, and Thailand are in the most favourable position. They not only have the largest numbers of Ph.D-level social scientists involved in population-related work, but also enjoy the best-developed research support facilities. Eleven government or university institutions engaged in population research are singled out in each of the three countries, with the Population Institute of the University of the Philippines and the Institute of Population Studies at Chulalongkorn Univsity being the best-known research and training centres in the region. Taiwan has demonstrated a capacity for population anlaysis and a policy-orientated concern with causes of demographic processes, while Singapore holds promise as a regional base for research through the Institute of South-East Asian Studies. Only Indonesia and Malaysia appear to be particularly weak in the social sciences. Although the situation is improving in the former, both nations are plagued by political problems that impede or jeopardize further development of population activities.

It should be pointed out that the impressive record of social-science research in several of these countries has been accomplished through collaboration with foreign scholars. In the Philippines, for example, the staff of the major research centres are regularly supplemented or headed by foreign consultants. Thus, the goal of achieving self-sufficiency in this area is far from being achieved.

Training for social-science research on population and development is available within the region primarily at the M.A. level through local-language

[24] This section is based on East–West Population Institute (1978), IRG Appendix 5.

programmes in Thailand, Indonesia, South Korea, and other countries, and through an English-language regional programme of study offered by the School of Economics of the University of the Philippines. Outside South-East and East Asia, the two institutions that have major programmes focusing on the region — the East–West Population Institute and the Australian National University — provide training at both the M.A. and Ph.D. levels. In terms of disciplinary orientation, economic demography is particularly strong in the Philippines; the behavioural sciences (especially psychology) are strongest in South Korea; anthropological approaches to population issues have been applied most frequently in Indonesia and in the Philippines; and social demography is strong in a number of countries, notably Thailand. M.A.-level regional training programmes of the latter type need to be supported and strengthened. The development of a programme with a broad social science orientation would be beneficial, especially one focusing on methodology for analysis of population-development interactions.

In addition to resources in individual countries, regional research networks and organizations with regional programmes must also be considered in an assessment of over-all capacity for research on population and development in South-East and East Asia. Foremost among regional resources is the East–West Population Institute (EWPI) in Hawaii. Its diverse programme includes fellowships for graduate study, awards for non-degree training, and collaborative research programmes. Studies currently under way deal with topics such as the value of children, marriage decisions and nuptiality patterns, internal and international migration, circular mobility, socialization for gender preference, and childspacing. In addition, EWPI is sponsoring numerous activities aimed at improving demographic measurement and analysis in Asia, with a current focus on the 1980 round of censuses.

The Department of Demography of the Australian National University (ANU) is another important resource for population research and training. ANU staff are involved in migration research in South-East Asia and are carrying out a broad programme of studies on the economic and social supports for high fertility.

Other regional organizations worthy of mention are the Council for Asian Manpower Studies (CAMS), the Association of South-East Asian Nations (ASEAN), and the Inter-Governmental Co-ordinating Committee in Population and Family Planning (IGCC). Two other groups, the Committee for Comparative Behavioural Studies in Population (COMBEP) and the Organization of Demographic Associates (ODA), once served to create linkages among Asian social scientists and population centres but are currently inactive. The South-East Asia Population Research Awards Programme (SEAPRAP) provides small grants for social-science research on population in South-East Asia, encouraging applications from junior faculty members in provincial universities. Finally, the UN and other international agencies are active in the region.

In summary, although some relatively strong research institutions exist in the region, their capacity to conduct high-quality research on population and development is limited in relation to present needs and none is likely to attain an optimal capacity in the absence of sustained and generous institutional support from the international donor community.

References

Aird, John S. 1978. 'Fertility Decline and Birth Control in the People's Republic of China.' Population and Development Review 4 (2), 225–53.

Caldwell, John C. and Caldwell, Pat. 1978. 'Population Policies and Their Implementation in South-East and East Asia.' Appendix 4 to the Final Report. El Colegio de México: IRG.

East–West Centre. East–West Population Institute. 1978. 'Capacity for Social Science Research on Population and Development in South-East and East Asia: A Report on Institutional and Human Resources.' Appendix 5 to the Final Report. El Colegio de México: IRG.

Goodstadt, Leo F. 1978. 'Official Targets, Data, and Policies for China's Population Growth: An Assessment.' *Population and Development Review*, 4 (2), 255–75.

Jones, Gavin. 1978. 'Social Science Research on Population and Development in South-East and East Asia: A Review and Search for Directions.' Appendix 3 to the Final Report. El Colegio de México: IRG.

Smith, Peter C. 1976. 'Asian Nuptiality in Transition.' Paper presented at the Seventh Summer Seminar on Population. Honolulu: East–West Population Institute.

World Bank. 1978. *World Development Report, 1978.* Washington, D.C.: World Bank.

PART II   THE DEMOGRAPHIC VARIABLES: KNOWLEDGE, GAPS, AND SPECIFIC RESEARCH RECOMMENDATIONS

Introduction

In the course of its work, the Group devoted considerable attention to assessing the state of knowledge on each of the demographic variables. Evaluating the state of this knowledge for each of the regions and subregions was one of the objectives of the regional reviews. Also, the Group had at its disposal and considered a number of reviews of the literature on the demographic variables that have been published in recent years. The workshops took up the implications for policy of the results of both previous and prospective research on mortality, fertility and migration.

The objective of this chapter is to present a summary evaluation of the state of knowledge of each of the four primary variables, examine the policy relevance of this knowledge, and, finally, to set forth some concrete recommendations for the 'variable-specific' research that the Group feels would be most likely to facilitate and influence policy formulation and implementation in the next decade.

In examining the state of knowledge, an attempt will be made to present answers to the following questions:

1. How much is known about the variable itself, in terms of levels, trends, and differentials, and also in terms of the component parts of the process that the variable represents?

2. To what extent have the factors that determine behaviour been identified? What are the elements of the local environment and the way it is perceived that influence demographic 'decision-making'? How are these elements influenced by the social, economic, and ideological trends occurring in the larger society?

3. What are the consequences of different types of demographic behaviour for individuals and families? For geographical communities and specific groups? For the nation as a whole?

4. What has been learned from experience with policy measures? What is known about the impact of public policies and programmes on the variable in question?

Policy relevance is an elusive matter. It is, however, central to the IRG's mission and terms of reference. Some of the questions that will be asked in this regard are: What are the implications for policy of the currently available knowledge? What kinds of research findings do policy-makers feel would be most useful to them? Is there disagreement or consensus as to what needs to be done? Is there a conflict between the indications for policy that have emerged from research findings, and what is actually being done?

With this discussion as background, the last step involves recommending a concerted research effort on a limited number of specific questions or hypotheses that have promise of yielding — in the near- to medium-term future — concrete results with a direct bearing on policy formulation.

6 MORTALITY

State of Knowledge

Levels, Trends, and Differentials

Information on levels, trends, and differentials in mortality is far from complete for many developing countries. Not surprisingly, the situation varies considerably among the different regions and subregions distinguished by the IRG. In many parts of Sub-Saharan Africa, estimates of mortality at the national level have only recently been constructed, and information on mortality trends and differentials is virtually non-existent (Mabogunje and Arowolo, 1978, pp. 15–17). Latin America, on the other hand, is in a notably better position. Complete or nearly complete vital registration systems, combined with regular decennial censuses, provide information on both levels and trends in mortality, and these estimates are often complemented by those obtained from demographic surveys. In addition, in a number of Latin American countries these data sources have been exploited for the purpose of estimating differentials in mortality both for geographical regions and for socioeconomic groups (Urzúa, 1978, p. 42). Estimates of mortality levels and trends are poor — often as poor as those in Africa — in much of the southern part of Asia: Saudi Arabia, the two Yemens, Afghanistan, Pakistan, Bangladesh, Burma, Kampuchea, Laos, and Papua-New Guinea. They are not much more trustworthy in Iraq, Iran, India, Indonesia, and some of the small states near the Persian Gulf. In Taiwan, both Koreas, Malaysia, Sri Lanka, Singapore, and Hong Kong the state of knowledge is probably comparable to that in Latin America; and in the Philippines, Thailand, and Vietnam, it is of an intermediate quality.

Almost universally, across the different regions and subregions of the developing world, more is known about levels, trends, and differentials in infant and child mortality than with respect to adult mortality. This is true in spite of the fact that vital registration is usually less complete for deaths occurring at young ages. The explanation lies in the development and application of powerful techniques for the indirect measurement of child mortality from census data that have been widely diffused in the course of the last decade.

In addition to knowledge of levels, trends, and differentials in a demographic variable, some knowledge of the 'process' that it consists of — that is, how the variable breaks down into its component parts — is basic to an understanding of its determinants and consequences. In the case of mortality, the component parts refer to the different causes of death. Conventionally defined in such a way that they are mutually exclusive and exhaustive, these are the biological variables through which all social and environmental relations must necessarily operate, and any variation in mortality from all causes is necessarily attributable to variations in mortality for one or more causes of death. Regrettably, information on cause of death is usually unavailable or highly unreliable in most developing countries.[1] Even in Latin America, data on cause of death are often suspect, except where a specific effort in either prospective surveys of a sample population or retrospective surveys of a sample of decedents has been made.

Relations Between Mortality and Development

The bulk of demographic research on mortality has been with respect to measuring and describing levels, trends, and differentials. Much less effort has gone into analysing the relations between mortality and development, although these relations have been the focus of considerable debate. Much of the available literature on these relations consists of attempts to sort out answers to three controversial and intriguing questions. The first and most important is: what was responsible for the dramatic declines in mortality that took place in the developing countries between 1940 and the late 1960s?[2] The bulk of the disagreement over this question has concerned the relative importance of the roles played by living standards and life styles on the one hand, and public-health programmes and access to medical services on the other. One of the interesting features of the debate over the reasons for the decline in mortality in countries such as India is that social scientists have identified the application of modern medical technology as the chief causal factor, while health scientists have claimed that public-health programmes have been too limited to have had such an impact and that therefore the responsibility must lie with economic development and social change.

[1] Normally, one of the main impediments to obtaining cause-of-death information is that someone with medical training must be available at the time of the event. To avoid this difficulty, some experiments are apparently now under way in the development of training materials and revised disease classifications that will permit or facilitate lay identification of cause of death. Work along these lines was recommended by participants in two of the three IRG workshops.

[2] An estimate of the over-all magnitude of this improvement by regions is as follows. On the basis of fragmentary evidence it appears that life expectancy at birth during 1935–9 was about 30 years in Africa and Asia and 40 years in Latin America. The respective levels in 1965–70 were of the order of 43, 50, and 60 (WHO, 1974, and UN Population Divison, 1973, cited in Preston, 1979).

While this issue is by no means resolved at the level of individual countries, a recent analysis and overview by Preston (1975 and 1979) has gone a long way towards identifying factors affecting mortality trends for the developing world as a whole. Part of his contribution has been to show the change that has taken place during the twentieth century in the cross-sectional relationship between national life expectancies and such indexes of living standards as national income per capita. His analysis demonstrates that factors exogenous to life styles and economic development have had a major effect on mortality trends in both less-developed and more developed countries.[3] Preston gives a comprehensive picture of what portions of the decline in mortality in developing countries can be attributed to declines in different diseases. Since diseases vary in the degree to which they are responsive to living standards or are capable of being controlled by medical technology, this analysis also affords a basis for affirming that both social-policy measures and higher standards of living have played an important role in the decline of mortality. On the one hand declines in the group of causes of death consisting of influenza, pneumonia, and bronchitis accounted for perhaps one-third of the mortality decline. No effective preventive measures have been deployed against these diseases (the effectiveness of immunization being minimal), and there are suggestions that antibiotics, sulfa drugs, and curative services are not widely enough available in developing countries to have substantially altered the disease picture. Therefore, environmental changes appear to explain the reduction in mortality caused by declines in these diseases. The decreased incidence of diarrhoeal diseases probably accounts for another 9 per cent or so of the decline, and the principal method of control has been improvements in water supply and sewerage that, because of their costs, are closely associated with economic development. It is likely that the prevalence of these diseases has been primarily affected by social and economic development, especially as reflected in water systems, nutrition, housing, and personal sanitary knowledge. On the other hand, in the case of diseases such as malaria, tuberculosis, smallpox, measles, and whooping-cough — declines in which may account for as much as one-half of the mortality decline in many developing countries — it would appear that programmes of a narrowly public-health nature that embodied inexpensive new techniques (especially vector control and immunization) have been the decisive forces in mortality reductions.

A second and closely related question around which discussion and research have centred is with respect to the role of private living standards versus the availability of health services and programmes in creating the patterns of sharp mortality differentials that appear to exist in most

[3] As Schultz (1979, p. 4) points out, there are some important difficulties with respect to the interpretation of these cross-sectional regression analyses. It is plausible that if more or better socioeconomic variables were included, the unexplained change in life expectancy that is attributed to improved technology might be reduced.

developing countries. The differentials that have been documented are for regional and urban-rural populations as well as for subsectors of the population defined on the basis of literacy, education, income, and other indicators of social class. Here again, there is a growing consensus that both sorts of factors are important determinants of mortality differentials, whether they be between geographically defined regions or between social groups. In the case of regional differentials, support for this conclusion comes from cross-sectional regression analyses that, in attempting to explain the variance in mortality across territorial subdivisions within countries, have been able to attribute significant portions of this variance to both economic variables and the availability of health services. Also supportive of the independent role of health services are the findings of the very few studies that have compared the level of mortality in individual communities similar in all respects except the availability of medical facilities (Orubuloye and Caldwell, 1975).

Significant rural-urban mortality differentials appear to exist in most developing countries, with urban areas enjoying the more favourable experience. Yet within urban areas there are often very great differentials, with low-income urban families having much lower life expectancy than the average for rural areas (Urzúa, 1978, p. 42; Jones, 1978, p. 56). It seems that among the poor and uneducated, inability to pay for medical care or for adequate food has prevented them from reaping the mortality-related advantages of urban living such as the proximity of medical facilities and a more even year-round food supply. It may also be that in many cities the conditions of sanitation and hygiene for the poor are worse, or at least no better, than in rural areas (Jones, 1978, p. 56).

There is as yet little solid evidence on which to base an interpretation of the very sizeable mortality differentials that are found between groups defined on the basis of education, literacy, or occupation.[4] While these variables are highly correlated with standard of living, they are also reflective of knowledge of medical facilities, a greater understanding of the need for a sanitary household environment, a more favourable attitude towards medical treatment, and, perhaps, more fundamental changes in the structure of familial relationships (Caldwell, 1979, p. 14). What is more, further progress in understanding the causal relations behind mortality experience, both with regard to differentials and to over-all mortality decline, would seem to hinge upon developing approaches to the problem that are considerably more sophisticated than those implicit in the 'either/ or' debate regarding the relative importance of developmental and technological factors. The antagonists on both sides are probably equally guilty of failing to address the behavioural questions concerning the

---

[4] Indeed, the slope of the relation between mortality and education within countries is generally so steep (especially at lower levels of development and life expectancy) that expenditures on education would, at first sight, appear to be an effective way to reduce mortality (Preston, 1978b, p. 13).

way individuals, families, and communities make the vast array of consumption and investment decisions that affect their health. For example, in spite of the accumulated evidence that maternal education plays a major role in determining the level of infant and child mortality, little has been done to explain this phenomenon except in terms of the role of education as a proxy for living standards. Caldwell (1979) has recently pointed to the need to examine maternal education as an important force in its own right. Among the various ways that education may have a 'direct' effect on health is by inducing mothers to break with tradition and adopt many of the alternatives in child care and the cure of illness that are becoming available in most developing societies. Educated mothers may also be more capable of manipulating the modern world, and more likely to be listened to by doctors and nurses. Finally, education may have an important effect on the nature of the family, ultimately pushing it towards 'child-centredness', with all that such a development implies for reducing child mortality.

In addition to in-depth sociological and anthropological analyses of the above question, there also seems to be a need to develop more comprehensive theoretical frameworks with which to analyse the relations between family or household economic endowments, community-level variables, and mortality in the cross-sectional data sets that are becoming increasingly available from population, housing, and agricultural censuses as well as special-purpose surveys. In such analyses, advantage should be taken of opportunities to identify the relative influence of various regional or community-level factors that are exogenous to the household and which affect the exposure to disease, such as climate and public-health programmes. There is also a need in such analyses to recognize the likelihood that a large number of the household characteristics that influence health — such as sanitation facilities and water supply, mother's age at marriage, and previous fertility experience — may be jointly determined by a limited number of variables having to do with the economic situation of the household.[5]

The third general question that has generated discussion and, occasionally, research on the relations between mortality and development is with respect to the social and economic consequences of improved health. For individuals, longevity is a universal value, and reduced mortality is clearly an objective for society to pursue in its own right. The issues considered here are rather the intended or unintended side effects (externalities) that result from mortality decline. These may be divided into consequences that operate at the aggregate level of the society or country as a whole and those that are felt at the individual level. Beginning with the former, there is no doubt that a decline in mortality rather than any substantial change in fertility was responsible for the sharp acceleration

[5] An interesting first approach to these problems is presented in Schultz (1979).

in population growth that took place in nearly all developing countries between 1940 and 1960. The effects on demographic, economic, and social processes of an increase in the rate of population growth resulting from a decline in mortality are quite different from those that result from an increase in fertility, because the two typically have very different effects on the age distribution of the population. The effects of a mortality-induced increase in population growth are usually thought to have fewer negative macro-level influences on the growth of per capita income. Yet, as will be argued later on, findings in this area are often challenged, and there is little certainty about the magnitude of the effects of mortality decline on capital supply, agricultural production, and so on. Mortality decline however has been and very likely will continue to be responsible for a significant part of the increase in the numbers of people entering young adulthood in developing countries; and that increase has very definite implications for the employment and unemployment prospects of most countries.

Of course, just as population growth is the main macro-consequence of mortality decline, the principal micro-level effect of reduced mortality is an increase in family size. What research is available on this question is mainly with respect to fertility and is discussed in the next section.[6] The effect that has received the most attention, however, is the suspected economic benefit deriving from greater labour productivity. But very few studies have been done in this area and there are difficult methodological problems with those that are available (Jones, 1978, p. 84; World Bank, 1975, chap. 3; Schultz, 1979). Some other possibly important positive effects at the individual level may stem from the fact that members of a population with lower mortality and morbidity can look forward to longer and more productive lives in which to reap the benefits of efforts at, and expenditures on, personal improvement.

The Impact of Specific Health-Sector Policies

In the area of health policy, far more is currently available in the way of prescriptions for the future than reliable evaluations of past policy experience.[7] This is unfortunate in that, while there is now nearly universal agreement within the community of international health experts about the need to introduce fundamental changes in the health-sector policies pursued by most developing countries in the direction of increasing the

[6] It seems likely that part of the reason why more attention has not been given to the issue of the influence of mortality change on family size and structure lies with the relative underdevelopment of the 'formal' demography of the family. See, for example, the evaluation presented in Ryder (1977).

[7] Certainly the 'Declaration of Alma Ata' is the most noteworthy set of recommendations as to the directions that health policy should take in the coming decade. This was adopted in the September 1978 WHO/UNICEF International Conference on Primary Health Care (WHO, 1978).

coverage of the health-care system and emphasizing preventive measures rather than hospital-based curative care, there is far less agreement as to specific ways to proceed.

In the current debate over how to utilize resources effectively and efficiently to improve the health of the poor, a central issue is whether providing primary health care[8] for the entire population should be the overriding strategic objective, or whether there is still a major place for disease-specific interventions that selectively attempt to prevent and treat those diseases responsible for the greatest mortality. Apart from these broader issues, the practical questions of how to organize and administer an effective health-care system are also in considerable dispute.[9]

Evaluations of the impact on mortality of specific health interventions are remarkably uncommon (Preston, 1978a, p. 12). Studies addressing the effectiveness of health programmes do, of course, face a number of problems. Over-all national experiences are difficult to assess both because there are apt to be limitations on the quality and quantity of available data and because there are so many influences unrelated to health programmes that are apt to be at work (Gwatkin, Wilcox, and Wray, 1979). Large-scale service programmes should be somewhat easier to evaluate, but it seems that especially in the nutrition area evaluation of programmes at this level has been 'sadly neglected' (Austin *et al.*, 1978, p. 15, cited in Gwatkin, Wilcox, and Wray, 1979). Those studies that have been done are principally with respect to those relatively well-organized and controlled field experiments that have provided general health and nutrition services to limited populations or that implemented certain disease-specific vector control or immunization campaigns among them. It seems clear, however, that of all the field experiments of this nature that have been undertaken in developing countries, only a few have made the effort to collect comprehensive data on mortality.

Gawtkin, Wilcox, and Wray (1979) have recently completed a review of the experience of ten 'well-recorded field projects which were directed toward alleviating the consequences of nutritional inadequacies and improving health' (p. 5). Infant and child mortality rates, utilized in the review, were the principal measures of health status available. The main conclusion reached by the authors is that health interventions of this sort

---

[8] According the the 'Declaration of Alma Ata', primary health care '. . . includes at least: education concerning prevailing health problems and the methods of preventing and controlling them; promotion of food supply and proper nutrition; an adequate supply of safe water and basic sanitation; maternal and child health care, including family planning; immunization against the major infectious diseases; prevention and control of local endemic diseases; appropriate treatment of common diseases and injuries; and provision of essential drugs' (WHO, 1978).

[9] For an up-to-date review and discussion of international health policy issues, see the background papers for the recent Bellagio Conference on Health and Population in Developing Countries (Rockefeller Foundation, 1979).

do have a notable impact on mortality.[10] In seven of the nine cases for which some information was available on mortality outside the experimental area, the data suggest that infant and child mortality fell more rapidly in the project than in the control areas. These impacts were generally achieved with quite modest expenditures. The annual per capita cost varied from about US $1.50 to US $7.50 in seven of the ten projects. The review also suggests that a number of factors, both with respect to specific project components (such as efforts to improve maternal nutrition) and to general considerations (such as reliance on paramedical personnel) appeared to contribute significantly to programme effectiveness. The authors, however, stress the tentative nature of their conclusions, noting that often the population in the experimental areas was small in size, that adequate control groups were not established and monitored, and that there was no conclusive evidence of direct causation.

In the above paper and in other recent contributions (e.g. Habicht and Berman, 1979), increased recognition is being given to the ways in which social structure affects and is affected by the effectiveness of health and nutrition interventions, especially since so many prescriptions involve shifting responsibility for primary care services towards local organizations. There does not appear to be much research specifically directed at these questions, but in various overviews of the issues surrounding the implementation of primary health-care systems there is open acknowledgement of the need for understanding how social factors affect the types of health services provided, the distribution of costs and benefits of services, and the impact that interventions have on local institutions (Habicht and Berman, 1979, p. 95).

Demographic Interrelations

Mortality is related in a number of ways to other demographic variables. There is a considerable literature on the behavioural and biological interrelations between infant mortality and fertility. Recent reviews of the evidence come to the conclusion that there is no reason to expect that a decline in infant and child mortality will be followed in the short run by a decline in the birth-rate that is anywhere nearly compensatory (Preston, 1978c). Mortality is also associated with fertility in that infant mortality varies with age of mother and, often, the length of the interval

[10] Preston (1978a) and the World Bank (1975) also cite a number of evaluation studies that have shown major programme effects on mortality. Of course, not all studies evaluating health interventions have come to such positive conclusions. A recent evaluation of one of the 'Taylor–Berelson' projects (Taylor and Lapham, 1974) prepared by Nancy Williamson (1979) was not able to detect any aggregate impact on maternal or infant mortality of a project to deliver basic preventive and curative health services to priority women and children in a remote rural area of the Philippines.

between births. A related point is that it seems that whether a child is breast-fed or bottle-fed may be a particularly important determinant of infant mortality. While the behavioural question of changing breast-feeding patterns in developing countries is of major importance, what is to be stressed here is that while there are strong indications of a major health advantage for breast-fed babies, firm estimates of the relative mortality risks have yet to be established (Knodel, 1977; Winikoff, 1978). The historical evidence for now-developed countries shows that the survival benefits of breast-feeding decreased over time with improved nutrition, environmental sanitation, and medical care; but where individual developing countries lie on this spectrum is still in much dispute.

Another question that is increasingly hard to overlook is the hypothesis that infant mortality may sometimes be a response to high and unwanted fertility. There is a certain amount of historical and anthropological evidence indicating that either conscious or subconscius control of mortality took place in some primitive and pre-industrial societies (Scrimshaw, 1978; Knodel and van de Walle, 1979, p. 230). For contemporary developing countries the case is less firm and relies principally on mortality differentials that 'appear to go beyond what might be expected biologically' (Scrimshaw, 1978, p. 388), especially as between male and female children.

Finally, mortality is related to the spatial distribution of population as Urzúa (1978, p. 47) points out, in that this can either impede or facilitate the implementation of effective national health policies. So, too, may mortality and health conditions affect migration patterns in important ways. In countries such as Upper Volta, freeing certain areas from endemic disease is an important component of resettlement programmes.

Towards Establishing a Policy-Relevant Research Agenda

The realization that the rapid decline in mortality that was occurring in some developing countries through the late 1960s appears to have tapered off significantly, together with indications that in most LDCs there are very pronounced differentials in health status between sectors of the population, lends urgency to discussions of the contribution of social-science research to the design of health and other development policies that affect mortality.

The preceding overview indicates that the mortality decline in LDCs was produced both by economic and social improvement and by the diffusion of preventive medicine and public-health measures. In this conclusion, the findings of broad cross-country studies are complemented by evaluations of specific health interventions. Furthermore, an understanding of the modes of transmission, methods of prevention, and treatment of the diseases that are responsible for the 'excess' or 'preventable' mortality in developing countries adds to the conclusion that both public-health measures and improved living standards are important, and that they are likely to be most effective in combination. The main questions for research in the 1980s are not of the either/or sort, but rather are with regard to the type of programme and the type of development that will have the greatest effect on morbidity and mortality.

But research priorities must take close account of the demographic and policy settings in individual countries. There is a great difference between the present allocation of resources within the health sector in most developing countries and that which appears to be needed to have an impact on the mortality of the bulk of the population and to reduce mortality differentials. By any mildly egalitarian standard, present policies appear to be both inefficient and inequitable. The litany of shortcomings in public health services and the mis-allocation of health resources has been elaborated in a number of WHO publications as well as in a Sector Policy Paper prepared by the World Bank (1975, pp. 32–40). The principal problem is usually the limited coverage of public-health services. Coverage extends to only a small proportion of the population, partly because total government expenditures on health constitute a small fraction of GNP (rarely in excess of 2 per cent), but mainly because the lion's share of both public and private expenditures is devoted to high-cost, individual curative medicine as opposed to environmental and preventive measures. The bulk of the limited government outlays for health go towards maintaining expensive, well-equipped hospitals staffed by highly trained medical personnel, and large numbers of people living in the countryside or city slums are allowed to remain beyond the reach of the modern medical sector. In contrast, there are a number of countries whose health policies represent notable exceptions to the rule. Among them are two countries that were represented at the series of IRG workshops, Sri Lanka and Cuba.[11]

It seems that the 'policy problem' at issue is not an absence of opportunities and indicators for remedial policy, but rather that in spite of such opportunities and indicators the remedial policies are not being implemented. The real question is: Why not? Several explanations have been put forward. The first is with reference to the lack of political avenues in most developing countries through which the poor can voice their demands, leaving little possibility for present priorities to be effectively challenged (Jones, 1978, p. 57). The second is in terms of the myopia of health sector policy-makers and the control exerted over them by the collective interest of physicians in the private sector. In all probability, both explanations are too simple. An important part of the problem

[11] Clearly, a number of important intermediate cases, such as India, may be found where governments have made an apparently strong commitment towards improving the health status of the poor, and where attempts to institute reorientated health schemes are just getting under way (Bose *et al.*, 1978).

may be a characteristic of the demand for health services common in both developed and developing countries: people are mainly interested in good health when they have become sick, and hence their 'felt needs' are primarily for curative services. Thus, whatever political demands the disadvantaged are able to make upon the system are apt to be for services that in the long run will do little to change their circumstances.

What can social-science research contribute in the near future towards breaking the impasse? Two complementary strategies appear to have some promise. The first would aim to increase the awareness of both policy-makers and the general public (both national and international) of the existing inequalities in health status between the rich and the poor in developing countries. The second would seek to establish more precisely the cost-effectiveness and likely mortality impact of reorientated health policies, and to make such results well known. Both involve attempts to provide more definite evidence combined with efforts to communicate the findings to policy-makers and the public at large. But a third strategy of realism also seems to be called for. It is self-evident that power relations in the society at large and in individual communities influence the allocation of resources and the establishment of priorities (Antonovsky, 1979). Research must be brought to bear on the very real question of the feasibility of reorientating health policies in the absence of broader changes in political and institutional structure.

Specific Recommendations

Measurement and Analysis of Mortality Differentials

Where they are not already available, there is a need for descriptive studies of mortality differentials by social class within individual developing countries. The least demanding and perhaps most promising way to produce such estimates is by deriving indirect estimates of mortality through the analysis of responses to retrospective questions included in censuses and surveys on the proportion of children surviving among those ever born to women of child-bearing age and on widowhood and orphanhood. Here the work done by CELADE on fifteen Latin American countries provides an example of what could be done in other regions (see Urzúa, 1978, pp. 42–3).

Also needed are complementary studies that apply multivariate statistical techniques to data on communities and families or households collected in censuses or surveys. If they included a rich set of independent variables and were undertaken in conjunction with the development of more complete theoretical frameworks, such analyses could test hypotheses about specific aspects of the relation between health and development with considerable policy significance.

While the associations uncovered by statistical analyses may be important by themselves, it is likely that in certain cases, such as the association between mother's education and child mortality, there may be considerable discussion about the way in which the variable actually affects mortality. To attempt to answer such questions, effort should be devoted to detailed exploration of circumstances potentially affecting health within the household, such as the organization of care for children and arrangements for preparing and eating food, as well as attitudes and priorities related to sickness and death and various forms of treatment.

Health Policy Studies

There is a need for a significant number of additional investigations to evaluate the mortality effects of a wide range of public interventions, ranging from those of a uni-sectoral public-health nature, such as vector control campaigns, to those with broader objectives, such as food and nutrition programmes and the provision of better water supply and sewage facilities by way of housing and urbanization projects. The need for evaluation exists whether the projects are carried out at the national level or on an experimental or pilot basis, but the possibilities of collecting detailed data on project inputs and mortality outcomes as well as for maintaining valid control groups — all at reasonable cost — are clearly greater for smaller projects. Given the wide variety of ways that primary health-care systems can be organized and the apparent importance of the role that administrative factors play in project success or failure, these issues as well as those related to local social structure should be addressed at the centre of evaluation designs.

It cannot be emphasized too strongly that evaluative studies in the health area require a collaborative effort by social and medical scientists. On the one hand, detailed knowledge of pathological processes and their physical correlates is needed in order to interpret developments and make recommendations; on the other hand, biostatistical and demographic expertise are required in the design and measurement stages, economic sophistication is needed for cost-benefit and cost-effectiveness calculations, and sociological insight is necessary for the analysis of the roles of culture and social structure.

In addition to intervention studies, also useful for the design of health policies would be more strictly demographic analyses of the influence of specific health factors where these are still poorly understood in terms of their actual quantitative impact on mortality. The relation between feeding practices and infant and child mortality would seem to be particularly ripe for further work of this sort. While the few studies now available on the effect of infant feeding practices on infant mortality in developing countries suggest that artificially fed infants have much higher death-rates than breast-fed infants, there is a need for further and more refined work on this topic. Most desirable would be a series of prospectively designed studies to measure relative mortality risks in a variety of health environments and socioeconomic settings.

Broad Political Analyses

To achieve a greater understanding of the reasons for the remarkable contradictions between current health policies and the present consensus as to how to reduce mortality differentials, research needs to be done on the political decision-making process that determines health policies in developing countries as well as on the role played in this process by specific interest groups. Of special interest are the forces sustaining the status quo as well as those groups or coalitions that are likely to be influential in supporting or demanding new policy initiatives.

Also needed are studies of the limitations imposed on the health sector in individual countries by the prevailing development strategy and the administrative and organizational structures on which it is based. Here, special emphasis should be given to questions regarding what changes in broader social and economic policy and in institutional structure might form advisable and/or necessary complements to changes in health policies.

In comparison with these lines of investigation, perhaps less priority should be given to further analysis of the side effects and consequences of reduced mortality. In contrast with the other demographic variables, mortality reduction is an end in itself; health represents a basic need that people in developing countries are, as individuals, disposed to make considerable sacrifices to attain. Although not much is known about the social and economic consequences of mortality decline, considering the available research leads, it seems unlikely that further research on the effect of more rapid population growth on various indices of welfare will yield results in the near to medium term that would be convincing enough to have a major impact on policy. The question of whether it would be worth while to devote considerable resources to investigating the effect of improved health and nutritional status on economic productivity is harder to answer. On the one hand, as noted above, the results that have been obtained so far are hardly conclusive, and severe methodological problems appear to stand in the way of accurate documentation of these effects. But, on the other hand, if major productivity gains could be shown either for specific interventions such as programmes for nutritional improvement or for more general efforts to improve health status, this demonstration could have a considerable influence on policy adoption.

References

Antonovsky, Aaron. 1979. 'Implications of Socioeconomic Differentials in Mortality for the Health System.' Paper prepared for the Meeting on Socioeconomic Determinants and Consequences of Mortality, Mexico City, June 1979. DSI/SE/WE/79.9.

Bose, Ashish, *et al*. 1978. 'An Assessment of the New Rural Health Scheme and Suggestions for Improvement.' Delhi: Demographic Research Centre, Institute of Economic Growth. Mimeo.

Caldwell, John. 1979. 'Education as a Factor in Mortality Decline: An Examination of Nigerian Data.' Paper presented at the Meeting on Socioeconomic Determinants and Consequences of Mortality, México City, June 1979. DSI/SE/WP/79.3.Rev.1. Geneva: WHO.

Gwatkin, Davidson R., Wilcox, Janet R., and Wray, Joe D. 1979. 'Can Interventions Make a Difference? The Policy Implications of Field Experiment Experience.' A Report to the World Bank. Washington: Overseas Development Council. Mimeo.

Habicht, J. P., and Berman, P. 1979. 'Planning Primary Health Services from a Body Count?' Paper prepared for the Conference on Health and Population in Developing Countries, Bellagio, Italy, April 1979. New York: Rockefeller Foundation.

Jones, Gavin W. 1978. 'Social Science Research on Population and Development in South-East and East Asia: A Review and Search for Directions'. Appendix 3 to the Final Report. El Colegio de México: IRG.

Knodel, John. 1977. 'Breast-Feeding and Population Growth.' *Science*, vol. 198, pp. 1111–15.

— and Etienne van de Walle. 1979. 'Lessons from the Past: Policy Implications of Historical Fertility Studies.' *Population and Development Review*, 5 (2), 217–46.

Mabogunje, Akin L., and Arowolo, O. 1978. 'Social Science Research on Population and Development in Africa South of the Sahara.' Appendix 7 to the Final Report. El Colegio de México: IRG.

Orobuloye, I. O., and Caldwell, J. C. 1975. 'The Impact of Public Health Services on Mortality: A Study of Mortality Differentials in a Rural Area of Nigeria.' *Population Studies*, 29 (2), 259–72.

Preston, Samuel H. 1975. 'The Changing Relation between Mortality and Level of Economic Development.' Ibid. 231–48.

— 1978a. 'Research Developments Needed for Improvements in Policy Formulation on Mortality.' Paper presented at the First IRG Workshop on Research Priorities for Population Policy, Colombo, Sri Lanka, 26–8 April. IRG/53.

— 1978b. 'Mortality, Morbidity, and Development.' Paper presented at the Seminar on Population and Development in the ECWA Region, 20 September.

— ed. 1978c. *The Effect of Infant and Child Mortality on Fertility*. New York: Academic Press.

— 1979. 'Causes and Consequences of Mortality Declines in Less-Developed Countries.' In *Population and Economic Change in Less-Developed Countries*, Richard A. Easterlin, ed. Chicago: University of Chicago Press.

Rockefeller Foundation. 1979. Background Papers. Conference on Health and Population in Developing Countries, Bellagio, Italy, April 1979. New York.

Ryder, Norman B. 1977. 'Methods in Measuring the Family Life Cycle.' In *Proceedings: International Population Conference, Mexico 1977*. Liège: IUSSP.

Schultz, T. Paul. 1979. 'Interpretation of Relations among Mortality, Economics of the Household, and the Health Environment.' Paper presented at the Meeting on Socioeconomic Determinants and Consequences of Mortality, México City, June 1979.

Scrimshaw, Susan C. M. 1978. 'Infant Mortality and Behavior in the Regulation of Family Size.' *Population and Development Review*, 4 (3), 383–403.

Taylor, H. C., Jr., and Lapham, R. J. 1974. 'A Program for Family Planning Based on Maternal/Child Health Services.' *Studies in Family Planning*, 5 (3), 71-82.

United Nations Population Divison. 1974. 'Recent Population Trends and Future Prospects.' World Population Conference Paper. E/CONF. 60/3.

Urzúa, Raul. 1978. 'Social Science Research on Population and Development in Latin America.' Appendix 11 to the Final Report. El Colegio de México: IRG.

Williamson, Nancy E. 1979. *The Bohol Project: Progress Report on an Experiment to Improve Rural Health & Family Planning in the Philippines*. International Programs Working Paper No. 5. New York: The Population Council.

Winikoff, Beverly. 1978. 'Nutrition, Population, and Health: Some Implications for Policy.' *Science*, Vol. 200.

World Bank. 1975. *Health: Sector Policy Paper*. Washington, D.C.: World Bank.

World Health Organization. 1974. 'Health Trends and Prospects, 1950-2000.' *World Health Statistics Reports*, 27 (10).

— 1978. 'Declaration of Alma Ata.' International Conference on Primary Health Care, Alma Ata, USSR, September 1978. ICPHC/ALA/78.10.

7   FERTILITY

State of Knowledge

Descriptive Knowledge

How much is known about the dimensions of fertility in the different regions and subregions of the developing world? The pertinent dimensions are with respect to both: (i) levels and trends in fertility in terms of such measures as the total fertility or crude birth rate, at various levels of disaggregation; and (ii) the various biological and social components of fertility and changes in levels of these components over time.

Levels, trends, and differentials. It bears reiterating that information on births and deaths is skimpy or simply unreliable for over three-fifths of the world's population. Somewhere between only 100 and 200 million inhabitants among the nearly 3 billion in the developing world are covered by proven or reliable fertility data (Stolnitz, 1978, pp. 4, 15). Despite this important caveat, fertility estimates of varying reliability, either from surveys or the application of indirect measurement techniques to census data, are now available for most developing countries.

As is the case with respect to mortality, Latin America is probably the region with the most complete information on levels, trends, and differentials in fertility, but there is considerable variation among countries. In fact, the largest country in the region, Brazil, is one of those with the least complete information. For the country as a whole and even more so for regions within the country, there is considerable dispute about the current level of fertility and how much of a decline has taken place in the past 15 years. While data on cumulative fertility from both censuses and surveys provide only rough indications of levels and trends, they do, however, indicate the existence of marked differentials in fertility between the different states and regions of that country.

In Middle South Asia, perhaps the only country with highly reliable statistics on levels, trends, and differentials in fertility is Sri Lanka. With respect to India, while there is uncertainty as to the amount of fertility decline that has taken place in the country as a whole, data collection efforts such as the National Sample Survey and the Sample Registration Scheme have provided estimates of fertility by states and for different population groups distinguished on the basis of socioeconomic indicators (Desai, 1978, p. 61 ff.). Other South Asian countries are not so well endowed with on-going mechanisms to collect data on fertility, but most have been the subject of special-purpose surveys such as those carried out in collaboration with the World Fertility Survey in Nepal, Bangladesh, and Pakistan. Special-purpose surveys are also the principal source of information on fertility in many South-East Asian countries such as Thailand, Indonesia, and the Philippines.

In West Asia and North Africa there are several countries with time-series data reliable enough to judge recent fertility trends. Egypt, Tunisia, and Jordan all fall in this category (Stolnitz, 1978, p. 16). Not surprisingly, Sub-Saharan Africa is the subregion with the most limited information on national levels, trends, and differentials in fertility. Available estimates have been based on censuses and, more frequently of late, special-purpose surveys, but the latter have not usually been based on nationally representative samples.

Fertility as a process. In a manner nearly analogous to the way mortality can be broken down into causes of death, fertility can be broken down into its different behavioural and biological components. The level of fertility in a population is directly determined by a series of variables that either as a matter of individual volition or indirectly through sociocultural practices interfere with or impinge on the biological conditions for birth.[12] In order of generality, the first of these is the proportion of the female population of reproductive age living in stable sexual unions, such as formal marriages and consensual unions. At a second level one can identify two factors associated with the control of fertility within marriage: contraception (defined as any deliberate practice, including abstinence and sterilization, undertaken to reduce or eliminate the risk of conception) and induced abortion. At a third level are two behavioural variables that affect fertility but which are not apt to be related to attained family size: lactational infecundability (determined by the length and intensity of breast-feeding) and the frequency of intercourse. Lastly, sterility, spontaneous intra-uterine mortality, and the duration of viability of ova and sperm are three variables that affect fertility in a physiological rather than a behavioural way.

Necessarily, any socioeconomic, cultural, and environmental influences that affect fertility must do so by producing a change in one or more of the above 'intermediate variables', yet in most cases relations between fertility and such influences have been studied without reference to the specific mechanisms through which they operate.

Looking briefly at the first of the intermediate variables, there is usually less complete knowledge about the age pattern and extent of marriage when nuptiality is changing rapidly or when there is a large percentage of consensual or informal unions, as in many Latin American countries. What is clear, however, is that changes in the age pattern of

[12] The classification that follows is developed in a recent paper by John Bongaarts (1978).

marriage sometimes account for a large share of substantial and rapid changes in fertility. Jones (1978, pp. 23–4) provides several examples from South-East Asia where rising age at marriage has played an important role in major fertility declines, and the case of Sri Lanka is well known. In Cuba in the early 1960s, following the revolution, a decline in age at marriage was responsible for a noticeable increase in fertility. As Urzúa (1978, pp. 54–5) notes, in the case of Latin America this factor is partially responsible for differentials in completed fertility that exist between rural and urban areas, according to occupational status and so on.[13]

While marriage patterns directly affect fertility, it is clear that they are determined by a series of factors that extend well beyond a couples' (or their relatives') intentions as to completed family size. But a large fraction of existing research on fertility virtually ignores marriage and/or the variety of purposes it may serve besides those having to do with fertility. Those research findings that are available on the determinants of marriage patterns *per se* are usually of the statistical sort that show a positive association between age at marriage and various social and economic indices such as education and urbanization.

Contraception and induced abortion, which make up the second category of intermediate variables, are mainly responsible for the low fertility that exists in most developed countries. They have also been the object of much of the voluminous research referred to below on the demographic impact of family planning programmes in developing countries. What is worth noting here is that in spite of the volume of that research, accurate estimates of the direct impact of contraception and abortion on fertility are often not available. While reliable data on the percentage of women currently practising different forms of contraception by age may be obtained with well-designed surveys, frequently the only available information is on accumulated acceptors of various methods from family planning programmes, with only rough estimates of how many of these women are still practising, or of how many women are practising contraception but not participating in a programme. Measures of the use-effectiveness of contraception are not as easily obtained from surveys, and while there is some international experience on which to base estimates, the situation is often far from ideal. The unreliability of current estimates as to the quantity of induced abortions in developing countries, other than those provided by official health services (often none), is well known.

Empirically the most important variable in the third category of

[13] A useful demographic distinction may be drawn between the 'permanent' effect of nuptiality on cohort fertility, with age at marriage and proportions ever married influencing eventual fertility, and the 'temporary' distortion of period fertility when age at marriage rises or falls. The Cuban experience is clearly an example of the latter type of effect, while the differentials in completed fertility in Latin America are an example of the cohort importance of nuptiality.

intermediate fertility variables is lactational infecundability. Of course, to directly obtain a reliable estimate of the length of time that elapses between birth and the resumption of ovulation or regular menstruation requires intensive observation in studies conducted over a length of time in a sample population. Very few such studies have been conducted in developing countries, and none of the samples is representative at the national level. It is usually the case in developing countries that information is also quite incomplete on the actual levels and trends for different sectors of the population in the mean duration of breast-feeding, yet lactational infecundability may be responsible for much of the large differences between countries in the level of marital fertility to be found among women not practising contraception or abortion (Bongaarts, 1978; Knodel, 1977). A related factor that appears to be of major importance in many Sub-Saharan African countries, and possibly in traditional or indigenous sectors of other developing country populations, is post-partum abstinence.

While the state of knowledge on both of these factors in Sub-Saharan Africa is more complete than in other regions and is improving rapidly, the same cannot be said with respect to the subfecundity and sterility that are prominent in the 'low fertility belt' of tropical Africa. Perhaps the one biological mechanism whose role is well documented is that of venereal disease in promoting sterility and spontaneous intra-uterine mortality.

Some Statistical Associations

A large part of social science research on fertility has been of a statistical nature, involving attempts to distinguish those aspects of development (as represented by socioeconomic indices of various sorts) that are most closely related to fertility. Often this type of research has been undertaken to determine the origins of fertility declines in the past or to account for regional differences in fertility. In many instances the results have been used to support the case for theoretical propositions that have varied in complexity from the most simple versions of demographic transition theory to the more sophisticated versions of the 'new household economics'. The statistical techniques employed have ranged in refinement from two- or three-dimensional cross tabulations to path analysis and highly sophisticated multiple-regression techniques, while the data have been both for individuals (collected in surveys) and for regions or countries (put together from a number of sources).

In the following paragraphs we will attempt to summarize very briefly some of the principal associations that have been reported in the very large number of such studies that were taken into consideration in the regional reviews prepared for the IRG.[14]

[14] These sorts of relations have recently been closely scrutinized in a number of other evaluation efforts. See Cassen (1976) and Ridker (1976); for education and female labour force participation, see Cochrane (1977) and Shields (1977), respectively.

In many analyses no other socioeconomic factor has a stronger negative correlation with fertility than educational attainment. Levels of education and/or literacy are found to be negatively correlated with fertility at the national, regional, and individual level, and the relationship holds over time as well as in the cross-section. A major complication is that the negative relationship does not always hold throughout the entire range of values for educational attainment, and that the 'threshold value', or the point at which the association becomes negative, varies widely between countries, between rural and urban areas within a country, and also through time. When the educational level of both men and women is considered, usually it is women's education that is found to have the greater correlation with fertility.

Female labour force participation is another of the variables usually found to be negatively correlated with fertility, whether the analysis is for individuals or for aggregates of individuals in regions or nations. But once again, across countries and regions the relationship between the two variables varies considerably. In particular, considerable female participation in urban occupations in Sub-Saharan Africa has been found to coexist with high and unchanging patterns of fertility (Mabogunje and Arowolo, 1978, pp. 22–3).

Income is a variable for which, when the influence of other variables is taken into account, an association with fertility often seems to emerge, whether income be calculated in per capita terms for a region, or per family or per household member or per wage earner in analyses of individuals or families. A major difficulty is that income is usually closely correlated with other socioeconomic variables associated with fertility, and thus attempts to separate out the particular role of income independent of education, female labour force participation, and so on, are by no means trivial exercises. The distribution as well as the absolute level of income have recently been shown to be related to fertility at the national level (Ahluwalia, 1976), with greater equality in distribution being associated with lower fertility.

The other variables that are generally recognized as having a negative association with fertility in cross-sectional analyses of regions or countries are urbanization and industrialization (or its rough complement, the percentage of the population earning a living in agriculture). Nevertheless, empirical results do not always support the generalization (Desai, 1978, p. 66). Certainly these two processes have a differential impact by social class, a fact that is often lost sight of in aggregate-level studies.

Finally, in cross-sectional analyses of countries or of political divisions within countries, the level of mortality (as measured either by the infant mortality rate or by the expectation of life at birth) is found to be a significant predictor of fertility.

Individual Attitudes towards Fertility and its Control

In the past two decades major efforts have been made in developing countries to determine individuals' knowledge of birth-control methods, attitudes towards fertility and its limitation, and the extent of unwanted fertility. Over a very wide range of developing countries, the early KAP (knowledge, attitude, and practice) studies provided results indicating that more people were interested in using contraception to limit fertility than were actually doing so. The conclusion was that there was a significant unmet demand for family planning services, and that if these were provided a substantial decline in fertility would occur. For a variety of reasons ranging from observation of certain historical experiences to dissatisfaction with the psychological premises underlying the highly simplified methodology, these results are now viewed with considerable scepticism.

The current of research that began with the KAP studies now seems to have forked in two quite different directions. The first of these is the pragmatic approach taken by the World Fertility Survey to continue measuring current reproductive intentions and actual contraceptive practice with a short battery of straightforward questions. One concept of unmet need for contraception that may be applied to WFS data is the proportion of currently married women who are exposed to the risk of conception (i.e. who are not pregnant or infecund by virtue of either a sterilization or natural sterility), who say they want no more children, but who are not practising contraception. The results of a number of World Fertility Surveys are just now becoming available, and like their predecessors, the KAP studies, they indicate a substantial number of women who apparently are disposed to terminate childbearing but who are not doing anything to prevent another pregnancy. Remarkably, the size of this proportion is very similar across the several developing countries for which results are available, although the amount of actual practice of contraception varies enormously between them. Westoff (1978, pp. 9–18) has presented a preliminary comparative analysis of results from Korea, Malaysia, Nepal, Pakistan, and Thailand, where the percentage of exposed women using a contraceptive method varies from 3 per cent (Nepal) to 46 per cent (Korea and Thailand). Among these five countries, unmet demand as defined above ranges only from 21 to 32 per cent. The same calculation for the WFS survey undertaken in the Dominican Republic shows a potential demand of 22 per cent. Of course, the principal question concerns the validity of the response to the question regarding the desire for additional children, but it may be noted that data of this type vary in a consistent and plausible way with age, parity, and other variables.

The second current of research that followed upon the KAP studies is one of considerable complexity that has involved developing and testing a conceptual framework for childbearing motivation and family size limitation. In the main it consists of an ambitious endeavour known as the cross-national Value of Children (VOC) Project, which began in 1972.[15] This research was carried out in six countries in its first phase: Japan, Korea, the Philippines, Taiwan, Thailand, and the US (Hawaii). In its second phase, the research no longer includes Japan but has added Indonesia, Singapore, Turkey, and the Continental US. The framework specifies that the meaning (value) of children to parents is based on the goals that children facilitate or frustrate. These goals may be categorized as social, economic, and emotional, and their relation with childbearing depends on the circumstances in which parents find themselves, including the alternatives to childbearing that are available. In addition, the VOC investigators have sought to go beyond an investigation of preferences alone to also include actual choice behaviour.

The results now available from the first phase of the project provide fairly convincing evidence that specific beliefs and values forming the basis of childbearing and child-limitation motivation can be identified. They also demonstrate how values and costs vary by parity, suggesting that appropriate communications could be designed to influence women of particular chosen parities. And they illustrate variations in values related to preferences for sons and daughters. While variations in both economic and emotional satisfactions from children by education, income, and urban residence have been shown, the research so far has not identified specific features of socioeconomic organization that are readily amenable to policy intervention. Finally, the relationship between the perceived value of children and fertility behaviour was only weakly demonstrated in the first phase of the project.

Research in the second phase of the project suggests that different patterns of values appear to be related to different fertility levels. Economic benefits of childbearing decline early in the fertility transition, the value of children for companionship and for reinforcing the marriage rises later in the transition, and the restrictions that children impose on parents become salient late in the transition (Bulatao, 1978). How these changes could be accelerated by policy instruments has not been fully discussed.

Theories of Fertility Change

Perhaps the most striking aspect of the present state of knowledge on fertility is the absence of an accepted theory of fertility change. The demographic transition has been an object of study in demography and related social sciences for over 25 years, and yet no satisfactory or proven theory is at hand to explain the phenomenon either in now-developed or in presently developing countries. Following, we present a rough

---

[15] The premises, progress, and the expected results of this research were recently reviewed in a paper by Alan Simmons (1977, pp. 157–80). See also Arnold *et al.* (1975) and Fawcett (1976).

summary of the present status of fertility theory and highlight the differences among some of the more important approaches to the demographic transition that are now competing for policy-makers' attention on the one hand, and additional research funds on the other.

One of the initial formulations of demographic transition theory was made by Notestein in 1953. In a now classic statement, he offered a summary explanation of the shift from high fertility — which was rational in its premodern context — to low fertility.

> The new ideal of the small family arose typically in the urban industrial society. It is impossible to be precise about the various causal factors, but apparently many were important. Urban life stripped the family of many functions in production, consumption, recreation, and education. In factory employment the individual stood on his own accomplishments. The new mobility of young people and the anonymity of city life reduced the pressures toward traditional behavior exerted by the family and community. In a period of rapidly developing technology new skills were needed, and new opportunities for individual advancement arose. Education and a rational point of view became increasingly important. As a consequence, the cost of childbearing grew and the possibilities for economic contributions by children declined. Falling death rates at once increased the size of the family to be supported and lowered the inducements to have many births. Women, moreover, found new independence from household obligations and new economic roles less compatible with childbearing.
>
> Under these multiple pressures old ideals and beliefs began to weaken, and the new ideal of a small number of children gained strength. (Quoted in Coale, 1973, p. 54.)

Numerous endeavours to analyse the relation between modernization and fertility were consequent upon this early formulation. Many, in a highly empirical fashion, set out to identify the aspects and levels of modernization that were required for the shift from one fertility regime to another. The terrain was at first largely confined to historical analysis of the transitions that took place some time ago in the now-developed countries, but as fertility decline and low fertility became a more frequent phenomenon in developing countries, efforts were launched to analyse the association of fertility with indices of modernization both across regions and over time in individual countries, as well as in the cross-section of all developing countries for which the requisite data were available. Both the developing country studies, reflected in the above subsection on 'Some Statistical Associations', and the studies of the now-developed countries, many of which were conducted under the rubric of the European Fertility Project, came to similar results in the sense that neither has been able to define anything close to a precise threshold — in Coale's words, 'a checklist of essential characteristics, or combined score on some socioeconomic scale' — of modernization that will reliably identify a population in which fertility is ready to fall (Coale, 1973, pp. 64–5).

The conclusion is not that fertility is not related to modernization and development — it very clearly is — but rather that the relationship is a loose one that varies among regions, countries, and cultures. As has often been pointed out, there is no doubt that fully modernized societies will have low fertility (Coale, 1973; Demeny, 1968). It is also clear, however, that fertility has declined substantially and at a very rapid pace in a number of countries that are by no means fully modernized, at least by comparison with the Western model.

Among other attributes, a more powerful theory of fertility would be able to discriminate between those developing countries where fertility is ready or about to decline and those where it is not, and would possibly suggest policy measures — other than general development — that could do much to speed up or bring on a fertility transition.

More recent approaches to the problem have been of two sorts. On the one hand, there have been further empirical attempts to identify the subset of developmental conditions that is sufficient to motivate fertility declines. Here the emphasis has been on the particular aspects of the development setting — such as female education or equality of income or opportunity — that are thought to be most closely related to reproductive behaviour. On the other hand, more theoretical approaches have concentrated on aspects of the decision-making environment that may constitute the direct links between the macrovariables that were relied on in previous work (or, more generally, between changes in the development setting) and fertility.

In the latter vein, following McNicoll (1978b), it is possible to distinguish somewhat arbitrarily three different routes or mediating variables through which changes in context may influence behaviour: '(1) through alterations in the array of economic benefits and costs associated with marriage and fertility; (2) through shifts in the organizational context of marital and fertility decision making that affect social and administrative pressures on individuals or couples; and (3) through changes in internalized values concerning marriage and fertility instilled by education, socialization, and acculturation.'

Economic costs and benefits. It is a shared tenet of those who first formulated demographic transition theory and almost everyone who works in the area today that fertility tends to respond to shifts in the balance of economic benefits and costs that childbearing entails. Among the elements or considerations that enter, consciously or not, into this calculus at the level of the individual or family are: the opportunity costs attached to time spent by parents or others in childrearing; direct costs such as those arising from expenditures on food, clothing, and education; the economic benefits derived from children, in terms of eventual monetary contributions as well as work contributed towards household maintenance; and, last, the costs attached to preventing or terminating pregnancy.

Changes in 'objective conditions' of various sorts can substantially affect the net economic benefit derived from balancing these different elements. Listed below, by way of example, are some of the more frequently mentioned contextual changes that presumably bear on the economic benefit attached to different levels of childbearing:

— A decline in mortality and improved health conditions mean not only that more children survive, but that planning horizons are lengthened and expectations of death or sickness are altered. If a given number of children made economic sense before, the same number can be achieved with fewer births in the new circumstances.[16]
— The proletarianization of the labour force and the decline of familial modes of production may increase the perceived cost of time devoted to childrearing as this activity begins to compete with opportunities to raise earnings outside the home.
— The increased availability of consumer goods introduces new consumption alternatives that, at least for the upwardly mobile, may compete for the time and resources previously devoted to children.
— When education becomes a possibility, it may be expensive. It also reduces the time that children can devote to household chores.
— Changes in family structure can radically restrict the possibilities for sharing the costs of raising children among the members of an extended family and lead to a new locus of authority for fertility decisions.
— Government-supported family planning programmes may serve to lower the direct economic cost of birth control.
— Welfare institutions, providing minimum subsistence, at least in food and support in old age, may constitute alternatives to children as sources of economic security.

Social and administrative pressures. The second route through which changes in context may influence fertility behaviour is less tangible and, perhaps for that reason, often overlooked. First of all, social pressure from kin and community are often felt not on the direct question of family size, but rather with regard to several related issues such as age at marriage, birth-control practices, coital frequency, breastfeeding, sex roles, divorce, remarriage, and so on. If the social groups that generate these pressures should weaken, then individuals and families face fewer sanctions in cases where self-interest diverges from social prescription whether in the direction of a greater or lesser number of children. To the extent that government takes an active stance in implementing policies to reduce fertility, however, new pressures arise that come to bear directly on

[16] Note that to the extent that in the original circumstances the desired number of children actually exceeded the number surviving, the previous level of fertility may still be advantageous (Tabbarah, 1971).

fertility. These may range in intensity and proximity from radio announcements promoting the benefits of a small family, to attempts to mobilize local administrative authorities to help meet family planning targets of various kinds.

Examples of contextual changes that affect local social relations are the following:

— Improvements in transport and communications are likely to expand the territory encompassed by markets for produce and labour, and thus reduce the cohesiveness and economic importance of rural village communities. Rural out-migration, facilitated by these same improvements, may also help to undermine the solidarity of villages.
— Changes in local political and administrative systems may remove the need for patronage or similar groups as a means to political power and economic position.
— Shifts in labour relations have social as well as economic implications. The significance of clan and other kin-based groups is likely to be eroded by the increased predominance of formal employer–employee relations.

Internalized values. The third route of impact is even less tangible than the second, but changes in attitudes and beliefs are held to be important factors, often independently of the institutional setting. The spread of a more homogeneous, urban-based popular culture is an almost inevitable phenomenon in today's developing countries. Part and parcel of this shift away from more traditional or indigenous cultural patterns is an increased awareness of alternative life-styles. The 'demonstration effect' produced by the consumption patterns of the rich, as well as the images that filter through from the world network of Western culture undoubtedly stimulate in a powerful way aspirations for new consumer goods. New tastes — in combination with the perception of the possibility of fulfilling them — can, as was mentioned above, come into conflict with high fertility. The second type of cultural change that may have an important effect on fertility is in attitudes towards spouse and children. The nuclear family as a distinctive emotional unit with a closer, more sentimental conjugal bond and more place given to the mother's maternal feelings may yield fertility decisions quite different from those that existed in the system of family relations that it replaced. A different sort of cultural change is in individual perceptions of freedom of action and the range of issues that require active decisions. When horizons of this sort are widened, matters such as contraceptive practice and family size may be among those that are no longer taken for granted.

What produces cultural change of the sorts described above is clearly an unresolved question — more a matter of opinion and argument than of proof by evidence. Among the contextual changes that may have an influence are the following:

- Improved transport and communication facilities are once again prominent. Increased mobility and the media are both responsible for exposure to 'new ideas' and life-styles.
- Expansion of formal education may give rise to a variety of challenges to traditional culture. Among other things, it has been said that the messages from the educational system are often Western and tend to teach age and sex equality.
- Family planning programmes attempt to instil a small family norm and legitimize the concept of family limitation and contraceptive practice.

The preceding paragraphs constitute a rather crude framework encompassing a variety of possible links between fertility and social and economic change. Besides demonstrating the complexity of the problem, it is useful as a means of classifying and assessing several of the more well-known approaches to fertility theory. These may be distinguished according to the different mediating variables that they take into account and the relative importance that is assigned to each.

The 'new household economics', for example, focuses squarely on the economic costs and benefits of children and ignores whatever effects may be generated by social arrangements. To the extent that tastes are subject to change, as in the work of Tabbarah (1971), Liebenstein (1974), and Easterlin (1978), the broader economic approaches actually incorporate some elements from the third set of relations included in the preceding framework.

In Caldwell's (1976 and 1978) recent theorizing on the demographic transition, the crux of the matter is seen as a reversal in the direction of intergenerational wealth flows. The stimulus for this change is mostly cultural and ideological — an acceptance of Western views of the family — but also takes into account changes in economic organization. This approach emphasizes the family as the main social group refracting environmental changes, and only slight importance is attached to pressures that may be generated by the supra familial social structure.

A quite different approach is taken by those who advocate institutional theories of fertility change. Here the focus is on the second set of relations included in the framework — inheritance rules, marriage customs, the system of local government, and so on. This approach has sometimes been associated with arguments in favour of community-level population policies that would seek to 'reduce the size of the group within which the costs of children are spread and to which the benefits of lowered fertility would accrue' (McNicoll, 1975).

Of the various Marxist approaches to fertility theory that are being developed today, probably the most well known is the Latin American 'historical-structural' school of thought. In some formulations (e.g. Singer, 1971) the main emphasis is on the demographic effect of a shift in the organization of economic activity towards capitalist modes of production.

The family is recognized as the main social group, which by adopting a 'survival strategy' attempts to cope by demographic and other means with the realities of its environment. The first set of relations included in the framework are, in the last analysis, those that receive by far the greatest emphasis in this perspective.

The last major approach to the demographic transition to be mentioned here is one that emphasizes the diffusion of ideas specifically concerned with reproduction as well as the diffusion of tastes and desires for consumer goods (Freedman, 1978; Knodel, 1977). This view recognizes the need for a certain minimum level of development as a precondition to demographic transition, but maintains that once it is achieved, the principal influences on fertility are those listed in the framework under 'internalized values'. These forces, once set in motion, are credited with generating very rapid declines in fertility that are not related to concurrent changes in objective conditions.

Most of the approaches to the demographic transition reviewed here appear quite narrow in comparison with the over-all framework set out earlier. The task of theory building, however, is clearly one of narrowing down the range of possible relations that are held to be important. In the present situation much of the narrowing has been done arbitrarily rather than on some systematic basis. Hence, there are major differences among the various schools of thought, and the emergence of a generally accepted paradigm seems to be a long way off. The proponents of one or the other approach have little difficulty in finding support from historical experience; indeed, it is common for the same fertility transitions to be used to support quite different 'theories'.[17]

One implication of this state of affairs is that the ability to predict fertility change with reasonable accuracy is severely restricted. In the general case there are just too many factors that might make a difference, one way or the other, for most people to be confident about the outcome. What, however, are the implications for policy analysis? There is certainly no shortage of hypothesized relationships with important implications for policy design. The problem would be easier if there were solid grounds for selecting among them; but, in practice, both thorough familiarity with the individual situation and political feasibility may provide sufficient criteria.

The Consequences of Alternative Patterns and Trends in Fertility

Not surprisingly, analysis of the consequences of fertility at the local, family, or individual level has much in common with issues and propositions that are identified above with regard to fertility determinants. Especially related are the consequences of family size for the health, education, and welfare of different members of the family, and the impacts

[17] For example, see the quite different lessons that are drawn from the Chinese case in McNicoll (1975) and Freedman (1978).

of different rates of increase in the membership of different local groups, both for the groups themselves and for others outside the groups. Not necessarily related, but certainly parallel are the consequences of different patterns of demographic change for certain 'structural' features of the local setting, which might include a change in the proportion of the population that is landless or that is employed in one type of activity or another, and the wages or returns that different activities are able to provide.

A proposition that is central to most approaches to the demographic transition is that high fertility and large family size is a sensible response to the objective economic and social conditions faced by a large proportion of families in developing countries. Yet, there is a considerable amount of literature in fields such as nutrition, psychology, and public health — often pulled together under the heading 'the micro-consequences of population growth' (e.g. Birdsall, 1977) — that purports to show negative effects of large family size on maternal and child health and child development, incorporating dimensions such as morbidity, physical development, and intelligence. In a review of literature of this type published in 1971, Wray concluded that 'the consistent trend of the consequences associated with either increasing family size or decreasing birth interval is striking and uniformly negative'. As Jones (1978, p. 87) points out, however, the extent to which the studies Wray refers to control for relevant variables besides family size is, on the whole, inadequate. Thus, there is room for doubt as to whether some of the ill-effects are caused by high fertility *per se*.

While there is an apparent discrepancy between the findings reported in the 'micro-consequences' literature and the results of the anthropological village-level studies that document the various ways in which children contribute to the economic well-being of the household (e.g. Nag *et al.*, 1977), to some extent this may be accounted for by the possibly exploitative nature of some intra-family relations and the presence of conflicts of interest between generations and between the sexes.

Relatively little work has been done on the impact of different rates of population growth on structural aspects of the local environment, perhaps owing to the underdevelopment of institutional analysis in comparison with mainstream micro- and macro-economic modelling (McNicoll, 1977, p. 30). Jones (1978, pp. 79–82) reviews findings that are available for countries in South-East Asia. There he contrasts Geertz's (1963) well-known characterization of the Javanese case, where by way of 'shared poverty' an ever-increasing work force has been accommodated to a fixed land area, with Geertz's critics, who emphasize the process of increasing class stratification based on differential access to land.

In the past, most analyses of the economic and social consequences of alternative trends in fertility were conducted at the macro or national level. The study of the relation between alternative rates of population growth and economic development has a long and chequered history. Much of this work, in accordance with the development objectives of the 1950s and 1960s, focused on income per capita as the relevant index of development and analysed the issue at highly aggregated levels, often with no disaggregation whatsoever. Early analyses came to the conclusion that a decline in fertility would result — in 15 years or so — in higher per capita income; but these results were later challenged on the grounds that various 'positive' effects of rapid population growth were not included and that a number of factors had been treated inadequately (e.g. Myrdal, 1968; Ruprecht, 1970). In short, no conclusive findings as to the quantitative relation between fertility and income per capita over time are available today. This should not come as a surprise, considering that agreement on, and understanding of, the factors responsible for economic growth in general are notably lacking. Today the fertility issue is no longer being tackled head on (with a few exceptions such as Simon, 1977 and Leontief, 1978). Rather, it surfaces from time to time in the development and application of economic-demographic models that claim many ambitious objectives besides analysis of the effect of fertility decline on GNP. (See, for example, the report on the BACHUE-Philippines model, Rodgers, Hopkins, and Wery, 1978.) Nevertheless, simulation exercises conducted with such models do in fact yield estimates of the influence of demographic change on per capita income. These tend to vary considerably between the different 'name' models, and they no longer receive a great deal of attention.

Sectoral impact studies that deal with the influence of alternative trends in fertility on particular parts of the economy (such as education, health, housing, transport, energy, and employment) constitute the second major area of research on 'macro-consequences'. Some of the most concrete results are with respect to education. A number of careful studies have been made of the additional costs involved in attaining improved school enrolment ratios under different demographic assumptions. Here the difference between high and low fertility becomes important after a 10-year period and very substantial within 20 years. With respect to employment, the analysis of the effect of alternative trends in fertility follows logically upon the completion of projections of both demographic and educational trends, requiring in addition projections of economic trends, employment structure, and manpower needs. The effects of different demographic assumptions show up clearly after a considerably longer period of time. The impact of a change in fertility on the health sector is felt almost immediately, however, owing to the fact that the demand for maternal and child health services constitutes a significant portion of total demand.

While the general nature of the relation between alternative trends in fertility and the feasibility of attaining targets related to the coverage of services in different sectors is by now quite evident from available case studies and simulation exercises, it is also clear that the specifics of such relations depend on the strategy that the country in question adopts to meet its objectives. In this sense, what is known about the impact of population growth on educational costs in, say, Thailand may not be readily transferable to Indonesia. Furthermore, the amount of attention that has been given to sectoral questions of this sort varies considerably among countries, in part due to the very uneven development of 'planning' in general among countries and regions.

One seemingly important question that has heretofore received relatively little attention from economists and demographers concerns the contribution of fertility change to income distribution problems. Several years ago the predominant hypothesis was that a decline in fertility would lead to greater income equality. The idea was founded on: (*a*) evidence from statistical analysis of the association between population growth and income inequality for a wide sample of countries at the same point in time but at different levels of development; (*b*) some elementary and perhaps naïve macro-economic logic regarding the 'labour share' of income; and (*c*) the assumption that fertility differentials between classes would tend to narrow rather than widen with a decline in fertility. Recently, however, it has been argued that in the Latin American context the third assumption is ill-founded.[18] In fact, the sharp declines in fertility that have recently taken place in the region have been very unevenly distributed among classes, and therefore the distributive effects of these declines may not be nearly as beneficial as once supposed. That is, the generally positive macro-level effects resulting from smaller (than otherwise) birth cohorts have to be counter-balanced with the effects of having a greater share of each birth cohort born into poor households (Potter, 1978).

Such discussion, due to an absence of both theoretical development and empirical testing, is only speculative. It does, however, point to two of the more severe limitations in many of the existing analyses of the effect of population change on economic development: their failure to distinguish between different groups within the population and their implicit assumption that fertility will decline evenly across all sectors of the society.

The last issue to be touched on in this subsection concerns the consequences of fertility trends for resource and environmental capacities. Fears of 'running out of resources' and concerns for loss of environmental amenities or, worse, ecological disaster, are age old. In the early 1970s, however, such concerns became surprisingly widespread in both the scientific community and among the public at large. It seemed, with the publication of *Limits to Growth* (Meadows *et al.*) in 1972, as if a new justification had been found for reducing population growth in both the

[18] It may, however, be a fair representation of much experience in South-East Asia.

developed and the developing countries. This study argued that the ultimate limits were sufficiently close to justify immediate action to stop world-wide population and economic growth. The subsequent debate served the useful purpose of creating interest in, and demand for, a longer-term perspective, but, in the final analysis, it left more questions than answers. Among these are: Are there limits to economic growth imposed by resource availabilities and environmental capacities? If so, how close are we to these limits? How important is population as opposed to other factors in moving us towards these limits?

A number of long-term growth studies attempting to answer these questions have either been recently completed or are near completion in a number of developing countries, several of them under the sponsorship of Resources for the Future (Ridker, 1978). On the whole they do not seem to have reached alarming conclusions. Some of the reasons why the limits to growth do not appear to be immediately in front of these countries are that: (*a*) unlike the developed countries, in many instances they can borrow technology that facilitates substitution away from scarce materials; (*b*) they are relatively unexplored and thus there is considerable optimism regarding as yet undiscovered resources; and (*c*) the potential for solving specific shortages through international trade appears to exist. The problem of analysing environmental constraints, as might have been expected, has proven to be the most intractable, and few hard conclusions about ecological deterioration appear to have been reached.

The other conclusion that seems to stand out is the importance of managerial, institutional, social, and political (both national and international) factors as impediments both to economic growth *per se* and to the achievement of increased equity.

The Impact of Family Planning Programmes

Family planning programmes have constituted the cornerstone of most antinatalist fertility policies in developing countries. The question of how much they have contributed to reducing fertility where it has declined is one of the most controversial within the IRG's field of interest.

There are basically three approaches that have been taken in attempting to determine the impact on fertility of family planning programmes. The first consists of accounting exercises in which a time-series of programme service statistics and information from surveys on contraceptive use are put together with information on nuptiality and natural fertility factors in a fertility model (TABRAP and PROJTARG are examples) to determine the impact of increased contraceptive use on fertility rates. This increase can in turn often be separated into the increment that was provided by the private sector and that provided by family planning programmes. Such exercises have been conducted with greater or lesser sophistication that usually hinged on the adequacy of the data base — both with respect to the use and effectiveness of contraceptives and to other elements of the fertility process. The point, however, is that the results provide only meagre indications as to the direction of causation — that is, whether the programme played an initiating rather than a facilitating role in the fertility decline — and what would have been the decline in the absence of the programme (see Urzúa, 1978, pp. 79–83; and Jones, 1978, pp. 25–49, for several references to studies of this type).

Recognizing the inconclusiveness of the 'accounting' evidence and responding to extreme claims put forth by one side or the other, it is not unusual for protagonists in the debate over the causes behind a given decline to engage in descriptive analyses of the changes that may have taken place in the 'socioeconomic setting' prior to and during the decline, in an attempt to argue either that the fertility decline was really initiated by socioeconomic change or that it was not.[19] (Again, Urzúa and Jones refer to several examples of analyses of this sort with respect to fertility declines in Chile, Colombia, and Costa Rica on the one hand, and Thailand, Indonesia, and Taiwan on the other). While 'reasoned' arguments and sociographic studies of this sort are unlikely to provide a definitive resolution of the issue, by making use of an eclectic mix of analytical techniques they may on occasion come as close to 'explanation' as anyone could hope to expect.

The third and final approach to analysing the impact of family planning programmes is through the utilization of multivariate statistical analysis. Taiwan was the first focus for this sort of research (Jones, 1978, p. 47). There, small-area data have been analysed in an attempt to disentangle the effects of social and economic factors and the effects of family planning programme inputs on contraceptive use and birth rates. More recently, Mauldin and Berelson (1978) completed a similar analysis at the international level using data on socioeconomic setting, contraceptive use, and an index of 'programme effort'. These studies have yielded results indicating that family planning programmes have a considerable influence on fertility decline. For the most part, they have made use of sophisticated statistical methodology, but not even the most powerful techniques can effectively distinguish the direction of causality (which in many other applications can be taken for granted on the basis of *a priori* theoretical grounds). To the extent that the 'programme effort' variable reflects underlying fertility determinants not grasped by the available socioeconomic indicators, its validity as an independent explanatory variable is severely compromised (Demeny, 1979, p. 149). In this regard it is worth noting that one extreme, but not entirely implausible, interpretation of the statistical evidence that has been assembled is that it is fertility decline in combination with an improving socioeconomic setting that has

[19] Often one of the key points in the position that socioeconomic change initiated the fertility decline is that fertility began to decline before the family planning programme was large enough to have had much of an effect.

a powerful effect on programme effort (Thomson, 1977). Another problem is that of distinguishing between 'demand' and 'supply' effects of the programmes themselves. One central hypothesis is that the 'availability' of contraceptive services makes an independent difference. Yet, so far, relatively little effort has been devoted to the definition and measurement of 'availability'. (For one of the few methodological studies, see Rodríguez, 1977.)

The Impact of other Interventions

Social scientists have attempted to analyse the impact of other policy interventions undertaken both with and without the expressed objective of modifying fertility. A limited number of policy measures or designs have been implemented to induce fertility change by influencing the 'demand' for children. These include incentive schemes, both pro- and antinatalist, and communication programmes. Often these form part, administratively, of family planning programmes. With respect to communication programmes, the empirical studies that are available on the effect of information (or propaganda) on fertility demonstrate some but not large impacts in isolation from other contaminating factors, plus resistance to influence in the absence of other life-changing conditions (Berelson, 1978, p. 13). It is notable, however, that a number of major communication projects such as that recently implemented in Mexico have not been the object of thorough evaluation (Simmons, 1977).

With respect to incentive schemes, there is substantial evidence that immediate monetary incentives of moderate size increase the acceptance of vasectomy in certain societies; the impact on fertility of disincentives or indirect incentives such as those implemented in Singapore regarding public housing and maternity fees, or deferred incentives as in the Taiwan educational bond scheme or the experiment undertaken on several tea estates in India has yet to be thoroughly evaluated.

Recently the possibility of evaluating the fertility impact of large projects to promote rural development in general, or rural electrification or irrigation in particular, has attracted much attention. The problem of developing a sound research design with which to carry out such endeavours is, however, clearly formidable. In one of the few available studies of this sort, it has recently been argued that part of the impact of a large rural electricity co-operative in western Misamis Oriental, the Philippines, was to raise the opportunity costs of children, and that this change, in combination with the availability of family planning services, led to a considerable decline in fertility (Herrin, 1979).

Towards Establishing a Policy-Relevant Research Agenda

In the preceding paragraphs we have tended to emphasize the inadequacy and incompleteness of the current state of knowledge on fertility. Indeed, considering the amount of research that has been done on this topic in the last 25 years, to an outsider it must seem surprising that there is so little agreement on the major questions that the field faces. Two extreme reactions to the situation would be to either set forth an impossibly long research agenda — in fact recommending 'more of everything' — or to pessimistically conclude that we know nearly as much about fertility as we will ever know.

In the following paragraphs, by pulling together what the IRG has learned about the major policy questions and the way policy-makers view these issues in the different regions and subregions of the developing world, we hope to demonstrate the logic behind the research recommendations that are made below, both in terms of what is included and what is not.

With Regard to Consequences

There is a tremendous difference between countries in the attitudes of policy-makers towards the need for additional research on the social and economic consequences of alternative trends in fertility with reference to their own country. The clearest division is between countries that have adopted a definite policy to reduce fertility and those that have not.

Let us take up first the case of countries strongly committed to reducing population growth. It became clear during the course of the first two IRG regional workshops that the participating policy-makers, the majority of whom were from countries strongly committed to reducing population growth, were not very interested in more definite or precise research results about the social gains to be achieved from reduced fertility, at least by further use of the methodologies currently available. For them, the need was rather to move ahead in determining how the goal of reducing fertility might be accomplished. This is not to say that there was any lack of interest in topics such as the influence of demographic factors on employment. On the contrary. But it seems that, to them, the policy relevance of research on such issues would be more in terms of what it could contribute to the design of, say, a more effective manpower and employment policy than in terms of what it might reveal about the need to reduce fertility (IRG 1978a and 1978b).

Among policy-makers from countries strongly or even moderately committed to reducing population growth, a similar attitude extended towards models. There was considerable interest in ensuring that demographic variables (and here the reference is to mortality and migration as well as fertility) were properly taken into account in both long- and short-term economic planning models. The emphasis, however, was on improving and using existing models rather than on developing new models and generating additional planning exercises.[20]

In contrast, policy-makers (and scholars as well) from several Sub-Saharan African countries, such as Nigeria, that do not have a definite fertility policy in the sense of being either firmly pro- or antinatalist took a quite different stance towards the need for more adequate knowledge on the effects that continued high fertility might have on development objectives. They were very much interested in the effects that alternative patterns and trends in fertility might have on achieving specific sectoral objectives such as increasing school enrolment ratios and on more general targets such as improving income distribution. However, these policy-makers expressed little or no interest in research attempting to provide more concrete data on the effect of population growth on growth of income per capita. They allowed that while simple sectoral analyses might be quite mundane and common endeavours in other parts of the world, that was not the case in Africa, and 'simple' applied research of this sort was a major priority for countries such as Nigeria. Like the policy-makers from countries more committed to reducing fertility, many of those from Sub-Saharan Africa were concerned and eager that demographic data be available for planning exercises as distinct from research in general.

In terms of research on consequences of fertility levels that could potentially make a difference to policy, two other types should be mentioned. The first is with respect to the economic value of children. As Mitra (1977) has recently argued, it is not sufficient to simply implement a policy for the sake of facilitating the attainment of various national objectives. To the extent that, in the present circumstances, survival of either households or groups depends on large families and rapid increase in numbers, the state must be committed to changing the national social and economic structure rapidly enough to guarantee the viability of the new demographic structure. In this sense, more complete and more widely recognized knowledge on questions such as the importance of children as productive elements in the household and as eventual hedges against risk could possibly help prevent the sort of policy débâcle that recently took place in India.

Another kind of research that could make a difference to policy is that which would shed light on the distributional consequences of reproductive behaviour. So far, possible gainers and losers have been identified

---

[20] The interest of some planners in models actually extended well beyond consequences in that they hoped for a tool that could provide a comprehensive overview of the relations between population and development. Ideally this would take into account two-way causation and the interlinking of determinants and consequences to provide the best possible understanding of the indirect effects of change in either economic or demographic variables on the other.

on the basis of the familiar demographic criteria of age and sex. But clearly there are other criteria for distinguishing groups that are differentially affected by existing demographic processes. Among them are social class, rural–urban or regional residence, kinship, occupation, and race or religion. What is more, fertility differentials surely have an important effect in terms of the composition of succeeding generations. The results of research that contributes to the development and testing of concrete hypotheses regarding questions such as these would be relevant to two sorts of policy. On the one hand, they could provide indications as to where (among what groups) efforts to implement fertility policy would be to the greatest national advantage (taking distributional goals into consideration). On the other hand, they might suggest the advisability of policies of other kinds that would attempt to adjust or compensate for the distributive outcomes of on-going reproductive patterns.

The Absence of an Accepted Theoretical Framework

Clearly, one of the major limitations in the current state of knowledge is evidenced by the disagreement that exists over which factors are most likely to cause fertility to decline. While the approaches to fertility theory now contending for attention have quite different implications for the kinds of measures that should be taken to induce fertility change, as was mentioned above, the impediment to policy analysis and design may not be correspondingly great. Although there is disagreement over the effectiveness of today's chief policy instrument – increasing the availability of contraceptive services through organized family planning programmes – and over the extent of the 'problem' that they are supposed to eliminate (unwanted fertility), there is every reason for a government seeking to reduce fertility to implement a comprehensive, continuous, and humane family planning programme. Only the harshest reading of the evidence implies that such a programme will not have a measurable effect on the birth rate, and the effort is certainly justified on other grounds. Much the same is true for a communications programme providing information about the availability and use of contraceptives.

The more difficult question remains, however, of what to do when family planning programmes are being pursued with all due diligence and yet the demographic change that results is judged insufficient. Certainly one response – and one that some governments have indeed resorted to – has been to apply administrative pressure. The previous review of the variety of ways that fertility may be linked to social and economic change seems to indicate, however, that there are a number of alternative ways to influence human reproduction. The problem is that more often than not the requisite policy analysis has yet to be performed.

Restructuring Development

One sort of policy advice that has been put forth by scholars is the recommendation that somehow development be 'restructured'. In a crude attempt to categorize the different ways people have suggested that this might be done so as to produce lower fertility (among other things), two general approaches can be distinguished. The first consists of placing greater emphasis on those features of development — such as increased levels of literacy, educational opportunities for women, higher rates of female labour force participation, and reduced infant mortality — that have been shown to be correlated with reduced fertility. One attractive aspect of such a strategy is that it involves promoting policies that are already desirable on other grounds. But, given the poor predictive power of existing fertility theory, it is not certain that indirect effects alone would provide an adequate case for modifying social policies so central to the existing style of development.

What is more, this approach is open to question on other, more fundamental grounds. The relationships picked up by regression analysis — upon which the argument for 'restructuring' is often constructed — are not necessarily causal ones, and lacking in some specific cases is a convincing explication of the mechanisms that lead to the changed demographic outcome. 'Education, for example, is a composite outcome of a particular bureaucratic structure, financing scheme, target population, and array of parental and student motivations (to mention only some more obvious components), in addition to a curriculum; each has its own ties to population processes' (McNicoll, 1977, p. 11). If such is the case, then more education could lead to either higher or lower fertility — or to no change — depending on the components of the intervention.

The second approach to 'restructuring development' involves focusing attention on the elements of social organization that mediate between the national government and the family or individual. Here, restructuring is taken to refer to the political strategy regarding what social structures are to be mobilized in the development effort, and at issue are how changes in this strategy could influence those aspects of the local economic, institutional, and cultural situation that determine the level of fertility that individuals and families find it necessary to sustain. In this perspective, 'restructuring' involves decisions affecting the organizational base for development. These, in turn, have 'a large impact on the nature and quality of socioeconomic change, influencing the pace of economic growth, how the costs and benefits of growth are allocated, and the kind of society that results' (McNicoll, 1977, p. 27).

In many ways, the second approach is even more ambitious than the first. And, too, has its weaknesses. To begin with, the task is one of enormous complexity. For it to become workable there is a need to identify which of the vast array of social groups and institutional structures, with their differing interests and access to power, strongly influence or create the incentives that bear on reproductive behaviour. The fewer these turn out to be, the more feasible a solution becomes; but as was noted above, the sort of analysis that is required to distinguish between what is relevant and what is not is at present not well developed. The second major difficulty is analogous to one pertaining to the first approach. Institutional change is politically difficult to initiate. Existing forms tend to have support within government and strong constituencies outside it. As Korten has said, 'it becomes realistic to consider such reforms only when they are also supportive of other social agendas that enjoy broad constituencies' (1979, p. 5).

In a broad sense the two approaches to restructuring development for the purpose of inducing fertility change are not totally incompatible. The discussion suggests that two kinds of policy can be distinguished: both attempt to influence the incentives that bear on the fertility decisions of households or families, one seeking to work through existing institutional arrangements, and the other seeking to change them.

Felt Needs of Policy-Makers

Faced with the panorama of policy implications that derive from current hypotheses about what is required to induce fertility change, what is it that policy-makers are concerned with and what seem to be their priorities for future research on fertility?

In those countries where governments have devoted a significant share of public resources to family planning programmes, there is a strong demand for analytical research to evaluate the demographic effect of the programmes, as well as for 'programmatic' research that would provide guidance as to how to make family planning programmes more effective. Similarly, policy-makers have a clear interest in estimates of the demographic impact of mass-communication efforts and programmes of sex education, as well as laws regarding age at marriage and regulations regarding abortion.

Besides this interest in evaluating and improving policy measures undertaken (usually) for the express purpose of reducing fertility, the government officials from Asia and Latin America participating in the first two IRG workshops made it clear that they also were eager to have indications, however rough, of the effect on fertility of specific programmes undertaken in areas thought to influence fertility, such as nutrition, education, and maternal and child health. In addition to the evaluation of the effects of on-going development projects and policies, these policy-makers were also interested in research that would indicate on a prospective basis what development activities should be emphasized in order to obtain a maximum depressing effect on fertility. In general, like most scholars, they were of the opinion that the familiar multivariate analyses linking particular aspects of development to fertility levels or changes had reached a point of diminishing returns. What they hoped for were research designs that would produce more definite estimates of the elasticity of fertility response to changes in the development factors or sectoral policies within their jurisdiction.

This pragmatism was complemented by a keen sense of the pressure of time. Policy-makers faced with imminent decisions and demands for immediate action, while ready to admit that theoretical advances were necessary, were insistent that in addition to research that would yield useful results, say, after two or more years of work, they needed a certain number of descriptive research studies that could be completed in a shorter time frame. As one person heading a unit charged with co-ordinating national development policies bearing on population put it: 'Such studies, carried out on a disaggregated or regional basis, will not provide much guidance towards identifying new and more effective approaches, but they will help us to focus present program effort where it is needed most.'

Specific Recommendations

Institutional Analyses

Demographic behaviour is usually seen in either macro or micro terms. National birth rates are the outcome of decisions at the family level, and the incentives and influences to which families are subject are determined by aggregate conditions. What has been notably lacking in prior research on fertility is a focus on understanding what happens between these extremes at the (intermediate) level of social organization and local institutions. A major objective of future research on fertility and development should be to remedy this shortcoming. There is a need to delineate the patterns of social organization in the particular society and examine how these patterns influence individual economic and demographic decisions. Of special interest are the adverse consequences of decisions or actions that are transferred to others.

While analyses of this sort will require a considerable analytical effort and a thorough familiarity with the nature of the particular society and its families, there is, in many cases, the advantage that much of the work already done in economic anthropology, social history, and peasant studies can be pulled together and utilized for this purpose.

The policy relevance of the studies recommended here would be greatest where the major decisions concerning the organizational base for development are being reconsidered and where there is the intent to broaden the scope of local participation in development programmes directed towards reducing unemployment and social and economic disparities. At their best, such studies would provide guidelines as to how major reforms could be undertaken so that they would be securely linked to fertility change.

Micro-Level Studies of Family Economy

In recent years some of the most important contributions of social-science research to the understanding of reproductive behaviour have been the small number of in-depth village-level studies that document the important economic roles of children in poor rural households. While some progress has been made in analysing family structure and the nature of economic and productive relationships within the family, the empirical work that has been done refers only to a few settings, and the number of hypotheses in need of testing is increasing at a rapid rate. Among other things at issue are the direction of intergenerational flows of wealth and labour, the possibly exploitative nature of some intra-family relationships, the relation between these and reproductive behaviour, and the role of ideology and attitudes as against objective economic and social conditions in promoting change.

It seems of considerable priority that work on these issues be continued and broadened. The relevance to policy is of several kinds. First, to the extent that in many countries programmes and policies to reduce fertility are built on the premise that families with fewer children will be economically better off, and to the extent that it can be shown that this premise is false, governments will be encouraged to adopt a more realistic posture with regard to what they can expect from family planning programmes, and what would be the reaction to programmes that would attempt to limit family size by fiat. Secondly, there is a strong likelihood that work on wealth flows and on the nature of the family will suggest a variety of new ways that governments may be able to influence reproductive behaviour. For example, there is now some evidence that any measures that served to increase the 'child centredness' of families would, in effect, increase the cost of children. Thus, the enactment of laws protecting children could have a demographic impact, as could public encouragement of greater child care. Besides more basic work on the relationships themselves, also needed are research projects that would attempt the very difficult task of measuring the impact on fertility of the 'family-related' policy measures now in effect, as well as analyses of how to make these or other policies as influential as possible.

Evaluation of the Fertility Impact of Specific Development Programmes

Given the demand by policy-makers for studies of the fertility impact of programmes and projects that governments are now carrying out, and the belief of at least some scholars that evaluative studies can produce meaningful results, resources must be devoted to increasing the amount of effort that is devoted to this kind of research. Nevertheless, it should be recognized that theoretically and methodologically sound quasi-experimental research designs for this sort of study have yet to be developed. The hope is that cumulative experience in this applied area may, in combination with hypotheses forthcoming from the two parallel research efforts discussed above, lead to a significant advance in the state of the art.

Empirical and Theoretical Work on the Availability of Contraceptive Services

An important problem with previous efforts to evaluate the impact of family planning programmes is a failure or inability to distinguish between increases in the number of acceptors resulting from an increase in the demand for as against the supply of contraceptive services. Part of the problem stems from the excessive attention given to the final rather than the proximate objectives of family planning programmes. The former usually includes both reducing the birth rate and improving maternal and child health. But, irrespective of the nature of the ultimate goal, the uppermost immediate objective of all family planning programmes is to increase the 'availability' of supply of contraceptive services. Significant progress could be made in this area if further efforts were made to define what is meant by availability and how it might be measured directly. Mauldin and Berelson (1978, p. 101) have posed the question: 'How many people in the community have available to them the specified means of fertility control (or some locally approved selection thereof) at a specified level of quality of service, at affordable cost, and within, say, 30 minutes travel time?' Clearly, an adequate definition of availability would refer to more than simply monetary prices, but would also include considerations of information, time, and distance. The emphasis would be on the consumer's perspective, and the effort she/he has to expend to obtain different services.

The benefits to be obtained from placing increased emphasis on this orientation are twofold. First, it provides a more reasonable criterion for evaluating programmes that can supplement the usual method of judging success in terms of the number of acceptors. Roughly speaking, the success or failure of the programmes should be and often is measured by the change in the proportion of the population that has the means of contraception 'available' to them, as well as by the change in the proportion of the population that actually makes use of programme services. Secondly, the data on availability generated by such evaluation efforts could then be fed into cross-sectional studies that would for the first time be able to evaluate the importance of availability in comparison with other factors in determining levels of fertility.

Consequences for Income Distribution of Alternative Patterns and Trends in Fertility

Many, but not all, of the declines in fertility that are currently taking place in developing countries appear to be associated with a widening of fertility differentials by social class. Considerable priority should be given to the study of the distributional consequences of this phenomenon, as well as to studies attempting to sort out at the macro-level how various groups, sectors, or classes are differentially affected by population growth.

If important distributive effects could be shown to exist, governments might be motivated to alter the focus or emphases of existing programmes to induce fertility change, as well as to take measures in other areas that would compensate for the effects of demographic processes.

Descriptive Research

In many countries there is a need to expand the amount of descriptive knowledge that is available on the dimensions of fertility. As was made clear in the first part of the section on 'State of Knowledge', levels, trends, and differentials in fertility have yet to be adequately documented in many parts of the developing world. What is more, there is often substantial ignorance as to the components of fertility and which of them are most important in determining levels, trends, and differentials in aggregate fertility rates. Better knowledge of dimensions and processes may or may not make major contributions to the design of new approaches to fertility policy, but if produced quickly, it will meet a demand by policy-makers for information that can help them steer their current programmes in the best possible direction.

References

Ahluwalia, M. S. 1976. 'Inequality, Poverty and Development.' *Journal of Development Economics*, 3 (4), 307–42.

Arnold, F., *et al.* 1975. *The Value of Children: Introduction and Comparative Analysis*. Honolulu, Hawaii: The East–West Population Institute.

Berelson, Bernard. 1978. 'Social Science Research for Population Policy.' IRG Appendix 1. to the Final Report. El Colegio de México: IRG.

Birdsall, Nancy. 1977. 'Analytical Approaches to the Relationship of Population Growth and Development.' *Population and Development Review*, 3 (1–2), 63–102.

Bongaarts, John. 1978. 'A Framework for Analyzing the Proximate Determinants of Fertility.' Ibid. 4 (1), 105–32.

Bulatao, Rodolfo. 1978. 'On the Nature of the Transition in the Value of Children in Asia: Cross-sectional Comparisons.' Paper prepared for the Conference on Comparative Fertility Transition in Asia, Tokyo, March.

Caldwell, John C. 1976. 'Toward a Restatement of Demographic Transition Theory.' *Population and Development Review*, 2 (3 and 4), 321-66.

—— 1978. 'A Theory of Fertility: From High Plateau to Destabilization.' Ibid. 4 (4), 553–77.

Cassen, Robert H. 1976. 'Population and Development: A Survey.' *World Development*, 4 (10–11), 785–830.

Coale, Ansley J. 1973. 'The Demographic Transition Reconsidered.' In *International Population Conference, Liege, 1973*, vol. 1, pp. 53–71. Liege: IUSSP.

Cochrane, Susan H. 1977. 'Education and Fertility: What Do We Know?' Mimeo.

Demeny, Paul. 1968. 'Early Fertility Decline in Austria-Hungary. A Lesson in Demographic Transition.' *Daedelus*, 97. 502–22.

—— 1979. 'On the End of the Population Explosion.' *Population and Development Review*, 5 (1), 141–62.

Desai, P. B. 1978. 'Social Science Research on Population and Development in Middle South Asia.' Appendix 2 to the Final Report. El Colegio de México: IRG.

Easterlin, Richard A. 1978. 'Fertility and Development: The Easterlin Approach.' Paper prepared for the Seminar on Population and Development in the ECWA Region, November 1978, Amman, Jordan. E/ECWA/POP/WG.12/BP.9. Mimeo.

Fawcett, J. T. 1976. 'The Value and Cost of Children: Converging Theory and Research.' Paper presented at the annual meeting of the American Psychological Association, Washington, D.C., 2–7 September.

Freedman, Ronald. 1978. 'Theories of Fertility Decline: A Reappraisal.' Modified version of the second annual Amos Hawley Lecture, 11 April. Mimeo.

Geertz, Clifford. 1963. *Agricultural Involution*. Berkeley and Los Angeles: University of California Press.

Herrin, Alejandro N. 1979. 'Rural Electrification and Fertility Change in the Southern Philippines.' *Population and Development Review*, 5 (1), 61–86.

International Review Group (IRG). 1978a. 'Draft Summary Report of the First IRG Workshop on Research Priorities for Population Policy.' Colombo, Sri Lanka, 26–8 April. IRG/63.

—— 1978b. 'Draft Summary Report of the Second IRG Workshop on Research Priorities for Population Policy.' Mexico City, 28–30 June 1978. IRG/66-E.

Jones, Gavin. 1978. 'Social Science Research on Population and Development in South-East and East Asia.' Appendix 3 to the Final Report. El Colegio de México: IRG.

Knodel, John. 1977. 'Age Patterns of Fertility and the Fertility Transition: Evidence from Europe and Asia.' *Population Studies*, 31 (2), 219–49.

Korten, David C. 1979. 'New Issues, New Options: A Management Perspective on Population and Family Planning.' *Studies in Family Planning*, 10 (1), 3–14.

Leontief, Wassily. 1978. 'Population Growth and the Future of the World Economy.' In *Conference on 'Economic and Demographic Change: Issues for the 1980s', Helsinki, 1978*. Liege: IUSSP.

Liebenstein, Harvey. 1974. 'An Interpretation of the Economic Theory of Fertility: Promising Path or Blind Alley?' *Journal of Economic Literature*, 12 (2), 457–79.

Mabogunje, Akin L., and Arowolo, O. 1978. 'Social Science Research on Population and Development in Africa South of the Sahara.' Appendix 7 to the Final Report. El Colegio de México: IRG.

Mauldin, W. Parker, and Berelson, Bernard. 1978. 'Conditions of Fertility Decline in Developing Countries, 1965–75.' *Studies in Family Planning*, 9 (5), 90–147.

McNicoll, Geoffrey. 1975. 'Community-Level Population Policy: An Exploration.' *Population and Development Review*, 1 (1), 1–21.

—— 1977. 'Population and Development: Outlines for a Structuralist Approach.' Centre for Policy Studies, Working Papers. New York: The Population Council.

—— 1978a. 'On Fertility Policy Research.' *Population and Development Review*, 4 (4), 681–93.

—— 1978b. 'The Demography of Post-Peasant Society.' In *Conference on 'Economic and Demographic Change: Issues for the 1980s', Helsinki, 1978*. Leige: IUSSP.

Meadows, D.H., *et al.* 1972. *The Limits to Growth*. New York: Universe Books.

Mitra, Asok. 1977. 'National Population Policy in Relation to National Planning in India.' *Population and Development Review*, 3 (3), 297–306.

Myrdal, Gunnar. 1968. *Asian Drama*. New York: Pantheon.

Nag, Moni, Peet, Robert C. and White, Benjamin. 1977. 'Economic Value of Children in Two Peasant Societies.' In *International Population Conference, Mexico, 1977*, vol. 1. Liege: IUSSP.

Potter, Joseph E. 1978. 'Demographic Factors and Income Distribution in Latin America.' In *Conference on 'Economic and Demographic Change: Issues for the 1980s', Helsinki, 1978*. Liege: IUSSP.

Ridker, Ronald G. 1976. *Population and Development. The Search for Selective Interventions*. Baltimore: Johns Hopkins University Press.

— 1978. 'Resource and Environmental Consequences of Population and Economic Growth.' In *Conference on 'Economic and Demographic Change: Issues for the 1980s', Helsinki, 1978*. Liege: IUSSP.

Rodgers, G. B., Hopkins, M. J. D. and Wery, R. 1978. *Population, Employment and Inequality: BACHUE-Philippines*. London: Saxon House/Teakfield.

Rodríguez, Germán. 1977. 'Assessing the Availability of Fertility Regulation Methods: Report on a Methodological Study.' World Fertility Survey Scientific Reports, Number 1.

Ruprecht, T. K. 1970. *Rapid Population Growth and Macro-Economic Development: The Philippines Case*. Bloomington, Indiana: International Development Research Centre, Indiana University.

Shields, Nwanganga. 1977. 'Female Labor Force Participation and Fertility: Review of Empirical Evidence from LDCs.' Washington, D.C.: Population and Human Resources Division, World Bank. Mimeo.

Simmons, Alan. 1977. 'The VOC Approach in Population Policies: New Hope or False Promise?' In *International Population Conference Mexico, 1977*, vol. 1. Liege: IUSSP.

Simon, Julian L. 1977. The *Economics of Population Growth*. Princeton: Princeton University Press.

Singer, Paul. 1971. *Dinámica de la Población y Desarrollo*. Mexico: Siglo XXI.

Stolnitz, George J. 1978. World and Regional Population Trends: Long Views and Current Prospects. Statement presented to the House Select Committee on Population, US House of Representatives.

Tabbarah, Riad B. 1971. 'Toward a Theory of Demographic Development.' *Economic Development and Cultural Change*, 19 (2), 257–77.

Thomson, Elizabeth J. 1977. 'The Role of Population Policy in Family Planning Program Acceptance and Fertility Decline.' Paper presented at the Annual Meeting of the Population Association of America, St. Louis, Missouri, 21–3 April.

Urzúa, Raúl. 1978. 'Social Science Research on Population and Development In Latin America.' Appendix 11 to the Final Report. El Colegio de México: IRG.

Westoff, Charles F. 1978. 'The Unmet Need for Birth Control in Five Asian Countries.' *International Family Planning Perspectives and Digest*, 4 (1), 9.

Wray, Joe D. 1971. 'Population Pressure on Families: Family Size and Child Spacing.' In *Rapid Population Growth: Consequences and Policy Implications*, vol. 2. Baltimore: Johns Hopkins University Press.

8   INTERNAL MIGRATION[21]

State of Knowledge

The rapid transformation of developing countries into urban societies is a common theme wherever the process of social and economic change occurring in these countries is discussed. Although a number of developing countries are already predominantly urban, while others will not reach that stage before the turn of the century, the overwhelming majority are experiencing annual rates of urban growth of between 4 and 6 per cent and will continue to do so well beyond the twentieth century (United Nations, 1975). At the same time, many developing countries are characterized by a trend towards increasing urban concentration and city primacy, with the largest city often being several times larger than the following three. Estimates of the contribution of migration to urban growth are by no means exact — usually they depend on some very rough assumptions concerning the difference in the rate of natural increase between rural and urban places and include reclassification of previously rural communities — but they indicate that migration accounts for about 42 per cent of urban growth in the developing world as a whole. This share ranges from about 34 per cent in some subregions to about 58 per cent in others (Findley, 1976).

The objective of this chapter is to set out briefly what is known about the patterns and dimensions of migration in developing countries, the determinants and consequences of internal migration, and the impact and efficiency of government policies.

Types of Internal Migration and the Migration Process

Rural-to-urban migration is only one type of population movement contributing to the pattern of, and trend towards, urbanization that may be found in a country. Other types of migration that it may be vital to take into account when analysing the migratory process in a country are seasonal, rural–rural, urban–urban, and return migration. When the perceived problem is the rapid growth of the largest cities, urban-to-urban movements are apt to be of special importance.

[21] This chapter draws on the workshop paper 'Internal Migration in Developing Countries: A Discussion from a Population Policy Viewpoint' prepared for IRG by Raúl Urzúa.

Unfortunately, knowledge about the various types of migratory movements is often dramatically inadequate. In large part, the problem lies with the limited amount and problematic nature of the migration data that have been collected in developing countries. Only recently have specific questions on migration begun to be included in censuses, and only a few specialized surveys have been undertaken on migration — at least in comparison to the number of fertility surveys that have been conducted in recent years. A large share of the migration estimates now available for developing countries are derived from the application of indirect techniques to the intercensal volume of population change. Such estimates refer only to net migration and provide no indication of the size of the flows of in- and out-migration to and from the region or city in question. As a rule the migration surveys that have been done have focused on individual spatial units of analysis, rural and urban, but particularly large cities and, therefore, do not capture many elements of the migration process in the country as a whole.

In addition, specific census questions on migration are usually made with reference to place of birth or place of residence at some previous time, thus restricting analysis to permanent migration. The situation becomes more critical when only limited numbers and kinds of census tabulations are made available. The limitations of the data base have been especially great with regard to determining the volume and nature of both seasonal and rural-to-rural migration. Return migration is in a similarly disadvantageous position, both because of the difficulty of obtaining estimates from census data and because it has been neglected in most specialized surveys (Urzúa, 1978). As a result of this situation, attempts to understand the migratory process as a whole and the mutual interrelations among the different types of migration are practically non-existent. Some analyses and interpretations address themselves to the links between rural–urban and urban–urban migration within the framework of the stepwise migration model; but even within this restricted view, the studies are few and the conclusions unclear.

The Determinants of Internal Migration

Ideally, population distribution policy should be based on knowledge of the effect that different factors have on the several particular types of population movement, as well as on migrants and potential migrants from different social classes. Most of the work that has been done on the determinants of internal migration, however, refers either to migration in general or to rural–urban movements in particular, and does not distinguish between socioeconomic groups.

The actual process of deciding whether or not to migrate, when to do it, where to go, with whom, and for how long has been a relatively neglected subject in the analysis of the determinants of migration. Lacking direct data, most studies assume that the decision-making process is an economically rational one and that people decide to migrate when the perceived costs of staying at their present place of residence are higher than the benefits of changing residence minus the costs of moving.[22] But an understanding of what is responsible for the difference between families and individuals in terms of their 'inertia' to move and strength of attachment to place of birth or current residence is notably lacking.

There is, however, a considerable amount of information regarding the motives for migrating that has been collected retrospectively from individual respondents to survey questionnaires. Although the relative importance of the reasons given by respondents is not necessarily the same, they basically fall into five main categories: (1) low income at the place of origin and expectations of increasing it at the place of destination; (2) unemployment, underemployment, or dissatisfaction with present job at place of origin and expectation of better employment opportunities at the place of destination; (3) the desire for better educational facilities/resources than those available at place of origin; (4) a number of other reasons such as marriage, death of a family member, presence of friends and relatives at the prospective new place of residence, and so on; and (5) the movement of a spouse or parents for any of the four previous reasons (Urzúa, 1978; Caldwell, 1968; Simmons *et al.*, 1977).

Most of the information available on the objective conditions and developmental factors that determine aggregate migration flows is from cross-sectional econometric studies of census data on net migration between administrative units and, occasionally, between rural and urban areas. The most recent reviews and evaluations of the findings from this type of study (Yap, 1976; Findley, 1976; Simmons *et al.*, 1977; Todaro, 1976; Shaw, 1975; Urzúa, 1978) confirm the importance of differences in average income or wage levels and in employment opportunities that previous reviews had already emphasized. Migration is positively associated with urban wages and negatively associated with rural wages. At the same time, the chances of obtaining employment (which are inversely related to the urban unemployment rate) are independently significant, but the distinction between opportunities in the modern or formal sector and in the traditional or informal sector does not seem to be of much importance (Yap, 1976). Other variables that usually obtain statistically significant coefficients in cross-sectional studies are the degree of urbanization, urban contacts, distance, and education.

These findings are consistent with those from surveys with respect to the reasons for migrating given by individual respondents in showing that rural–urban migration, as well as other types of internal migration, is

---

[22] The classical formulation of this model is found in the often-quoted paper by Sjaastadt (1962). Similar assumptions are made in the well-known Todaro model (1969) and its successive modifications.

responsive to opportunities for economic improvement. But, while wage differentials, the probability of finding a job, and the other factors mentioned above are clearly the immediate factors determining migration, these in turn clearly depend on, among other things, the spatial allocation of economic activities and patterns of regional and sectoral development, which are the result of both government policies and decisions made in the private sector of the economy (where this exists). Within this framework an important question is, what are the identifiable aspects of overall development that tend to promote or retard migration to urban areas? By and large the answers that are presently available are the product of logical argument rather than empirical comparative analyses.

Perhaps the most basic hypothesis is that migration rates will be higher where economic growth is more rapid. The argument usually turns on rising levels of personal income in combination with income-inelastic demand for agricultural products and greater efficiency of urban as opposed to rural configurations in production and consumption of non-agricultural products. It is widely recognized, however, that a number of other features of development will modify the rate and the pattern of urbanization. Among those frequently mentioned are: (*a*) unbalanced technological changes (say, between primary and secondary activities); (*b*) international economic relations (affecting the pattern of import and export specialization); (*c*) population growth rates and differentials (affecting the relative abundance of, and returns to, labour in rural and urban areas); (*d*) institutional arrangements governing relations among factors of production (land tenure systems, financial and credit mechanisms, and price and tax distortions, usually in favour of urban activities); as well as (*e*) biases in government services, especially health and education (Preston, 1978). Increasingly, it is also being recognized that such fundamental aspects of an economy do not vary at random but are closely linked to (and contribute to the definition of) a country's style of development.[23]

Certainly one approach to verifying hypotheses regarding the influence of patterns of development on migration and urbanization would be comparative cross-sectional studies utilizing data for a large number of countries. As Preston (1978) suggests, probably the main reason these studies have not been conducted is the absence of an internationally comparable set of data on rural–urban migration rates.

---

[23] For example, one hypothesis with considerable currency in Latin America is that the pursuit of economic growth through import substitution-led industrialization often combines a number of these factors in such a way as to produce massive movements to a few urban centres. This is apt to be the case when economic decision-making is closely tied to a centralized bureaucratic apparatus, leading to a concentration of political power and government institutions in a few industrial centres. Inherent in the unbalanced centre-periphery relations that emerge is sharp inequality of opportunities between the largest cities and the rest of the country.

The Consequences of Internal Migration

Until a few years ago much of the literature on the consequences of migration for individual migrants was characterized by a pessimistic view about the opportunities cityward migrants had in their places of destination. Their difficulties in adjusting to an urban environment and culture, their economic disadvantages compared to the native population, their inability to move upward socially in the cities, and their frustration and the political radicalization derived therefrom were a constant theme. But, viewed from the perspective of the empirical results of studies undertaken in recent years, as well as from more careful analyses of past surveys, that pessimistic image appears to lack factual support, to be highly exaggerated, or to be empirically wrong.

One of the most common assumptions about migrants' adaptation to their new environment was that they encounter great difficulty in finding employment. The evidence indicates that this is not so, at least for the majority. Not only is their search for employment shorter than was expected, but also their unemployment rates do not differ significantly from those of natives (Simmons *et al.*, 1977; Urzúa, 1978; and Findley, 1976). Studies from three very different parts of the world — Taiwan, Kenya, and Brazil — also support the generalization that migrants receive higher incomes in their place of destination than in their place of origin (Spears, 1971; Harris and Rempel, 1976; Yap, 1976). Similarly, there is very little evidence showing that migrants suffer social and psychological maladjustments in their new environment.

All told, if one considers only the fate of migrants themselves in the cities, attempts to reduce cityward migration cannot be justified on grounds of improving their lot.

Migration may, of course, influence the welfare of the population that remains in the places of origin or that is already present in the places of destination, but the consequences of internal migration for sending and receiving areas have proved difficult to evaluate. Among the economic effects of migration that have been taken into consideration are those on economic growth and productivity, on wages and employment, and on technological change. With regard to sending areas, the empirical association between rural out-migration and declines in agricultural productivity has given rise to the hypothesis that migrant selectivity by age, education, and skill level (a common finding in all the regions reviewed) results in a drop in productivity (Schulz, 1976; Skinner, 1965; Martínez, 1968; and Chi-Yi-Chen, 1968). The other explanation is that both the out-migration and the productivity decline are the result of third factors, such as soil erosion and increasing population density (Simmons, *et al.*, 1977). Another debate has been with regard to the nature of the relation between technological change (mechanization) in agriculture and rural out-migration (Urzúa, 1978). With regard to the impact on rural wages, there is some evidence that these are higher than they would be in the absence of migration (Gaude, 1976). Remittances from migrants to their communities of origin, either in cash or kind, constitute another mechanism through which migration has an economic effect on sending communities (Caldwell, 1968; Johnson and Whitelaw, 1974; Simmons *et al.*, 1977; and Connell *et al.*, 1976).

The economic effects of migration on the receiving cities are even more difficult to unravel. Increases in urban unemployment and underemployment, fragmentation of the urban labour market into traditional and modern sectors, increased congestion and environmental pollution, and greater expenditures on and/or greater shortages of public services are some of the consequences considered to derive either directly or indirectly from urbanward migration.

Different social and cultural consequences of migration between rural and urban areas that have been mentioned are: rural losses in the capacity for social change that result from the selective character of rural out-migration, the 'ruralization' of cities due to the maintenance of rural life patterns in the urban environment, and the 'modernization' of rural areas through seasonal rural-urban migration and return migration.

Although there is little research available to demonstrate the point, migrant selectivity by age and sex can have a recognizable effect on nuptiality in both places of origin and of destination. Data on the characteristics of migrants from all three developing world regions confirm that rural–urban migrants are predominantly young adults. In Latin America, more women than men migrate from the rural areas, while the contrary seems to be the rule in Africa, the Middle East, and South Asia. The situation in other parts of Asia appears to vary from country to country: women have recently caught up with men in South-East Asia, with the exception of Indonesia, and have surpassed men for over two decades in East Asia.

The negative statistical association found between urbanization and fertility gave rise to the hypothesis that rural-to-urban migration has a depressing effect on the national fertility rate. The issue, of course, turns on the question of whether the fertility of female migrants would have been higher had they remained in a rural area. Research on the topic has usually involved comparing migrants with rural women of similar characteristics, and for the most part the latter have more children at an equivalent duration of marriage. Such results have occasionally been cited to support the case for rapid urbanization (Currie, 1971).

In addition to the issues raised by rural-to-urban migration in general, in recent years the question of migration to the largest metropolitan cities – whether from rural or other urban areas – has been gaining special attention. Until a few years ago it was almost an article of faith among economists, sociologists, and social planners that both urbanization and metropolitanization were postively associated with higher productivity, industrialization, and social integration. Proponents of the thesis that large cities have a positive role in development have pointed to the advantages that firms or businesses receive from access to larger markets for their products as well as for labour and other inputs; the advantages that urban residents enjoy in terms of access to better social services; the benefits deriving from the diffusion and adoption of a culture more attuned to the needs of development; and the value of the more organized participation in the political process that comes with increased urbanization.

In recent years, however, unqualified endorsements of urbanization have become much less frequent, and social scientists of quite different ideological and theoretical persuasions have become increasingly concerned with the possibly negative effects of high city primacy and the concentration of economic activity and population in the huge metropolitan agglomerations that now exist in many developing countries. An ever-growing concentration of industrial development in one, or at most a few, pre-existing large cities creates, according to some authors, a type of internal division of labour and asymmetric 'centre-periphery' relations that help to perpetuate dependency on developed countries and wide inequality in the distribution of income and opportunities within and between regions of a country. This dependency and inequality, in turn, contribute in a recursive way to further concentration and metropolitanization. The 'over-urbanization' that results is associated with widespread unemployment and underemployment in addition to all of the problems of environmental pollution, lack of social services, marginality, and traffic congestion that plague most cities in the developing world (Geisse, 1978, pp. 31–3).

In large measure, however, the debate over whether or not urbanization cum metropolitanization is beneficial has come to rest on the empirical but elusive question of whether the largest cities in a country have become 'too big' in the sense that diseconomies of scale have set in. There are several aspects of this issue. The first is in regard to the demand for and cost of publicly provided services such as water, electricity, and waste disposal. It is argued that, up to a point, the larger the city (or town), the more efficiently (cheaply) these can be provided. Beyond that point the marginal and average cost of providing such services rises sharply. Attempts to estimate these relations are at an early stage in developed countries (Carlino, 1978) and are just beginning in developing countries. In the latter, however, there are a number of clear examples — such as Jakarta and Mexico City — where this sort of diseconomy may have been important for some time. Also, there is the secure impression among policy-makers that providing services in 'medium-sized' cities is cheaper than in the very largest (IRG, 1978).

The second aspect of the agglomerative economies question refers to production. After taking into account the cost and availability of public services, there are still other considerations — such as a larger and more efficient labour market and reduced transportation costs — that make larger cities more efficient in producing goods and services. The point at which such economies diminish and then become negative is unknown for both developed and developing countries. It is an empirical question, but one that seems very hard to get a grip on (Alonso, 1975).

The Impact and Efficiency of Government Policies

Government policies designed to modify or guide the spatial distribution of population take a wide variety of forms, and are, of course, complemented or frustrated by policies and programmes implemented with no consideration as to their effect on migration.

Direct policies. Among the most direct policies to affect the spatial distribution of population are colonization and resettlement schemes to induce migration to selected rural areas. Although these programmes are often multi-purpose in their conception, agricultural development is a dominant and recurring objective (Mabogunje, 1978). They are perhaps most common in Sub-Saharan Africa, but are also found with some frequency in Asia and Latin America. Two of the most well-known projects of this type are the Tanzanian programme of villagization and the resettlement of Javanese on the outer islands of Indonesia. The former is undoubtedly the most thorough-going programme to influence the spatial distribution of population in recent times, involving the resettlement of about half the population of Tanzania.

Measuring the initial impact of colonization and resettlement is usually quite straightforward in that the responsible agency is apt to collect reliable statistics on the number of families or individuals that have been relocated. What return migration may occur after relocation is often much harder to estimate and has considerable bearing on the 'success' of the programme. More often than not, thorough evaluations of colonization projects are lacking.[24]

Legal controls, enforced by the police, are another quite direct way in which governments may try to influence migration. In China, for example, passes are required to leave a rural area, to enter an urban area, to secure the transfer of use of food ration cards, to move within the transport system, and to secure accommodation in an urban area; police checks at the entry point to the city, as well as periodic pass checks in urban areas, are used to make this regulation effective. In Indonesia a slightly simpler regulation governs Jakarta — the legal prohibitions against moving to the city are used as a method of intimidation rather than as an enforceable law. Comparable controls of one form or another have also been used in Tanzania and South Africa. Less direct controls have also been implemented.

[24] A notable exception promises to be the case of the AVV (L'Autorité de l'Amenagement des Vallées des Volta) programme in Upper Volta (Sawadogo, 1978).

For example, in order to move to Havana, Cubans must present evidence that they have secured housing with a certain minimum area of floor-space per member of the family.

How successful such policies are in limiting migration depends largely on the amount of influence government is able to exert at 'street' level; laws are likely to be evaded, enforcement officers are likely to be bribed, and exceptions sought as an illegal black market in the labour supply emerges (Weiner, 1975). Such policies may also have an important political cost, but so far there are no comprehensive studies of both the political and demographic impact of major policies of this type.

Indirect policies. Government policies to influence migration often take the form of 'doing things differently' for the sake of avoiding the negative effects of a too rapid or too concentrated pattern of urbanization. Indirect policies of this nature are of several kinds:

— Efforts to narrow the rural–urban wage gap. These usually involve incomes policies to keep urban wage rates from rising and price supports for agricultural products to raise rural incomes, as in Kenya. More generally, rural development programmes that generate employment opportunities in rural areas serve to raise incomes relative to those in urban areas and, perhaps, reduce the pace of rural–urban movement.

— Attempts to increase the relative disposition of public services in rural areas and medium-sized cities. These are another aspect of many integrated rural development programmes that incorporate sectoral inputs in areas such as transport, electrification, and education. In urban and semi-urban areas, housing may be an important good that is provided by government and that may serve to attract population. Housing policy has apparently been used extensively and with great effect to guide the spatial distribution of population in Cuba.

— Administrative decentralization and relocation. Policies of this sort range in magnitude from the relocation of a few government offices, to major programmes to decentralize the administration of public programmes to state and district-level capitals. Building an entirely new national capital as in Brazil and, more recently, Nigeria would also fall in this category.

— Regional development and industrial location policies. These usually have as part of their stated purpose the redirection of migration towards selected new or medium-sized towns or cities — either as a matter of planned metropolitanization or of creating so-called 'growth poles' at a considerable distance from existing industrial centres. There are important examples in India, one of the best known being the policy implemented in Maharashtra State (Harris, 1978). Algeria and Egypt have undertaken important efforts to disperse industrial activity away from the capital. Colombia has implemented a policy whereby investments in industrial plants by foreign capital may only be made in cities other than the principal urban centres (Bogotá, Cali, Medellin, and Cartagena).

— General town-planning principles. Regulations in this area are often designed to curb as well as rationalize urban growth. Measures include the creation of green belts around cities, zoning laws, and land use and density controls.

The efficiency and effectiveness in reorientating migration of most of the indirect policies mentioned above have, in general, not been researched.[25] Part of the problem is that the redistributive aims of many policies were never clearly stated, and often the policies themselves were never fully implemented. Clearly one important factor is the amount of control that the state has over economic activity in general. When there is a large private sector subject to few controls, the implementation of policies to influence migration has usually met with considerable difficulty.

Towards Establishing a Policy-Relevant Research Agenda

Pulling together the strengths and weaknesses of the knowledge base and taking into account the policy-making context, certain considerations seem to be critical in terms of the contribution that social science research can make to migration policy in developing countries.

The Nature of the Problem

As was indicated above, there are few 'hard' empirical research findings with regard to questions such as how fast should urbanization proceed, when are cities 'too large', and what is the most appropriate spatial distribution of the population, although these are hotly debated issues among scholars, many of whom have very firm opinions in this regard. This lack of consensus is in marked contrast to the understandable uniformity of opinion among most politicians and officials responsible for providing public services in the largest cities, who believe that rapid rural–metropolitan and urban–metropolitan migration should be curtailed.

An important complication is that even if the facts of the case were clear, the matter of whether urbanization is proceeding too rapidly or not would be seen from different perspectives by different groups, and there would clearly be no single answer to the question. What appears to be important is to concentrate on learning more about the proximate consequences of migration, placing special emphasis on determining the costs

[25] See, however, Simmons (1979) for a stimulating analysis and overview of Asian policy experience.

or effects that are not borne or felt by the migrants themselves (and their immediate or extended families), but which rather 'spill over' on to the public sector and different population groups resident in the place of destination, or on to the population remaining in the place of origin. Clearly, such spill-over effects are not negligible — and this, for many, provides the justification for public intervention — but analysis and quantification have not yet proceeded far.

Jurisdictional Issues and the Current State of Planning

The wide variety of governmental actions that were earlier identified as migration policies usually lie within the purview of a number of ministries or governmental departments. With increasing frequency, a special ministry or agency has been given authority to co-ordinate or develop a national 'human settlements' policy. What is of some relevance to the need for, and the role of, social-science research in this area is the type of ministry or agency where such authority is apt to be placed, In the main, these tend to be the departments responsible for housing and public works. Their co-ordinating function and authority is usually exercised jointly with the planning agency or budget office. The point, however, is that the people who develop such plans are mostly engineers or architects, or administrators used to relying on professional inputs from these fields. Social-science inputs are often given short shrift or are not considered. Often, the 'comprehensive' planning document that such departments produce meets with a cool reception from social scientists who are quick to point to its technical deficiencies and lack of social content, and who argue that the proposed policy measures are of a piecemeal sort, doomed to failure in the absence of a major shift in development strategy.

Felt Needs of Policy-Makers

At the series of IRG workshops, policy-makers expressed quite definite preferences with regard to priorities for research on migration. Not surprisingly, uppermost on their list was evaluation. In the case of countries where direct policies have been implemented and quantitatively significant redistributions have taken place, such as Tanzania, the chief interest of policy-makers was in evaluating the extent to which the programme had accomplished its ultimate social objectives. In the case of countries where indirect policies have been implemented, such as Kenya and Colombia, the interest was more in the first-order question of how much migration flows had actually been altered by the policy.

Latin American policy-makers were quick to recognize that for a long time governments in the region had neglected rural development, while concentrating their energies on industrialization by way of import-substitution.

They also claimed, however, that recently the majority of these governments had taken important steps to correct this bias and had implemented many of the indirect policies listed above with the intent of achieving a more 'rational' pattern of urbanization; but that so far the demographic impact of most of these measures had not been studied seriously.

A second major and related concern expressed by most policy-makers was with regard to the lack of detailed information on the size and character of the migratory flows taking place in their countries.

Specific Recommendations

Consequences of Internal Migration

There is a need for additional knowledge on the consequences of migration. The fact that so little has been accomplished to date is an indication that the issues are complex and not easily quantified. For this reason, initial efforts should be directed towards investigating the most tractable questions about consequences. One priority topic should be measuring the economies and diseconomies of agglomeration in the provision of public services. Beyond that, attempts should be made to identify and quantify the most important spill-overs or externalities that immigration to major metropolitan cities has for different population groups already resident in those cities and for rural residents left behind. Where feasible research designs are forthcoming with respect to analysing the effects on productivity, both in the receiving and the sending area, of population redistribution, these too should be supported.

Work along these lines will not produce finely-honed estimates of the different costs and benefits of alternative patterns of migration. It could however, introduce some quantification into an area of policy debate that up to now has been an empirical vacuum. No simple answers will emerge, but the inevitable political decisions that will be taken on migration policy in the next 10 years could then be based on a more accurate appreciation of who the affected parties are and what it is that they stand to lose or gain.

Links between Migration Patterns and Over-all Development Strategy

Among the seemingly most consequential hypotheses that have been advanced by scholars in the field is that the pattern or style of development is what in the final analysis determines the spatial distribution of population and changes therein. An implication or corollary is that most of the indirect policy measures available to governments will either never be effectively implemented or will have little impact unless there is also a change in the mechanisms responsible for rural–urban and inter-urban differentials in wages and employment opportunities.

These hypotheses merit further investigation that should be carried out at different levels. First, detailed studies of individual countries should be undertaken to determine the nature of the mechanisms and forces at work in concrete situations. These studies should pay particular attention to how changes in social and economic structures are affecting the levels of living and employment opportunities of particular social groups in specific rural and urban places. Secondly, international comparative studies should be attempted that make use of comparable data on migration and indicators of development style for as large a sample of countries as possible. This type of comparative analysis would follow on and expand the scope of research that has recently been undertaken by the Population Division of the UN.

Evaluation of Migration Policies

In the past 15 years or so, such a wide variety of direct and indirect policies have been adopted with the objective of modifying migration flows that there is at present a pressing need for studies to evaluate their success in affecting the spatial distribution of population, as well as their ultimate impact in terms of improving social welfare.

One project that would constitute an important first step and a foundation for further work would be to prepare a comprehensive descriptive and evaluative inventory of policies adopted during this period in developing countries to curb rural-to-urban migration. Attention could be focused on some of the more important cases (Indonesia, Tanzania, India, Nigeria, Colombia, and Cuba), appraising the degree to which the policies adopted were actually implemented, to what extent they achieved the stated purposes, and whether what was achieved was desirable. This review would describe the design and mode of operation of these different policies and assess their costs — economic, administrative, and otherwise. In short, it would attempt to answer the question of what has been tried and how it has worked. Such a broad and comparative overview would not pre-empt but would rather complement detailed studies of programmes and policies that should be undertaken in the context of individual countries.

Descriptive Research

As was described above, basic knowledge of the various dimensions of the migration process is notably deficient in most developing countries. While data are generally available on the net transfer of population from rural to urban areas, reliable estimates of return, seasonal, and rural-to-rural migration are usually not available. This represents an important impediment to policy design as well as to further understanding of the determinants and consequences of the migration process itself.

A large part of the blame lies with the bluntness of the instruments (especially censuses) that are presently relied on to produce data on migration flows. One venturesome suggestion put forward in the IRG workshop for Latin America was to conduct a preliminary investigation of the feasibility of establishing a system of indirect population registers that, while avoiding the potential for abuse and political control inherent in a population registry such as that existing in Sweden and other European countries, would use information collected by the various public agencies or services with whom migrants come in contact. While this suggestion is far from constituting a well-developed proposal, it bears following up.

References

Alonso, William. 1975. 'The Economics of Urban Size.' In *Regional Policy: Readings in Theory and Applications*. John Friedmann and William Alonso, eds. Cambridge, Mass.: MIT Press.

Beier, George, *et al.* 1975. 'The Task Ahead for the Cities of the Developing Countries.' Staff Working Paper no. 209. Washington, D.C.: IBRD.

Caldwell, J. C. 1968. 'Determinants of Rural–Urban Migration in Ghana.' *Population Studies*, 22 (3), 361–77.

Carlino, G. A. 1978. *Economics of Scale in Manufacturing Location*. Leiden: Martinus Nijhoff.

Chi-Yi-Chen. 1968. *Movimientos Migratorios en Venezuela*. Caracas: Instituto de Investigaciones Económicas de la Universidad Católica Andrés Bello.

Connell, John, Dasgupta, Biplab, Laishley, Roy, and Lipton, Michael. 1976. *Migration from Rural Areas: The Evidence from Village Studies*. Delhi: Oxford University Press.

Cornelius, Wayne. 1976. 'Outmigration from Rural Mexican Communities.' In *The Dynamics of Migration: International Migration*. Occasional Monograph Series, no. 5, vol. 2. Washington, D.C.: Interdisciplinary Communications Programme, Smithsonian Institution.

Currie, L. 1971. 'The Exchange Constraint on Development – A Partial Solution to the Problem.' *Economic Journal*, December.

Findley, Sally Evans. 1976. *Planning for Internal Migration: A Summary of the Issues and Policies*. Washington, D.C.: Centre for Advanced Studies.

Gaude, J. 1976. 'Causes and Repercussions of Rural Migration in Developing Countries: A Critical Analysis.' Working Paper. Geneva: International Labour Office, Rural Employment Research Programme.

Geisse, Guillermo. 1978. *Ocho Tesis sobre Planificación, Desarrollo y Distribución Espacial de la Población*. Santiago: CELADE. DS/28–3.

Harris, Nigel. 1978. 'Memorandum: Policies Addressed to Modifying the Spatial Distribution of Population – Asia and Africa.' Paper prepared for the Third IRG Workshop on Research Priorities for Population Policy, Nairobi, 6–8 September. IRG/67.

Harris, John, and Rempel, Henry. 1976. 'Rural–Urban Labor Migration and Urban Unemployment in Kenya.' Manuscript.

International Review Group (IRG). 1978. 'Draft Summary Report of the Second IRG Workshop on Research Priorities for Population Policy.' Mexico City, 28–30 June. IRG/66–E.

Johnson, G. E., and Whitelaw, W. E. 1974. 'Urban–Rural Income Transfers in Kenya: An Estimated Remittances Function.' *Economic Development and Cultural Change*, 22 (3), 473–9.

Mabogunje, Akin L. 1978. 'Research Priorities for Population Re-Distribution Policies in Africa South of the Sahara.' Paper prepared for the Third IRG Workshop on Research Priorities for Population Policy, Nairobi, 6–8 September. IRG/69.

Martìnez, Hector, 1968. 'Las Migraciones Internas en el Perú.' *Aportes*, no. 1.

Preston, Samuel H. 1978. 'International Comparison of Net Rural–Urban Migration Rates.' In *Conference on 'Economic and Demographic Change: Issues for the 1980s', Helsinki, 1978*. Liege: IUSSP.

Sawadogo, P. 1978. Personal communication.

Schulz, G. E. 1976. 'Out-Migration, Rural Productivity and the Distribution of Income.' Paper presented at the Research Workshop on Rural-Urban Labor Market Interactions. Washington, D.C.: IBRD.

Shaw, P. R. 1975. 'Migration Theory and Fact.' Bibliography Series no. 5. Philadelphia: Regional Science Research Institute.

Simmons, Alan. 1979. 'Slowing Metropolitan City Growth in Asia: Policies, Programs and Results.' *Population and Development Review*, 5 (1), 87–104.

—, Díaz-Briquets, Sergio, and Laquian, Aprodicio A. 1977. *Social Change and Internal Migration: A Review of Research Findings from Africa, Asia and Latin America*. Ottawa, Canada: International Development Research Centre. IDRC-TS6e.

Sjaastadt, Larry A. 1962. 'The Costs and Returns of Human Migration.' *Journal of Political Economy*, 70 (5), 80–93.

Skinner, E. P. 1965. 'Labor Migration Among the Mossi of the Upper Volta.' In *Urbanization and Migration in West Africa*, Hilda Kuper, ed. Berkeley and Los Angeles: University of California Press.

Spears, Alden, Jr. 1971. 'Urbanization and Migration in Taiwan.' Taiwan Population Studies, Working Paper no. 11. Ann Arbor: University of Michigan.

Todaro, M. P. 1969. 'A Model of Labor Migration and Urban Unemployment in Less-Developed Countries.' *American Economic Review*, 59 (1), 138–48.

— 1976. *Internal Migration in Developing Countries: A Review of Theory, Evidence, Methodology, and Research Priorities*. Geneva: International Labour Office.

United Nations. 1975. *Selected World Indicators by Countries, 1950–2000*. New York: United Nations. ESA/P/W.P.55.

Urzúa, Raúl. 1978. 'Social Science Research on Population and Development in Latin America.' Appendix 11 to the Final Report. El Colegio de México: IRG.

Weiner, Myron. 1975. 'Internal Migration Policies: Purposes, Interests, Instruments, and Effects.' Migration and Development Group, Working Paper MDG/75-1. Cambridge, Mass.: Centre for International Studies, MIT.

Yap, Lorene. 1976. 'Internal Migration and Economic Development in Brazil.' *Quarterly Journal of Economics*, 90 (1), 119–37.

9   INTERNATIONAL MIGRATION [26]

State of Knowledge

International migration has often been referred to as the neglected step-child of demography, a discipline that is very prone to the simplifying assumption of a 'closed population'. Yet international migration has played an extremely critical role in the economic development of many now-developed countries and is thought to have been and will continue to be, important to the development of many poor (and also 'newly rich') countries. In fact, it has been and is an important component of total population growth in many of these nations.

The pattern and also the determinants and consequences of international migration seem to vary enormously between regions and often between countries, as well as over time. For the moment at least, no set of general propositions — say, a theory of the international migration transition — has acquired any meaning in the field. While the variable appears to be one that can best be approached by analysing specific cases in all their particulars, it is not unlikely that there are important generalizations waiting to be discovered.

It is well to recognize that not all of the policy issues presented by international migration are ones that can be coped with adequately within the framework of national policies and bilateral agreements. In the future there may be increasing pressure exerted by the nations of the densely populated regions to take up the more general question of the global inequality in the distribution of manpower over the land areas of this earth and the ethical dilemmas that are raised by the present situation. At least, the issues of a new economic order for international labour and the human rights of migrant workers are almost certain to gain increasing attention in international forums.

Measurement of the Flows, Stocks and Characteristics
of International Migrants

Unlike migrants who move from one place to another within the same country, international migrants are usually obliged to fill out forms, present identification and, often, a previously obtained visa when they

[26] This chapter draws on the paper 'Some Thoughts on International Migration: Questions and Research prepared for IRG by Riad Tabbarah.'

cross national boundaries. The information collected at points of entry and exit provides an abundant amount of data on international migration. Unfortunately, in the case of migration between developing countries or between developed and developing countries, this information does not always present an accurate picture of the true situation. The main problems are, first, that such statistics are heavily dominated by short-term movements which, when procedures for processing the data are imperfect, means that longer-term or permanent migration may be difficult to sort out with any accuracy; and, secondly, that international migration is sometimes clandestine or 'illegal', in which case it is impossible to know the exact magnitude of people involved.

The basic source of data on international migration continues to be the population census, which includes questions on place of birth and nationality that are later cross-tabulated with certain socioeconomic characteristics. It does, however, present several limitations. First, some countries in which international migration is an important phenomenon have not conducted censuses. Even in countries where censuses do exist, some have not asked the appropriate questions while others fail to publish the necessary tabulations. Secondly, a census provides a view of migration at a particular point in time and as such permits an estimate of the stock rather than the flow of migrants. Finally, censuses are not generally undertaken simultaneously in different nations of a region — a practice which would constitute a source of information allowing the construction of an 'input-output table' of international migration.

Obviously, detailed data regarding the effect of migration on the welfare of the migrant's family, the impact of remittances, the volume and nature of return migration, etc. — all important factors for an understanding of the determinants and consequences of international migration — can only be obtained through specialized surveys. But such surveys, which could also supplement census information by providing additional reference points for estimating intercensal migration trends, are quite scarce. Furthermore, unlike the case of internal migration, neither the survey nor the census is able to interview out-migrants; only in-migrants and return migrants are present in the country in question.

In terms of estimating flows, stock, and characteristics of international migrants, the greatest difficulties are with respect to illegal migrants. There is little hope that illegal migrants will either be fully represented in the censuses of the country of destination or that if interviewed they will respond truthfully to questions on country of birth and place of earlier residence. The illegal or clandestine migration between a large number of Latin American and Caribbean countries and the US certainly represents one of the most blatant examples of the unsatisfactory nature of quantitative information on this type of movement. At the moment, there is nothing that could be considered as even approaching a reliable estimate of the number of Mexican citizens currently residing in the US

(Keely, 1977). One approach that seems to hold some promise of improving this situation is intensive interviewing in the country of origin in an attempt to identify out-migrants on the basis of information obtained from relatives.

The Determinants of International Migration

The reasons why most people move from one country to another often appear to be similar to the reasons why people move from one place to another within the same country. Economic motivations are uppermost — migrants are attracted by higher wages and greater probability of finding a job as well as, on occasion, better educational opportunities — in short, the chance to improve their standard of living. There are, however, important exceptions where economic motivation is not or may not be of importance, as in the case of political or religious refugees.

But such considerations constitute only one side (and probably the least important side) of the equation. Immigration laws and the provisions for their enforcement in the receiving countries to a large extent determine the amount and character of out-migration. Changes in the immigration laws of most developed countries in the past 15 years have had an important influence on the composition of migratory flows from the Third World. The changes, which in general relaxed restrictions on race and country of origin and placed greater emphasis on skills, greatly exacerbated the so-called 'brain-drain' or loss of highly skilled manpower by the developing countries (Appleyard, 1977, p. 291).

The other major change that influenced the pattern of international migration to and from developing countries in this period was the opening up of substantial differences in wages and standards of living among developing countries due to differential rates of economic growth. These increased differences had the effect of intensifying migration between countries in the same region. The most extreme case is that of West Asia, where rapidly rising oil revenue led to spiralling wages in a few countries, while much of the region was untouched by this bonanza (Tabarah, Mamish, and Gemayel, 1978). Important differences in economic growth among countries in both Latin America and Africa have led to increased intra-regional migration in those areas, too.

One point that deserves emphasis is the close relationship that often exists between internal and international migration. Indeed, the difficulty of distinguishing between the two is often noted in the African context. Both form part of the migration 'process' in a given country, and it is usually advantageous to incorporate them in the same theoretical framework.

The Consequences of International Migration

When discussing the consequences of international migration, it is custo-
mary to distinguish between the migration of manpower with limited
skills (migrant workers) and that of highly qualified personnel ('brain-
drain'). This distinction is observed below, but it should be recognized
that the intermediate case, corresponding to skilled workers in construction and other trades, is becoming increasingly important. In both
cases, the issues can be analysed from three points of view: that of
the sending countries, that of the receiving countries, and that of the
migrants and their families.

Migrant workers. From the point of view of the receiving (and generally
more-developed) countries, it has been argued that it is not in their best
economic interest to voluntarily permit or encourage such migration
since the migrant workers are often not badly needed and compete with
native workers in categories where unemployment in the receiving countries is often highest, such as among the least skilled youth entering the
labour force and poorly educated minorities. It is further argued that, even
if the labour shortage is real, there are better ways of dealing with it —
for example, by tapping the large reserve of women outside the labour
force (Davis, 1974, p. 104). On the other hand, it has been observed that
migrant workers generally occupy employment levels that are being
vacated by the native labour force as it continually moves into more
skilled jobs or jobs involving less personal hardship. More important, in
most receiving countries, unemployment among native labour in the
main occupations of the migrant workers is generally not high (Kayser,
1977, p. 9) and is, at any rate, much less than the volume of migrant
workers in the country. Even in the US, where it is certain that some
competition exists between the large number of illegal or seasonal migrants
and the national agricultural labour force, it has been argued that the
large majority of these migrant workers are filling jobs that would not
have been taken by American citizens (Tabbarah, 1977, p. 308). In a
dynamic perspective, however, such propositions may lose some of their
force: the fact that the low-level, poorly paid positions exist at all is
related to the present availability of migrant workers to fill them. If
migrant workers were not available, a quite different structure of employment might emerge. At the present time, analysis of this sort is not well
developed and definite conclusions about the economic repercussions of
sizeable inflows of migrant workers are not available.

From the point of view of the less-developed sending countries, the
emigration of workers is sometimes thought to constitute a welcome
relief to unemployment, a source of foreign exchange, and a means by
which to increase the skill level of labour (Tabbarah, 1977). Yet in countries where migrant workers abroad constitute a sizeable proportion of
the domestic labour force, there is also apt to be concern for longer-term

problems related to the eventual reintegration of migrants and the opportunity costs that may be attached to having some of the country's most able workers spend the prime years of their productive lives abroad. In some countries, such as the Yemen Arab Republic, where as much as 20 per cent of the labour force is working abroad, there may even emerge a concern for labour shortages among national planning authorities.

Finally, from the point of view of the migrants and their families, the serious dimensions of the problems created by the policies of developed countries to regulate migration according to their fluctuating need for foreign labour are too obvious and well known to be elaborated here. The resulting insecurity of employment, the separation of families, and other related issues have, in fact, been the subject of many resolutions of the ILO in the past several years (Bohning, 1977, pp. 314–8).

The 'brain-drain'. As already mentioned, the changes in immigration laws of the 1960s in the developed, receiving countries, which favoured education and skills rather than national and ethnic origin, resulted in a sudden upsurge in the migration of skilled and professional workers from less-developed countries. It seems clear that the developed receiving countries are benefiting from the immigration of highly qualified manpower from developing countries and that, on the other hand, the developing countries are losing very costly resources. It does not necessarily follow, however, that legal restrictions should be placed on this type of migration by the developing countries. For one thing, many of the highly qualified emigrants are specialized in fields where few or no employment opportunities exist in their home countries, at least at wage levels commensurate with the living standards these individuals aspire to. Legal restrictions of this type may also raise questions of human rights or result in frustration on the part of the potential emigrants that would negate the benefits derived from keeping them in their native country.

The questions of which country benefits, which country loses, or whether both gain or lose from international migration constitute intricate problems in welfare economics that have attracted considerable academic attention in recent years. Some of the earlier theoretical analyses of the 'brain-drain', which were based on pure neo-classical assumptions with little or no institutional content, came to the happy conclusion that international migration of this sort did not constitute a problem for either the sending or the receiving country. More recent treatments, however, include richer and more plausible assumptions regarding how labour markets operate and the way that education is financed in developing countries, introduce additional considerations such as national pride in the presence of technical personnel *per se*, and reach much less comforting results regarding the welfare of those left behind in the country of origin (Bhagwati and Rodríguez, 1975).

But empirical questions may be even more important than appropriate theoretical development in evaluating the impact of international migration of both skilled and unskilled labour. The chief example concerns remittances that migrants may make to relatives at home and the savings they return with if their migration is temporary. Information on such transfers is understandably scarce and rarely 'representative' of all migrants. Yet there are indications that average annual remittances by migrant workers in Western Europe exceed US $1,000 and that lesser but still substantial amounts are remitted by migrant workers in the US and Canada (Bohning, 1977 and Cornelius, 1976).

While nearly all attention regarding the consequences of international flows of highly educated labour has been directed towards movement from less-developed to more-developed countries, it is worth noting that there also exist flows in the other direction. This counterflow to the 'brain-drain' — which is not well investigated as to size, characteristics, or consequences — is of a quite different nature, being made up largely of individuals on assignment with developed country organizations (businesses, governments, international organizations, donors, and so on) rather than individuals seeking improvements in their standard of living or a wider range of opportunities.

International Migration Policies

Government policies directly related to international migration are implemented by both the receiving and the sending country. Clearly the principal policies of the receiving countries are immigration laws and the provisions for their enforcement, which can be designed to either promote or limit different types of migration. But another, albeit drastic, policy alternative that has been used by some receiving countries is the expulsion of immigrants who are already legally or quasi-legally settled. Foreigners have been expelled from several African countries, the most notable example being the expulsion of large numbers of Nigerians residing in Ghana.

In the case of legal migration, the direct impact of changes in immigration laws, treaties, and enforcement provisions on migration to the receiving country is readily apparent. What, of course, remains largely unknown is the impact of changes in laws and enforcement provisions on clandestine migration.

The other sorts of international migration policies are those that are implemented by the sending country. At one extreme, these can include the negotiation of international agreements whereby a country will seek permission to send a part of its population abroad. (El Salvador is currently involved in efforts of this sort). More frequently, developing countries formulate less explicit policies to promote or at least facilitate the temporary emigration of manpower to comparatively lucrative employment in either developed or newly rich developing countries. At the other extreme are policies designed to promote the repatriation of skilled manpower residing abroad or to limit and control the emigration of qualified personnel. The former are by now quite common in developing countries, yet few country-specific or comparative studies of the effectiveness of such programmes have been undertaken. Increasingly there is a tendency for governments to seek ways of gaining control over the export and import of unskilled and semi-skilled labour in an attempt to guarantee the economic rewards accruing to the state from this migration. Some primarily receiving countries such as Singapore and Kuwait have placed very strict limitations on the rights of migrants. The restrictions are more often than not aimed explicitly at the rights of migrants to marry and have children. On the other hand, a growing number of primarily sending countries such as the Philippines and South Korea are organizing and promoting group contract labour schemes in which remittances can be paid directly by the employer to the sending state.

Another policy approach hinges on the entire issue of taxation in relation to the flow of highly skilled manpower from developing to developed countries. The compensation argument, which provides a rationale for generating flows of resources from the North to the South, has been voiced most convincingly by Bhagwati (1978). In a similar vein the Crown Prince of Jordan (1977) recently proposed the establishment of an 'International Labour Compensatory Facility' that would divert resources from labour-importing countries to developing labour-exporting countries 'in proportions relative to the estimated cost incurred due to the loss of labour'.

Towards Establishing a Policy-Relevant Research Agenda

The importance of international migration to governments often exceeds its quantitative importance in terms of numbers of people and strictly economic impact. A whole series of issues come into play, involving a country's international image, its foreign policy, and its leverage in international negotiations. Emigration of 'indocumentados', for example, tends to expose in a dramatic way the apparent failure of a country's national development policies to provide for the basic needs of its population, as well as to constitute a sort of liability in terms of its bargaining power with the receiving country since the latter always has the option of attempting to deport illegal residents. The problems created for the receiving country are perhaps equally sensitive. There is apt to be considerable popular and political controversy as to the correct course of action regarding any sort of international migration, and sudden changes in or 'vigorous' attempts to enforce immigration statutes may involve cruelty and infringement on the human rights of immigrants.

In many ways the policy issues raised by international migration lie somewhat to one side of the social sciences. Critical aspects are related to ethics, law, diplomacy, and international relations as much as to sociology, economics, or demography. The one policy area that is directly affected by international migration and that is closely tied to the social sciences is manpower planning. It is often claimed that the principal long-term solution to the 'brain-drain' is the design and implementation of educational and training programmes that will prepare people to perform the jobs that are available and need to be done in their native country.[27]

Responsibility for international migration policy is usually not localized in a specific government agency or ministry, but rather is generally shared among a number of departments. The ministry of foreign relations clearly plays a major role in defining and protecting the interests of nationals residing in other countries, and the interior ministry is apt to have the primary responsibility for setting policy on who should be admitted into the country and on what terms. The IRG was understandably not able to involve representative policy-makers from such ministries in its work, but from what was said at the three regional workshops regarding international migration issues and what is generally known about the priorities of individual countries in this area, we can be reasonably sure that governments of primarily sending countries are eager to have both data on number and types of migrants, amount of remittances, and so on, as well as more complete knowledge about the impact of different public policies that affect international migration either directly or indirectly.

The interests of policy-makers in the primarily receiving countries in more and better research on international migration is less obvious. What is clear is that in many of these countries myths and misinformation about the quantitative importance of the phenomenon and the economic roles played by migrants, whether legal or illegal, are exploited for a variety of political purposes, almost always in ways that are prejudicial to the interests of the migrants themselves who to a greater or lesser degree are used as scapegoats. In these countries social scientists would seem to have an independent responsibility to conduct research that would lead to a fair appreciation of the situation and an upgrading of the level of policy debate.

Before turning to the Group's specific recommendations in this area, it is well worth pointing out that here, as in the discussions of the influence of policy on the other demographic variables, there is the issue of how to 'restructure development'. In this case, however, the question refers to the pattern of international development and the appropriate division of effort between rich and poor countries in the production of labour as against capital-intensive goods. In some measure, migrant workers go to developed countries to produce labour-intensive goods that the developed country might otherwise import from the sending country.

[27] It must be noted, however, that policy-makers from a number of countries — India is prominent among them — are sometimes inclined to view the emigration of highly skilled manpower as a process beneficial to the national economy, not necessarily reflective of a misallocation of domestic resources.

The tariffs and quotas on imports of manufactured goods and agricultural exports from LDCs that developed countries incorporate in their trade policies are thought to be among the factors responsible for the enormous difference in wages between developed and developing countries.

Specific Recommendations

Measurement of International Migration

There is no question as to the priority that should be attached to obtaining more and better data on international migration. In particular, special efforts should be devoted to developing and applying methodology for obtaining indirect estimates of the stocks and flows of clandestine migrants to and from developing countries. The most promising lead seems to be interviewing the population resident in the sending country, both with specialized survey questionnaires and special questions included in censuses. As soon as an acceptable set of questions and the corresponding techniques for deriving estimates have been developed,[28] support should be provided for experimental testing and eventual full-scale application of this methodology.

Specialized surveys of international migration applied on either a national basis or in selected areas of the sending country can provide a remarkable amount of information on migration other than indications as to its volume. Surveys of this type can be used to determine reasons for migrating, the average length of stay, the amount of remittance and returned savings, the costs of migration, and the characteristics of the migrant — all of which can be used to clarify often factless discussions of the determinants and consequences of the phenomenon. As evidence of the interest that policy-makers have in this sort of information, it is worth noting that the government of México is now spending about $900,000 on a national survey of migration to the northern border and to the US.

Consequences

There is a general need for further research on the consequences of international migration in those developing countries that experience sizeable migratory flows, either temporary or permanent, of skilled or unskilled manpower. Projects on this topic should not be undertaken with a view to determining the net benefit or cost to the country concerned, but rather should focus on the particular aspects of the phenomenon — social, economic, or political — that seem to be most important in the case at

[28] The IUSSP has recently formed a working group under the direction of Jorge Somoza that is at work on this topic.

hand. Especially in need of investigation are the economic and social effects of the recently initiated flows of skilled and semi-skilled workers from several Asian and African countries to the oil-rich countries of the Middle East. Part of the justification for such research is the insights such studies might provide as to measures that the sending countries could take to increase the benefits obtained from this migration by both the places of origin and the migrants themselves.

Policy Evaluation

Efforts on the part of developing country governments to modify international migration have become sufficiently widespread and are of a sufficiently diverse nature that a comprehensive evaluative study of a comparative nature — such as that recommended on policies to modify internal migration — seems called for. In particular need of comparative evaluation are the wide variety of measures that have been taken to induce highly trained nationals to return home. So, too, are the emerging policies that a number of countries are adopting with regard to the organized export of unskilled and semi-skilled labour. Once again, the questions to be answered are: to what degree was the policy actually implemented, what was the design or mode of operation, to what extent was the stated purpose achieved, and how beneficial were the end results for the different parties concerned. Finally, there is a pressing need for a comprehensive comparative evaluation of the legal rights accorded to non-citizen residents in both developed and developing countries as a prerequisite for the redefinition of international codes to protect the human rights of migrant workers and refugees.

References

Appleyard, Reginald T. 1977. 'Major International Population Movements and Policies: An Historical Review.' In *International Population Conference, México, 1977*, vol. 2. Liège: IUSSP.

Bhagwati, Jagdish. 1978. 'The Brain Drain: Compensation and Taxation.' In *Conference on 'Economic and Demographic Change: Issues for the 1980s.' Helsinki, 1978*. Liège: IUSSP.

— and Rodríguez, Carlos. 1975. 'Welfare — Theoretical Analysis of the Brain Drain.' *Journal of Development Economics*, 2 (3), 195–221.

Bohning, W. R. 1977. 'The Migration of Workers from Poor to Rich Countries: Facts, Problems, Policies.' In *International Population Conference, México, 1977*, vol. 2. Liège: IUSSP.

Cornelius, Wayne. 1976. 'Outmigration from Rural Mexican Communities.' In *The Dynamics of Migration: International Migration*. Occasional Monograph Series, No. 5, vol. 2. Washington, D.C.: Interdisciplinary Communications Programme, Smithsonian Institution.

Davis, Kingsley, 1974. 'The Migration of Human Population.' *Scientific American*, 231 (3).

Kayser, Bernard. 1977. 'L'échange inégal des resources humaines: Migrations, croissance, et crise en Europe.' *Revue Tiers-Monde*, janvier-mars, p. 9.

Keely, Charles B. 1977. 'Counting the Uncountable: Estimates of Undocumented Aliens in the United States.' *Population and Development Review*, 3 (4), 473–81.

Tabbarah, Riad. 1977. 'International Migration and National Population Policies.' In *International Population Conference, México, 1977: Proceedings*. Liège: IUSSP.

—— Mamish, Muji A. and Gemayel, Youssef. 1978. 'Social Science Research on Population and Development in the Arab Countries,' Appendix 9 to the Final Report. El Colegio de México: IRG.

Thomas, Brinley. 1973. *Migration and Economic Growth*. Cambridge: Cambridge University Press.

10 OVERVIEW: GUIDELINES FOR FUTURE RESEARCH

In the preceding chapters, for each of the demographic variables, the state of knowledge, policy considerations, and recommendations for future research were set out in an all too compartmentalized way. There are, however, a number of conclusions that can be drawn with regard to research on all, or nearly all, of the population variables that delimit the IRG's field of interest, and that suggest six general types of analysis worthy of emphasis in future research.

The Processes of Demographic Change

One conclusion that emerges from the examination of the state of knowledge on each of the demographic variables is that there has been a tendency to ignore the complexity of demographic processes, concentrating attention on variations in the level of a single index, such as total fertility or net rural–urban migration. Only slight attention seems to have been paid to the determinants and consequences of the different components of the demographic process and to how changes in an over-all index break down into changes in its component parts. This limitation seems to apply equally to fertility, mortality, and internal migration. The only exception might be international migration, where considerable attention has been given to the composition of flows by skill levels and to distinguishing between seasonal and longer-term migration.

In chapter 7 stress was placed on the need to analyse fertility in terms of its distinct behavioural and biological components, in part because many of these respond to influences, preferences, and interests that have little to do with the 'ultimate' question of family size.[29] The other essential point is that, just as the components of the fertility process

[29] While no specific recommendations were made with regard to the determinants of changing patterns of breast-feeding and nuptiality – two components of great interest from a policy perspective – it is the Group's strongly held opinion that these mechanisms of fertility change should be an integral part of the analyses recommended on pp. 112–115 under the headings 'Institutional Analyses', 'Micro-Level Studies', 'Evaluation of the Fertility Impact', and 'Descriptive Research'; and that where governments have undertaken policies that attempt to modify marriage or breast-feeding patterns directly, social scientists should contribute in every way possible to their evaluation.

respond to considerations other than the number of children a woman will eventually bear, so too do they have consequences that extend far beyond total fertility.

Nearly analogous points can be made about mortality and migration. With respect to the former, the different causes of death clearly respond to different sorts of environmental changes and policy interventions. They also have different consequences in that incidence by age, sex, and social group varies among them, as may the degree of associated morbidity. In the case of migration, a different sort of decomposition is also extremely relevant. That the causes and effects of, say, rural–rural migration are different from those of rural-to-urban movements hardly needs elaboration.

In these three cases, some portion of the neglect stems from the absence of the necessary data. While in many cases there are a number of serious financial and/or technical impediments to collecting data on the components of demographic processes — the problems with obtaining useful information on cause of death or rural-to-rural migration are familiar examples — it is also often the case that the reason more and better data are not available is that there has not been a compelling rationale for collecting them. Given the likely pay-off to attempting to analyse the determinants and consequences of demographic change in terms of the components of those changes rather than in net or aggregate terms, it seems to the Group that efforts to improve and refine procedures for obtaining the necessary data on various components of demographic processes are more than justified.

Descriptive Research

In recent years, the term 'descriptive' has acquired an increasingly pejorative connotation in the social science research community, and many recommendations on population research have been to 'go beyond' descriptive research into more analytic work on interrelations between population and development. The distinction is a valid one in that one type of activity seeks to present information while the other is after knowledge; but it is easy to downplay the need for information on demographic behaviour, for policy-making as well as for research.

In the previous chapters of this report it has been shown that information on levels, trends, and differentials in each of the demographic variables is either not available or is unreliable in a rather large proportion of the developing countries. The absence of information is due to two quite different reasons. In some cases, the data simply have not been collected; censuses and demographic surveys have not been undertaken and vital registration or sample vital registration systems have not been set up. In other cases, the data are available but have not yet been analysed with the appropriate techniques for demographic estimation or at the required levels of disaggregation.

Besides the obvious need for demographic data as a foundation for much of the analytic work recommended in the previous chapters, the need that policy-makers have for such information became very clear to the IRG in the course of its work. In cases where governments have clearly defined population policies, information on changes or trends in demographic behaviour — both in the aggregate and for different regional and socioeconomic groups — is necessary to answer the persistent question of how things are going. 'Answers' of this sort do not constitute a valid evaluation of the impact of government policy, but they do provide an indication of whether 'more policy' is required and where. What is more, as was emphasized earlier, policy-makers more often than not are faced with decisions that have to be taken in the very near future on the basis of the information and knowledge that is available to them. In such situations the policy-maker has little alternative to making the most extensive use possible of whatever data are currently available or that can be collected quickly.

Evaluation of Public Policies and Programmes

One of the most insistent needs voiced by policy-makers at the series of IRG workshops was for studies to evaluate the demographic impact of past and present public policies and programmes. The appeal for evaluation extended from those programmes and projects with immediate demographic objectives, such as family planning programmes and specific public-health measures, to those thought to be strongly linked to demographic behaviour but without specific demographic objectives, such as education, nutrition, and rural development programmes.

At present, considering the state of knowledge on the determinants of population variables, there are only limited grounds for believing that social scientists will be able to tackle such a task successfully. The one kind of population-related evaluative activity with which there has been extensive experience is the evaluation of family planning programmes. The regional reviews of social-science research undertaken for the IRG were able to point to a few cases where attempts have been made to evaluate specific health measures, but only a very limited number of instances were located in which social scientists have attempted to evaluate the impact of migration policies. In short, due to the limitations of both theory and experience, the methodology to support broader attempts at demographic evaluation is extremely underdeveloped.

It is the Group's opinion that this situation can and should be considerably improved in a relatively short period of time. One way of approaching evaluation is to view public policies as natural experiments: to be measured are the intensity, quantity, and duration of the intervention, as well as the previous and subsequent behaviour of the population that is affected (Ilchman, 1975). Control groups often result from the variable application and implementation of policies. But taking an experimental approach to evaluation is only straightforward when the intervention in question is narrow in scope and directly focused on promoting demographic change. In the case of more diffuse multi-purpose projects the problem is much more difficult. It is here that there is a need for complementary theoretical developments. On the one hand, there is such a wide variety of policies and projects that are candidates for evaluation that there is a need for sharper criteria for choosing among them. On the other hand, because such interventions introduce a multiplicity of changes in the decision-making contexts of individuals and families, to have some chance of success, one must be able to concentrate on at most a few of these on the basis of *a priori* considerations.

Developing Sound Theoretical Frameworks

In the past 20 years considerable progress has been achieved in discovering the nature of the relations between population and development. Perhaps most noteworthy are the number of major misconceptions that have been disproved. It seems clear, though, that the present state of knowledge on the determinants and consequences of demographic behaviour is somewhat uneven: there remain several important areas where no central paradigm has emerged and several different views or schools of thought are in competition with one another. Perhaps the three most important un-resolved questions are with regard to the determinants of fertility, the consequences of internal migration, and the consequences of alternative trends in fertility.

Disagreement on these questions remains not because they have not attracted attention, but rather because they are extremely complex issues that have resisted simplification. The IRG has suggested what seem to be promising ways of tackling each of them in the future, but what is to be stressed here is that these approaches and others will have to be followed with persistence and determination over a consider-able length of time if the present gaps in knowledge are to be reduced in size.

The more complete knowledge and sounder theoretical frameworks that will be the result of such efforts should make important contributions to the design of population policy. In the case of determinants, the major pay-off should be in terms of new policy options, while more complete knowledge of the consequences of demographic behaviour will lead to better-informed population policy decisions as well as policies in other areas to compensate for the adverse effects of certain patterns of demographic behaviour. An active attempt to develop and test the policy leads that emerge from 'basic' or 'theoretical' research is clearly a very important adjunct to this enterprise.[30]

Analysis of Political Processes

There is frequently a very naïve quality to much of the existing and proposed research on population and development that purports to be 'relevant for policy'. The *naiveté* consists of an excessive confidence in the ability of research and the new knowledge it produces *per se* to have a direct influence on the design and implementation of public programmes. One common line of reasoning is that if research succeeds in identifying the relationship between the demographic variable in question and different economic, social, and cultural indicators of development (and the former can be expressed as a function of the latter), then a tool will have been obtained for use in decisions regarding policies and plans. But that is as far as it goes. 'Policy relevance' is not attached to a thorough analysis of how, in fact, government policies eventuate and the decision-making processes that are involved. There is little or no consideration of the roles of different interest groups and of the use that they in turn make of research findings in their efforts to influence government policy.

Better knowledge of the politics of population policy-making would, in the first place, provide criteria for analysing what kinds of research would strengthen the hands of the various contending groups that are attempting to influence population policy decisions and thereby could play a role in helping to break the political impasse preventing the adoption or implementation of a certain type of policy. This sort of consideration comes up, for example, with regard to setting priorities for research on mortality. Which would have the greatest chance of legitimizing policy changes that would reduce the inefficient and inequitable nature of most developing country health care systems: more research to determine the cost-effectiveness of different sorts of health measures, or research that would simply set out in as clear a way as possible the existing differentials in health status between social classes?

A second and related purpose of political analysis would be to identify needs and deficiencies with respect to research utilization. It may be the case in some countries, for example, that a disproportionate amount

[30] In passing, it may be noted that the question of whether the study of the influence of variables such as population growth and internal migration on the rest of the economy properly fall within the IRG's field of interest was discussed at some length at several of the Group's meetings. At least one member of the IRG feels that such issues are the province of experts on the dependent variable and should not absorb financial and human resources available for 'population and development'.

of effort is being spent on communicating research results to planners when they, in fact, have less influence on the design and implementation of population policies than a great many other elements within a government.

Finally, accurate political analysis is a precondition for determining which government organizations are best able to take on the responsibility for both developing and advocating policy options. As Korten (1979) has emphasized, such decisions should be based on a thorough knowledge of how government decisions are arrived at, where the centres of influence are located, and which of these have an inherent interest in effective population policy.

Styles of Development and Population Policy

It is little more than conventional wisdom to say that population and development are related. There is, however, considerable difference of opinion as to the strength and nature of the relationship. One extreme but quite widespread view is that demographic processes are such an integral part of the more global mechanics of development that there is only a minimal possibility of altering the course of demographic trends without undertaking a major change in development objectives or the means by which they are pursued. The hypothesis is that the more proximate economic and social determinants of the individual population variables are very closely linked to broader social and economic processes and to the political and policy options behind them. This hypothesis was set out in some detail in Chapter 8 with respect to the spatial distribution of population and patterns of internal migration, but it also has considerable relevance to the other demographic variables. In the case of health policies and family planning programmes success depends on, among other things, providing services. In this respect, the amount of 'participation' attained by different sectors of a society may be crucial.

The probability of a family planning programme significantly reducing fertility differentials is directly related to the proportion of the population with high fertility that it serves. How high that proportion can be is to a considerable extent determined by the degree to which government institutions — especially those that are part of the health-care system — have penetrated into the different regions of the country and levels of the society. These institutions not only provide the means of distributing contraceptive services, but also a range of complementary services such as adult education, food supplements, and maternal and child health care. But an integral aspect of the development styles that characterize many developing countries is that sizeable fractions of the population are excluded from both participating in more than a marginal way in the productive structure and receiving the benefits of public services. The groups most likely to be excluded — recent migrants to the cities, families living in squatter settlements, agricultural labourers, and small farmers — are among those most likely to have fertility that is considerably higher than the national average, at least in countries where fertility declines have been under way for some time.[31]

Commercial channels and, especially, community organizations are often presented as alternative vehicles for the distribution of contraceptive services. Commercial channels, however, are not likely to be well developed in rural areas or urban slums; and although spectacular successes are often cited with regard to certain 'community based distribution programmes', they may turn out to be the exception rather than the rule in settings where social mobilization is limited and strong community organizations are viewed as a threat to order and authority.

Clearly this example is but one of many that could be used to demonstrate the general point that the larger developmental context may often impose severe limits on the kinds of population policies that may be implemented. The question of just where these limits lie in individual countries is an extremely important one and should constitute a priority topic for future research.

References

Hakim, Peter, and Solimano, Giorgio. 1978. *Development, Reform, and Malnutrition in Chile*. Cambridge: MIT Press.

Ilchman, Warren F. 1975. 'Population Knowledge and Population Policies.' In *Comparative Policy Analysis*, R. Kenneth Godwin, ed. Lexington, Mass.: Lexington Books.

Korten, David C. 1979. 'New Issues, New Options: A Management Perspective on Population and Family Planning.' *Studies in Family Planning*, 10 (1), 3–14.

[31] These same points have recently been made with considerable force by Hakim and Solimano (1978) with respect to nutrition programmes.

PART III   INSTITUTIONAL AND HUMAN RESOURCES FOR SOCIAL-SCIENCE RESEARCH ON POPULATION AND DEVELOPMENT

Introduction

The implementation of the research recommendations set forth in Part II of this Report will require, among other things, the expansion and the strengthening of the institutional and human resources for social-science research on population and development in all developing regions. Future efforts to overcome the present scarcity of researchers with the required qualifications will necessarily have to rely to some extent on the experience accumulated in the recent past on matters related to institution building and personnel training. But new schemes and programmes will have to be instituted, not only to cope with the growing demand for knowledge in the population field, but also to ensure a continuous flow of qualified personnel into the field.

In the first chapter (11) of Part III there is an examination of the situation prevailing in the respective developing regions and some suggestions are advanced useful for the difficult task of defining national priorities for personnel development in the population field in each of them. This first chapter ends with a review of some of the factors that have contributed to the development of research capacity in various regions. The second chapter (12) discusses some of the major questions concerning the amount and direction of future support, and ends with some general guidelines for future efforts to develop institutional and human resources for policy-orientated analysis and research.

11 A REVIEW OF THE PRESENT SITUATION

From the brief regional overviews of institutional and human resources for training and research contained in Chapters 1–5, the detailed examination undertaken for three of the regions,[1] and the partial review for some West African countries undertaken by one of the IRG's members in connection with another project (Planning Studies Programme, 1977), it is obvious that in none of the regions with which the Group was concerned have these resources achieved a level of self-sufficiency, and that there are important differences between regions and between countries within regions. These differences do not refer only, as might be expected, to the numbers of qualified personnel and institutions engaged in population studies. They refer also to the existing institutional arrangements and the general environment for research provided by them; to the type of professionals available and to the amount of contact and communication among them; to the predominant disciplinary orientation of the research; and, to some extent, to the links with developed country institutions and scholars.

The Arab Countries

A comparison between regions shows clearly that the Arab countries have the lowest level of institutional development. It is also among them that the insufficiency of personnel capable of analysing and interpreting the relations between demographic phenomena and the process of socio-economic development is the greatest. Within the region the largest concentration of professionals in the population field and therefore of related research products occurs in Egypt. But well-known academic institutions in the region that have been operating for many years, such as the American Universities in Cairo and Beirut have had no success in attracting professionals capable of organizing research and training programmes in demography and population studies. Although the Cairo Regional Demographic Centre has been in operation since the late 1950s, it has had a limited influence in the region. The training given by the Centre has remained for the most part at the junior and intermediate levels and is

[1] See East–West Population Institute, Appendix 5, for South-East and East Asia; Hill, Appendix 10, for the Arab Countries; and Urzúa, Appendix 12, for Latin America.

essentially limited to techniques of demographic analysis. Furthermore, graduates from the Centre have been very unevenly distributed among the countries of the region, and a significant number of those trained are not actually working in the population field.

Until recently, channels of communication among the small group of Arab scholars working in the population field have been extremely limited. Previously they had to rely almost entirely on the *CDC Newsletter* issued periodically by the Cairo Demographic Centre and its technical publications. The vacuum has now been partially filled by the publication of a periodic bulletin, together with the issuance of other technical documents, by the Population Division of the Economic Commission for Western Asia (ECWA).

In the past, the Arab countries received limited foreign financial and technical assistance for population research and training, mainly from US sources. This situation has changed with the strengthening of the ECWA Population Division, thanks to UNFPA support, and with the programme being developed by the Population Council, particularly the Middle East Awards (MEAWARDS) fellowship programme in which the Ford Foundation is also collaborating.

In the case of the Arab countries it is indispensable to break the vicious circle that makes the existence of teaching and research programmes at a high academic level almost impossible due to the lack of personnel with the required qualifications to undertake them. It is clear from the report prepared for the IRG by Allan Hill (Appendix 10) that there is a dearth of professionals with the training needed to undertake research of the nature being recommended by the IRG. If this situation is to change, it is evident that the environment within which population research is undertaken must be greatly enhanced if it is to provide the support conducive to an improved situation both in terms of quality of scholars attracted to the field as well as in terms of the topics to be addressed. Here, perhaps more than in any other region, it will be necessary to resort to foreign academic institutions to train a number of professionals at the postgraduate level who, upon returning, would constitute the necessary critical core that, with financial support and perhaps technical advice continued for some time, could organize programmes of teaching and research in population with various disciplinary orientations in selected universities of the region. These programmes should include an element of interinstitutional collaboration. Until more qualified personnel are available it would be advisable for government departments to hire some of the junior- or intermediate-level demographers who already exist in some of these countries. These technicians could undertake the analytical exploitation of numerous data sets that remain unexamined or only partially studied. This step could be instrumental in promoting the development of some of the descriptive research recommended in Part II of this Report.

The Cairo Demographic Centre could undoubtedly play a role as a regional training and research facility, provided the Centre expands the coverage of its activities to as many Arab countries as possible. There also appears to be a need for follow-up mechanisms that would give former fellows continued support upon returning to their countries, in order to help ensure that they continue to work in the population field. If the links of the Centre with Cairo University were strengthened, perhaps a larger number of diploma students could go on to post-graduate studies leading to a higher university career that would combine population studies with another social-science discipline.

ECWA's programme of population research has already expanded beyond purely descriptive studies, and could possibly continue to fill the important role of serving as a forum in which basic population issues are identified by governments, thus offering guidance both to the work of its own Population Division and interested Arab academic institutions. At a subregional level, continued support to the Association Maghrebine pour les Études de Population would not only help to keep population and development research active in the three member nations but could also have multiplying effects in other Arab countries.

Sub-Saharan Africa

If the regions are classified in order of lack of capacity for population teaching and research, Sub-Saharan Africa should probably be placed second after the Arab countries. There are, of course, clear distinctions between the capacities in West and in East Africa. Within the former, one can also find significant differences between anglophone and franco-phone countries. In anglophone West Africa, the countries best endowed with university resources for research in population and development are Nigeria and Ghana. Support for activities in this field were initiated as early as 1960 in Ghana and in the 1970s in Nigeria, with the support of several US foundations. In Nigeria, five universities (Ibadan, Ife, Lagos, Nigeria-Nsukka, and Ahmadu Bello) have at least one department, Institute, or programme doing research in population and related subjects, and in several instances they have collaborative relations with a post-graduate teaching programme in demography or sociology with a strong curriculum in population. In all of these universities, there is a core of professionals — albeit sometimes small — with postgraduate training abroad in demography, statistics, economics, or sociology. A certain number of Nigerian professionals in the population field can be found serving abroad, either in international organizations or in other African countries. In Ghana developments have been more modest, but there are two distinct programmes at the University of Ghana embarked on demo-graphic research. It is also expected that the UN Regional Demographic Centre in Accra will have a beneficial influence in promoting population research in other Ghanaian universities.

Although some government departments in these two countries are interested in population issues and research on them, the bulk of the efforts in this area is entrusted to the university institutions, with which some of these departments have established working relationships. In some cases academics also hold government appointments.

Population teaching and research activities within academic institutions in other anglophone West African countries are either very incipient or almost non-existent. More recently an important resource for the training of anglophone West African demographers and for the execution of pertinent research was created: the UN Regional Institute of Population Studies (RIPS), located at the University of Ghana.

It appears that in anglophone West Africa most of the researchers presently engaged in population studies were trained originally in sociology or geography, although a few economists and anthropologists also seem to be active in the field. A base, therefore, exists for promoting and developing among them research of the nature included in the agenda being recommended by the IRG in this Report.

In the francophone West African countries, university-based population training and research are of very recent origin (early 1970s). Perhaps the more important developments are occurring in the Ivory Coast, where the Centre for Research and Scientific Studies includes a Department of Demography, and in Zaïre, where the National University established a Department of Demography in the early 1970s. In general, however, population research activities in francophone countries are carried out primarily in government departments. Such is the case, for example, in Upper Volta, where the Volta River Basin Resettlement Project (AVV) has undertaken several studies of population movements and other studies needed in connection with its plans.

The francophone countries are better endowed with regional institutions than the anglophones. Besides the regional UN Demographic Centre, L'Institut de Formation et de Recherche Démographique (IFORD), in Cameroon, the Overseas Office of Scientific and Technical Research of the French Government (ORSTOM) has local offices in several francophone African countries, Ivory Coast, Togo, and Upper Volta. Little is known at this date about the potential contribution to demographic research of the newly established Sahelian Institute in Mali, but it is another regional facility that in the future could undertake population studies.

Population training and research in East Africa is even less developed than in West Africa but two countries, Kenya and Tanzania, have achieved some capacity for demographic research. In both countries support from abroad (mainly the Population Council) has been instrumental in developing and giving continuity to two university-based institutes. One is the University of Nairobi Population Studies and Research Institute and the other the Demographic Unit of the Bureau of Resource Assessment and Land Use Planning (BRALUP) of the University of Dar-es-Salaam.

If the existing West and East African academic institutions interested in population studies continue to receive external support both for training personnel locally and abroad and for strengthening available facilities for conducting research, we can expect significant progress in population research in Sub-Saharan Africa, since there is already a critical minimum core of professionals to build upon. Means of promoting communication between scholars both within and among countries appear to be badly needed. Particularly beneficial would be an improved dialogue between francophone and anglophone scholars working in the population field. Perhaps intellectual communication of this sort can be fostered through the African Population Association, which publishes the quarterly *Jimlar Mutane*.

Efforts to initiate, expand or improve on-going research activities in West and East African countries other than those mentioned above might well be able to rely primarily on technical assistance from institutions and scholars from within the Sub-Saharan African region. Such efforts should, of course, include assistance from the two UN regional centres. In order to be able to organize a concerted regional programme of institutional development, financial support from abroad is indispensable. Technical assistance from developed country institutions and scholars will also be needed, but it would probably be more effective and profitable if integrated with the efforts mentioned above. The training facilities available within the region can be utilized by those countries that lack a well-developed system of higher education to build a core of junior- and intermediate-level professionals, from among whom those with the greatest potential for future professional development should be selected for postgraduate training abroad.

Middle South Asia

India, the largest country of this region, was the first to have received significant external support for the development of training and research capacities in population. In early 1957 a biannual *Population Review* was begun by the Indian Institute for Population Studies in Madras with the support of a joint Canada–US grant. In that same year the UN established in Bombay the first regional demographic centre to be organized in a developing country. In early 1971 the Indian Association for the Study of Population was formally founded, and towards the end of 1972 it began publishing the quarterly review *Demography India*. By the middle of 1973 the Association had more than 200 members, including Indian population specialists working abroad. By 1975 there were at least ten teaching and research institutions in India having population as their major field of interest.

Despite the early appearance in India of institutions, organizations, and publications in the population field, as well as the prior tradition of social-science research, population research in India has not developed to the high level of quality and coverage of topics — particularly those more closely related to development issues — that one would expect. *A Survey of Research in Demography*,[2] sponsored by the Indian Council of Social Science Research and published in 1975 by P. B. Desai, concluded that 'it would appear that at no time during the period was any serious thought given in any quarter to the development of demography as a discipline' (p. 72) and that 'what emerges from the foregoing review of the 'demographic' literature and its research content is a rather apologetic and disquieting conclusion that our knowledge of the demographic processes and conditions in India is very limited, peripheral and even superficial' (p. 85). The report adds that 'with regard to the present state of demographic research, it is apparent that one of the reasons why its course has not been orderly is the lack of personnel with training in the field' (p. 80). It further recommends that 'in the light of the importance that demographic research clearly merits in the context of official policies and programmes as well as of the critical situation we find ourselves in, it would be useful to expand training facilities for the benefit not only of new recruits but also of those who are now struggling to pursue it' (p. 81).

It is well known that statistical and survey methodology is reasonably well developed in India. We can conclude that human resources for formal demographic analysis and teaching of these techniques is probably adequate for the needs of the country and even for providing technical assistance to other Asian countries less developed in this field. In other words, descriptive research of the nature being recommended by the IRG could expand with very little difficulty. What seems to be required is the development of research programmes that bring together sociologists, economists, and other social scientists to undertake analysis of the interrelations of demographic and other factors along lines identified as prioritary in the Indian context. Postgraduate students in associated fields could be attached to these programmes when preparing their theses or dissertations and together with some of the more experienced researchers, could constitute the basis for reorientating present graduate-level training in population towards a more interdisciplinary approach that would also be based on sounder theoretical frameworks. Doctoral and post-doctoral training abroad should be considered as an integral part of a co-ordinated approach. Technical support from selected foreign institutions and scholars, in many instances of a short-term nature, would also be advisable for guiding certain aspects of given research areas or simply as a means of opening up avenues for the discussion of on-going research projects or particular topics currently receiving attention in the population field. With the existing core of distinguished Indian population scholars, the government

[2] Of the literature reviewed, 94 per cent was published between 1951 and 1970.

support of demographic research centres that has been traditional in India, the collaboration of the Indian Social Science Research Council and the Indian Association for the Study of Population, and continued support from international donors, it should not be very difficult, as the Council has recommended, 'to nurse the development of demography [in India] in order that it matures into a viable basic social science'. If progress can be accomplished in this direction, India could well serve as a place for training population specialists from other Asian countries. In this connection, the role to be played by the International Institute of Population Studies should be re-examined.

In four other countries of Middle South Asia — Bangladesh, Nepal, Pakistan, and Sri Lanka — the short-term development of population research activities appears to depend more on government-sponsored institutions, such as the Bangladesh Institute of Development Studies and the Pakistan Population Planning Council, or on private centres such as the Marga Institute in Sri Lanka. Some possible foci for the development of academic training in demography and eventually the organization of research programmes in these countries are Dacca University in Bangladesh, the Department of Sociology of the Punjab University in Pakistan, and the Faculty of Arts of the University of Sri Lanka; but more continued and significant technical and financial assistance from abroad seems to be needed in order to achieve self-sustaining development. The need to train more professionals abroad at the postgraduate level is also evident.

South-East and East Asia

Over all, there is a very substantial capacity for social science research on population and development in South-East and East Asia. This is described in some detail in the report that the East–West Population Institute prepared for the IRG. The report correctly points to the considerable variation among countries, singling out the Philippines, South Korea, and Thailand as the countries where the supply of trained researchers is relatively good and where the best-developed research support facilities exist.

Intracountry contacts and communication among social scientists working in the population field are rather scarce; more contact seems to exist at the interregional level. The *Asian-Pacific Population Programme News*, issued quarterly by the Division of Population and Social Affairs of the Economic and Social Commission for Asia and the Pacific, is a means of keeping abreast of some of the developments in the population field. Unfortunately, very little coverage — if any — is given in the *News* to academic activities in the field.

While links between university and governmental institutions tend to be rather weak in Sub-Saharan Africa, the opposite is the case in several

East-Asian countries. Rather strong linkages exist between population research institutions and central planning agencies in Thailand, South Korea, the Philippines, and Indonesia.

The region appears to be reasonably endowed with regional institutions, although some of the regional networks such as the International Committee for Applied Research in Population (ICARP) and the Committee for Comparative Behavioural Studies in Population (COMBEP) do not seem to be solidly established. The Institute of South-East Asian Studies in Singapore appears to be a promising base for developing regional activities in the future. It already serves as Secretariat to the South-East Asia Population Research Awards Programme (SEAPRAP), which receives financial support from the Ford Foundation and the International Development Research Centre (IDRC). The recently established Association of South-East Asia Nations (ASEAN), which has defined priority areas for collaborative research on population and development, offers some promise of significant progress in the future if the initial support granted by UNFPA and FAO is continued. For several years the region has received substantial support both in terms of training and research from two institutions on the periphery of the region, the East–West Population Institute in Hawaii and the Department of Demography of the Australian National University in Canberra.

In the recent past, most South-East Asian countries do not seem to have had difficulty in securing external technical and financial support. In fact, in some cases foreign donors appear to have been in somewhat competitive positions, a situation that, if it still exists, calls for co-ordination among them. More recently in other cases — such as South Korea — external support has begun to diminish or has been entirely withdrawn. What appears to be needed in the region is a substantial continued commitment on the part of donor agencies so that the Institutions that appear to be well established will be able to achieve a level of development that will ensure their continuation. There is a diversity of disciplinary approaches being taken by the different institutions in the region. This diversity should continue to be encouraged as a means of ensuring that population phenomena are studied from the many angles pointed to in the IRG research agenda and that are identified by scholars from the region as prioritary under the conditions of their countries. The general upgrading of social-science research by ensuring, among other things, that South-East and East Asian institutions are enabled to retain their professional personnel by improving working conditions, career incentives, and local facilities for publication is a goal to be supported both from inside sources and outside donors.

While there are important capacities within the region for postgraduate training in population, the continuation of fellowship support for study abroad at the doctoral and post-doctoral level would seem to be an important element of a programme to further the progress already attained.

Latin America

There is a marked disequilibrium in Latin America between the capacity for training and that for research in population, with rather limited facilities for training, particularly at the national level, and a significant array of social science centres embarked on population and related research. Local university graduate-level training in demography was never very active in the region, and even after many years of national efforts and outside support, only the Centre for Economic and Demographic Studies, El Colegio de México; the Catholic University of Lima, Perú; the Centre for Regional Development and Planning, University of Belo Horizonte, Minas Gerais, Brazil: and the Centre for Demographic Studies, University of La Habana, Cuba, appear to have solidly established graduate programmes. To some extent, this explains why the Latin American Demographic Centre (CELADE) at its two locations in Santiago, Chile and San José, Costa Rica has played and continues to play such an important role in the training of professional personnel at different levels for both governments and universities. More recently CELADE has been joined in these efforts by another regional institution in the social sciences, FLACSO, with which it conducts jointly a masters programme in Social Sciences and Population. The disequilibrium between training and research activities has become even more acute during recent years due to the crises through which the universities in several countries have been going. As a result, many social-science research activities have been forced out of their former milieus. The majority of centres undertaking population research in the region are private institutions, and they perform practically no training activities.

While demographic research in Latin America was initially mainly composed of descriptive studies and paid considerable attention to measurement and projection, present research activities cover a rather wide spectrum of topics paying particular attention to the study of population and development. It is probably the region where the most attention is being given to the study of the role political processes play in shaping particular aspects of population dynamics and policy.

With very few exceptions, such as the Corporación Centro Regional de Población (CCRP) in Colombia, a major limitation of the present situation is the absence or weakness of relations between private research institutions and the government departments that are among the natural consumers of the research findings produced by these institutions. To some extent this lack of dialogue explains why in Latin America one finds more frequently than in other parts of the world (with the exception of francophone African countries) that government departments, particularly those entrusted with the formulation or the implementation of population policies, undertake a significant amount of demographic research, especially of a descriptive nature. In this connection CELADE has also served a useful purpose because it constitutes, for most countries, the main resource not only for the training of government personnel but also for technical assistance for the development of government research programmes.

Contact and communication between Latin American scholars working in population is facilitated through several mechanisms. The most important of them is the Programme of Social Science Research on Population (PISPAL), which both funds research projects and provides professionals working on particular themes the opportunity to meet in workshops and other technical meetings. The Executive Secretariat of PISPAL also issues a quarterly bulletin that is widely distributed in the region and keeps scholars abreast of what is happening not only within the programme itself but at a good number of the social science research centres in the region. Another group that actively fosters communication and collaboration between researchers in the region is the Commission on Population and Development of the Latin American Social Science Council (CLACSO), which operates through three working groups dealing with the processes of population reproduction, internal migration, and sociodemographic data. These groups meet periodically to discuss papers prepared on the topics with which they are concerned and to examine common theoretical and methodological problems. Meetings bringing together scholars attached to government institutions have also been organized by CELADE and other international organizations working in the region. Finally, there are several regular specialized publications: *Demografía y Economía*, published by El Colegio de México; *Notas de Población*, published by CELADE; and the *Boletín Demográfico*, published by the Brazilian Institute of Geography and Statistics. Additionally, at least eighteen research centres periodically issue reports of research findings.

Latin America appears to possess the needed research facilities and a good number of the professionals required to undertake a research agenda of the nature being proposed by the IRG. The weakest link in the chain is sources of training. For lack of formal training programmes, there is heavy reliance on informal in-service training by research centres of the young professionals they take on. Training at the doctoral level within the region is almost non-existent, and considering the present situation of Latin American universities, it is difficult to envisage that a strong base could be developed in the very near future for this type of training in public academic institutions. Perhaps such an undertaking could be attempted by private institutions like El Colegio de México after their present staff is strengthened both quantitatively and qualitatively. With this purpose in mind, an effort should be made to strengthen those faculties presently awarding M.A. degrees in demography, or in economics and sociology with a specialization in population and to continue training abroad at the doctoral level professionals who can return to these programmes and eventually help organize doctoral degree programmes. In the meantime, teaching and research programmes can be strengthened by the seconding by developed country institutions of staff for extended periods of time. This practice, which has been used in the M.A. programmes at CEDEPLAR and El Colegio de México among others, should be continued and enlarged, and representatives from donor agencies should be alert to possibilities of this nature arising within the institutions with which they are related in the region.

How We Got There

Some understanding of the different means that have been used in the recent past to help the developing countries create or improve population training and research capacities is needed before one can evaluate the degree to which they have succeeded and chart future steps addressed at expanding, strengthening or, if necessary, redirecting the course of capacity building in the Third World.

Institutional Development

In the late 1950s and throughout the 1960s several of the important donors in the population field allocated considerable resources towards what was then labelled 'institutional development'. After 20 years of effort the results in the different regions and countries vary considerably. They have been moderately successful in some South-East Asian Countries. Reference is made in the East–West Population Institute Report (IRG Appendix 4) to some of the institutions that received such outside support and are at present contributing effectively to population research activities in those countries. The success was more modest in Latin America: after considerable investment on the part of certain donors, institutional facilities remain insufficient. The attempts in Sub-Saharan Africa are of more recent origin, and in general they seem to be producing modest results, although at a somewhat slower pace than expected.

Institutional development as a means of providing an academic environment with a certain continuity and a high level of proficiency for the development of social-science research in population -- or for the development of any scientific endeavour — is an extremely logical and worthy idea. It is, nevertheless, not easily implemented. That the level of academic institutional development in developing countries leaves much to be desired not only in the population field but generally is due to a combination of factors (the political situation, style of development and importance attributed to higher education, tradition of academic research, etc.) that cannot easily or quickly be changed by the mere availability of external technical and financial resources, although these can, of course, be helpful.

Three factors appear to be basic to the success of the 'institutional development' approach. First, the institution must be 'built' at a pace and in a way that will avoid friction and antagonisms with organizations already established. Some initial adaptive capacity from the new institution is required. Pushing or trying to force the development of the 'ideal' organization in a milieu not yet prepared for such an organization has often led to failure. Secondly, external support should continue for an extended period of time, even when it appears at first sight that the institution can continue without it. Premature withdrawal of support also explains certain cases in which institutional development efforts failed or did not live up to expectations. Thirdly, a strong programme of fellowships for study abroad must continue for some time to ensure an adequate supply of qualified personnel, as well as to make up for the inevitable loss of trained professionals who move to other institutions, government service, or abroad. Although fellowship programmes have contributed considerably in the past to building important academic institutions and private research centres in many developing countries, donors seem to have cut these programmes too short and too soon.

Regional Demographic Centres

Both in Part I and in the preceding section of this Chapter, reference has been made to the regional and subregional demographic centres that with UN support have been operating in the developing regions for periods varying from 5 to more than 20 years. There are, at present, five of these centres working in developing regions (one of them, CELADE, with two headquarters) and one in a socialist country (Romania), which serves primarily francophone African countries.

While no over-all comparative evaluation of the UN-supported regional demographic centres seems to exist — or at least has not come to the attention of the IRG — there appears to be consensus among most evaluators of the different centres that they have in general performed up to now a very useful function. For some countries they have been the sole or most important provider of junior- and intermediate-level personnel.

Development of Population Assistance

When the international donors community was already evaluating the results of their efforts at institutional development, the gains obtained through the fellowship programmes that had been operating for years, the value of regional research networks being sponsored, and the usefulness of the UN-supported regional centres, the international population field was shaken from some of its previous positions by events at the World Population Conference held in Bucharest in 1974. There, the developing countries, having as background some of the basic demands already aired by them when discussing the establishment of a New International Economic Order, at a UN General Conference argued forcefully for the sovereign right of each nation to determine the manner in which to cope with problems arising from population growth and for considering population policy as an integral part of a country's overall development strategy. The stance taken at Bucharest by the developing countries implied that to understand or attempt to modify the population dynamics of a given country, it is indispensable to understand and explain how they interact with other socioeconomic phenomena. To some extent, this meant a rejection of some of the research models that had been promoted by certain developed country institutions and scholars.

This rejection, along with the noticeable increase in the number of developing countries with population policies that explicitly envision co-ordinating demographic and other development objectives, and whose policy-makers, government consultants, and administrators pose continuous demands for information and knowledge on which to base decisions, actions, and evaluations, led to a change in the emphasis being placed by developed country institutions and scholars on research topics that concentrated mainly on fertility and on the effects of family planning programmes on reproductive outcomes. The result has been a greater convergence of concerns, which to some extent is reflected in the research agenda being recommended by the IRG in this Report.

How has international financial assistance in the field of population behaved in the recent past, and is it responding to the new climate created by the World Population Conference?

It is difficult to make reliable estimates of the size of international financial assistance in the field of population, but Gille (1977, p. 4) has estimated that it grew from US $2 million in 1960 to 18 million in 1965. The second half of the 1960s witnessed a considerable increase in funds being granted for population assistance. By 1970 expenditures had grown to 125 million. From then on, there was a continuous expansion. Gille estimates that from 1971 to 1976 assistance increased in real terms (1970= 100) from US $148 million to 214 million, a growth of more than 44 per cent in a 6-year period. Official governmental population assistance as a proportion of total official international development assistance also grew from 0.1 per cent in 1961 to 2.3 per cent in 1974. This proportion varied among governments, ranging in 1974 from 9.5 per cent in Norway to 0.1 per cent in Belgium.

While the figures cited above give a positive picture of the growth of over-all international financial assistance in population, unfortunately, because of their aggregated nature they do not tell us much about how the level of assistance for different sorts of activities has evolved. The increasing emphasis that was placed on providing support for action programmes in the population field during the decade prior to the World Population Conference must have led to a proportional narrowing of the range of other activities that were originally being supported, particularly by private foundations. This narrowing affected primarily the availability of support for the broader social-scientific research on which this report has focused and for fellowships to train personnel with that orientation. All this was happening precisely at a time when the action programmes being supported were generating needs for new and more disaggregated information on fertility and additional knowledge concerning the interrelations between fertility and other aspects of development policy. One result was that in many cases the attention being paid by social scientists to migration and mortality actually decreased.

In the early years most of the external financial and technical assistance in population granted to the developing countries was explicitly assigned to family planning programmes and other closely related activities. Some support was also given to the gathering of basic demographic data and to the training of demographic analysts. As stated earlier, some donors, particularly private US foundations, began to grant support in the 1960s for the development of academic institutions and the training of social scientists with specialized knowledge of population. In the early 1970s more funds became available for social-science research in population, particularly through regional or subregional consortiums of national research institutions and through other award-granting mechanisms. This support helped to expand significantly the research being undertaken in many developing countries on the relations between population and development, but the expansion was relatively small in comparison with enormous increase in programmatic activity to which the bulk of international financial assistance was being directed.

Since the World Population Conference in 1974 emphasized so strongly the need to take into consideration the interrelatedness of population and development and because of the growing number of governments adopting broad population policies, it seemed to many observers that new orientations in the type, direction, and size of international technical and financial assitance would be needed in the 'post-Bucharest' era. Furthermore, the World Population Plan of Action adopted by the Conference called for a 'considerable expansion of the international assistance in the population field . . . for the proper implementation of this Plan of Action' (UN, 1975, p. 25, paragraph 104).

Over all, what occurred in the 2 years following the Conference was a *decrease* in the proportion that population assistance represented of total official development assistance. It declined from 2.3 per cent in 1974 to 2.1 per cent in 1975 and further to 2.0 per cent in 1976. On a national level the proportion increased considerably in the cases of Australia, Finland, and Sweden and somewhat in Norway, but it declined in Canada, Denmark, Japan, the United Kingdom, and the US (Gille,

1977, Table 3). The reversal of the previous trend since 1974 can also be appreciated by comparing the 20 per cent average annual growth in resources available for international population assistance during the period 1970–4 with the 11 and 8 per cent increases for the years 1975 and 1976 respectively. A decline in purchasing power resulting from world-wide inflationary trends and the devaluation of the US dollar to a large extent offset this growth. Measured in constant US dollars (deflated by the consumer price index), the annual increase since 1974 has been limited to from 1 to 2 per cent.

The main factor in the slowing down of the trend in resources for international population assistance was that the largest donor, the United States, did not continue to make substantial increases in its population assistance as it did in the late 1960s and early 1970s, but actually reduced its annual contributions from year to year in the period 1972 through 1975.[3] An upward trend appears to have begun in 1976, but the amount of assistance for that year was still below the 1972 level. Although a number of other donor Governments of developed countries at the same time showed a growing recognition of the importance of population assistance by increasing substantially their contributions, these increases were not large enough to maintain the overall growth rate of resources available for population assistance. (Gille, 1977, pp. 5 and 6.)

Prospects for the future seemed more promising by the middle of 1977, with probable increases in the funds for international population assistance from the US, Japan, and other donor countries that had been increasing their annual contributions all along.

The donor community has already demonstrated its willingness to broaden the scope of activities deserving support. Greater recognition is being given to the need to better understand the manner in which demographic and socioeconomic factors interact as a means of providing a sound basis for explicit population policies. The creation of the IRG can be taken as an example of the move in that direction. But an increased level of external technical and financial assistance is required for this recognition to be translated into actual support for social-science research on population and development and for the expansion and upgrading of facilities for the training of personnel. The need is even greater than is immediately apparent if one considers that support for programmatic activities will continue to grow in the coming decade (UNFPA, 1977, Report of the Executive Director). If an increase in both local and foreign funds for research and training is not forthcoming in the immediate future, one can expect that the gap between the supply and the demand for a sound analytical basis for policy decisions can only widen.

[3] An amount of $146 million is estimated for 1977 and around $160 or higher for 1978 (footnote in original).

References

Desai, P. B. 1975. *A Survey of Research in Demography*. New Delhi: Indian Council of Social Science Research.

East–West Population Institute. 1978. 'Capacity for Social Science Research on Population and Development in South-East and East Asia: A Report on Institutional and Human Resources.' Appendix 5 to the Final Report. El Colegio de México: IRG.

Gille, Halvor. 1977. 'Recent Trends in International Population Assistance.' Paper presented to the Fourth Bellagio Conference on Population. 6–9 June 1977. New York: UNFPA.

Hill, Allan. 1978. 'Population Research and Training Institutions in the Arab World.' Appendix 10 to the Final Report. El Colegio de México: IRG.

Planning Studies Programme. 1977. 'Institutional Capacity and Follow-up Action in West Africa.' Ibadan, Nigeria: University of Ibadan. IRG/48.

The Population Council. 1975. *A Survey of Institutional Development Needs and Capabilities in Developing Countties*, vol. 1 (January). New York: The Population Council.

UNFPA. 1977. *Report of the Executive Director*. New York: United Nations Fund for Population Activities.

United Nations. 1975. Report of the United Nations. World Population Conference, 1974. E/CONF.60/19.

Urzúa, Raúl. 1978. 'Population Research and Training Institutions in Latin America.' Appendix 12 to the Final Report. El Colegio de México: IRG.

12 SOME MAJOR QUESTIONS CONCERNING THE AMOUNT AND DIRECTION OF FUTURE SUPPORT

There are a number of important questions that persons and institutions interested in strengthening the institutional capacity for research on population and development will have to ask themselves. The variety of strategies that could be adopted to accomplish this end is considerable, and there are a number of different ways that certain of the more obvious problems could be attacked. In what follows, a number of central questions — both strategic and tactical — are set forth and discussed in an effort to identify the major choices that have to be made and the considerations that should be taken into account in each case.

Before tackling these specific issues on an individual basis, there is one very general question that cannot be easily neglected. Does population constitute a privileged field within the social sciences? In the series of IRG workshops a number of scholars pointed out that however difficult or precarious was the situation of researchers working in the population area in their countries, such individuals were often considerably better off in terms of the resources that were made available to them than their colleagues, even in the same basic discipline, who were working on other problems. They argued that this situation often led to imbalances and conflicts that had a prejudicial effect on the over-all development of the social sciences, and represented a problem that should be taken into account by those institutions, both national and international, that provide support for social-science research.

The question of whether population actually constitutes a privileged area within the social sciences is not one that the IRG is in a position to address. Considering the magnitude of the research agenda that the IRG is recommending, there is no room for shifting resources away from population. Rather, to the extent that it exists now, the problem will continue to exist in the future. Ideally, heightened awareness might go some distance towards alleviating the difficulties that this unequal relationship entails.

Projects Versus Institutions

One of the most fundamental strategic choices facing donors is whether to direct support towards specific research projects or to provide 'institutional' support for research centres carrying out a programme of research in population and development. Clearly, the issue is not one of choosing either one or the other course of action, but of arriving at an appropriate balance between the two, and of considering as well a number of inter-mediate strategies that may be available. To begin with, however, it may be worth while to contrast the strengths and weaknesses of the two extreme strategies in as stark terms as possible.

We begin by characterizing the selection procedure that is employed in each case. Project grants are usually made on a competitive basis. The donor agency may define the area of research in which proposals are to be accepted as narrowly or as broadly as it chooses, but the breadth of the area is usually related both to the amount of funding that is available and the size of the 'market' from which proposals are solicited. The actual selection of projects for funding may be made either by the agency's staff or, as is more frequently the case, by a review panel composed of professionals in the field. Perhaps the most notable characteristic of the procedure is its prospective nature. In the review of individual pro-jects some attention may be given to the researchers' prior experience and accomplishments, but inevitably the greatest emphasis is on the quality of the proposal itself. Other important characteristics of the procedure are that it is orientated towards individuals rather than in-stitutions and that its time horizon is apt to be short, with most funding directed towards projects that will be completed within a year's time.

The procedures involved in making grants for institutional support are less clearly defined, but they differ in a number of ways from those employed in selecting projects. In the first place, the submission or pro-posal may be less specific, referring to the general direction of a programme of research rather than to a collection of specific projects. Responsibility for carrying out the proposal rests with the institution rather than with individuals, and the funding period is usually considerably longer than in the case of project proposals. Within such funding arrangements, the allocation of research funds among specific projects rests in the hands of the recipient organization. In evaluating individual proposals — both with regard to initial grants and to the continuation of support — donors are apt to rely more on actual performance than on statements about what will be accomplished in the future.

In practice, institutional grants are often made to newly formed centres in the hope that the funding will permit them to mature rapidly to the point where they can compete effectively for project funds and no longer require 'core' financing. But there is no apparent reason why this has to be the case. To the extent that donors are going to provide support over the long term for research on population and development, institutional grants may constitute just as viable an option as project support.

Both of these funding mechanisms have evident advantages and dis-advantages. By way of project funding donors may exert considerable leverage on the subject areas and also the methodology of research. What is more, such funding should produce foreseeable results in a relatively short period of time. In other words, it is not very risky. Donors usually have a good idea at the start of the nature and reliability of the results that will be obtained.

But what may be advantageous from one perspective may be prejudicial from another. To the extent that donors have less than perfect vision of what kinds of research need to be done, project funding may involve them too closely in the selection and definition of research areas. To the extent that funding agencies are apt to change their minds about priority areas of research every couple of years or so, the possibilities of realizing cumulative research on given topics over a longer period may be severely jeopardized. Finally, project-funding mechanisms often tend to ignore, or at least take for granted, the allocation of researchers and research funds among research centres or universities as well as the institutional context in which research is done.

The weaknesses of project funding are by and large the strengths of institutional support, and vice versa. Institutional grants can have a direct influence on the environment in which research is done. In addition to having a direct bearing on the personnel and facilities that are available to support researchers, to the extent that such grants are made for longer periods and with relatively broad mandates, they can provide a certain amount of both security and independence for researchers. In the best of circumstances, these conditions will yield the cumulative research that narrower, shorter-term project funding is unlikely to produce.

In a particular country or subregion, research activities may tend to be either highly concentrated in a single or at most a few large research centres in the capital city, or excessively dispersed in a number of smaller centres and universities spread throughout the country or area. While both extremes may be perfectly understandable as responses to given rules of the game in individual countries, they are likely to be inefficient. Institutional incentives may also prevent or at least hinder the establishment of centres made up of researchers from different primary disciplines. Explicit consideration is given below to questions regarding the sorts of institutions that it might be advisable for donors to promote and support, but the point to be made here is that it is through institutional rather than project grants that donors can best exercise a positive influence on the allocation of research activity between centres and attempt to overcome some of the institutional constraints that may be having an adverse effect on the present situation.

The provision of institutional support also has a number of potentially important drawbacks. From the point of view of donor agencies, institutional grants are apt to be considered somewhat frightening propositions. Coupled with the uncertainty of the outcome are the size and length of commitment that is involved. There is also the danger that on occasion generous institutional support may make life too comfortable for a select group of researchers, with a consequent decline in productivity.

An important intermediate strategy for donors that lies between project and institutional funding is supporting regional consortia composed of a fairly large number of research centres. Typically, in such an arrangement, the consortia submits a relatively broad proposal to the donor agencies indicating what sorts of research they consider prioritary, but the actual selection of projects for funding is made on a competitive basis by the officials of the consortia and any review panel that it may appoint. Perhaps the most important advantage of such a scheme is that it permits scholars in the region to play the major role in determining what lines of research should be given highest priority. Another advantage is that consortia provide a framework which, in the best of circumstances, can encourage cumulative if not necessarily continuous work on a selected and relatively narrow range of topics. The disadvantage or problem with consortia seems to be that they are only apt to appear spontaneously in regions where there is both considerable communication and solidarity among researchers; and, once established, their success seems to be highly dependent on the administrative ability of the co-ordinating secretariat or whatever unit is established to implement the programme.

Three Types of Research Institutions

Once the decision has been taken to make a concerted effort to develop or improve the institutional base in developing countries for social-science research on population, the question arises as to what sorts of institutions should be given priority. In this regard a useful distinction may be drawn between universities, independent or private research centres, and research units within government agencies. What are the organizational strengths and weaknesses of these three institutional settings? What sorts of research are best done in each? Although there are no universal answers to such questions and much depends on the particular situation in individual countries, in the following paragraphs some very modest generalizations are set forth in this regard.

Universities

The IRG is convinced that universities should play a major role in the production of knowledge on population and development. This conviction is based not only on an appraisal of the functional advantages of carrying out research in a university environment, but also on a belief that universities have a moral obligation to orientate their research activity towards problems with important implications for national development policy. What seems to vary enormously between countries and regions, however, are the relations between universities and the government.

In Latin America, for example, universities are usually extremely critical of the government, and relations are as often based on antagonism as on co-operation. In some parts of Asia, on the other hand, links between universities and the government are quite close, with the latter quite dependent on the former for research that is 'relevant' to up-coming decisions (see East–West Population Institute, 1978, p. 9, for a discussion of the situation in the Philippines). The nature of the prevailing relationship has a lot to do with the type of research universities can be expected to do as well as the impact it is likely to have on policy.

In at least two respects universities are particularly well-suited sites for the location of population-research activities. The first advantage is that offered by the presence of research infrastructure such as a library and, often, a computer centre. The second refers to the mutual benefits that can derive from integrating research with teaching. These are apt to be most important with respect to graduate training: students can be integrated into on-going research efforts once they reach the thesis stage, and regular graduate-level teaching assignments can be valuable stimulae for researchers to stay abreast of their fields of specialization. A related consideration is that, in the long run, without the direct transmission of ideas and methods from the most prominent researchers to those newly entering the field, the over-all possibilities for continuity and cumulativeness in research will be vastly curtailed.

A third advantage enjoyed by some universities is their independence and capacity to analyse on-going policies in a critical way. In some cases, however, independence may not really exist or the university may be so fundamentally opposed to the government that their criticism will be virtually ignored by policy-makers.

Universities, of course, often suffer from some appreciable handicaps in comparison with other institutional bases for population research. One is that working conditions are often far from ideal in Third World universities due to low salaries and heavy teaching loads that are coupled with the absence of incentives to produce research (Demeny, 1972). A second disadvantage that is often mentioned is the bureaucratic impediment to multidisciplinary work constituted by the traditional departmental organizational framework that predominates in universities throughout the world.

Independent Research Centres

In some developing countries (and also in some developed countries) a considerable amount of social-science research on population is conducted in research centres or consulting firms that are neither attached to universities nor directly incorporated within a government agency. In some cases research on population may be the principal activity of the organization, while in others it may form part of a larger programme of social-science research on development. Independent research centres of both sorts are particularly important in Latin America, where some of the hemisphere's most prominent scholars are working in institutions such as the Brazilian Centre for Analysis and Planning (CEBRAP) in Brazil, the Centre for Population Studies (CENEP) in Argentina, and the Regional Centre for Population Studies (CCRP) in Colombia.

On many occasions, the formation of such centres is a response by researchers to adverse conditions or developments in the universities that leave researchers little alternative but to seek to do their work elsewhere. On other occasions, however, centres may be formed as a sort of entrepreneurial response to the ready availability of funding, either domestic or foreign, for research in particular areas. In propitious circumstances, independent research centres are able to provide better salaries and working conditions than universities and can thereby attract highly qualified researchers. To some extent these attributes are compensated by a lesser amount of security in that private or quasi-private centres are typically highly dependent on relatively short-term project funding. This latter circumstance sometimes constitutes an important impediment to realizing continuous and cumulative research on a specific line of investigation. Certainly one of the main drawbacks of independent research centres is that, unless they regularly incorporate a significant number of younger scholars, they contribute very little to training future generations of researchers.

Government Research and Evaluation Units

The sort of institution that is playing an increasingly prominent role in conducting social-science research on population and development is the research and/or evaluation unit that is located within a government agency that has responsibility for the co-ordination or implementation of part or all of the national population policy. While evaluation units have most frequently been created in connection with family planning and maternal and child health programmes, recently units with a considerably broader mandate have been formed as governments have adopted more comprehensive policies and have sought to co-ordinate a wide range of activities that impinge on the growth and distribution of population.

Research units located within government agencies are subject to a number of constraints that are not shared by universities or independent centres, but they also enjoy some special advantages, especially with regard to the impact their work can have on policy. Their ability to attract good analysts and researchers is, of course, related to the level of salaries that the government pays civil servants in comparison with those offered by competing institutions. There seems to be a substantial variation among countries in this respect. For instance, in México the salaries of government research jobs are considerably higher than those offered by universities, while in the Philippines the reverse seems to be true.

The most obvious advantage of doing research within government is that it is likely to have a greater and more immediate impact on policy. Since policy-makers are directly involved in its design, such research will very likely to be highly responsive to their needs for knowledge and information. An important disadvantage may be that the pressure of political circumstances may affect the intellectual climate in which the work is undertaken and stand in the way of critical analyses of existing policies.

An Appropriate Division of Research

Implicit in the preceding discussion of the strengths and weaknesses of each type of institution is the idea that each is therefore likely to enjoy a comparative advantage in some kinds of research activity and to suffer from a comparative disadvantage in others. With respect to three of the broad kinds of research distinguished by the IRG — descriptive, evaluative, and causal research — some very rough indications are apparent as to which of these activities are appropriate for each type of institution.

Government research units would appear to be particularly well suited to undertake both descriptive and evaluative studies. Research of both types is usually in urgent demand by policy-makers, and there has some- times been a tendency for academic researchers to avoid this work. University and independent research centres, on the other hand, are likely to be in a better position than government centres to undertake the longer-term work that needs to be done on the determinants and (perhaps to a lesser extent) consequences of demographic behaviour. There may be, however, some important exceptions to this generalization. It may be well for independent centres and, to a certain degree, universities to involve themselves in evaluative work because they may have a greater capacity for detached analysis of programmes, because the availability of government funding for such work may increase their economic via- bility, and, lastly, because the work that needs to be done exceeds the capacity of the existing government research units. Furthermore, the analytical difficulties involved in constructing and carrying out many evaluative research designs are such that this work is not easily distin- guished from research on determinants, for which it may have important implications.

Another quite particular situation that deserves special mention is the research role that can be played in some of the larger developing countries by regional or provincial universities (as distinguished from those located in the capital city). These institutions are likely to have a strong compara- tive advantage in doing descriptive work on the demographic processes in their area of the country, and in evaluating the impact of government pro- grammes on a regional basis. Because of their special advantages in this re- gard, their over-all research capacity may warrant strengthening.

Training

The overview presented in the previous chapter identified some fairly specific and immediate needs for training. These needs, and also the more general and longer-term question of how to assure an orderly and sufficient recruitment of talented persons into the field as a whole, raise a host of questions about the amounts and kinds of training that should be provided. The situation is somewhat more complex today than it was, say, 10 years ago in that the range of alternatives has broadened considerably. In determining priorities and establishing courses of action for equipping people to work on topics such as those outlined in Part II of the Report, fundamental judgements must be made about the skills that are needed and the ways that those skills can be best acquired. Questions have to be answered regarding such matters as the level of training, subject-matter and disciplinary orientation, where training should be provided — at national, regional, or developed country institutions, whether degree or non-degree programmes are most appropriate, the role that can be played by special *ad hoc* courses, and so on. Similarly, there are important choices to be made concerning under whose auspices and on what terms fellowships and other grants for training should be made available. Although there are no definitive answers — at least at a global level — to questions such as these, it does seem worth while to take up briefly some of the issues that arise in connection with the different sorts of skills and associated training that would seem to be needed to accomplish the research agenda that the Group is proposing.

Demographic Analysis

Perhaps with the exception of Sub-Saharan Africa, the regions with which the IRG has dealt appear to have a reasonable supply of junior- and intermediate-level personnel with the capacity to undertake basic demographic analysis useful, mainly, for descriptive purposes. Creating this capacity has been the principal training role played by the UN-supported regional centres, and some local universities' undergraduate training programmes have contributed as well. For countries where these analysts are still in short supply this type of training should be continued. The availability of these technicians facilitates the first steps of a diagnosis of the population situation. The experience already accumulated in the regional centres make them logical candidates for support to continue these activities. The organization of *ad hoc*, on-site training courses with the collaboration of the pertinent regional centre is an alternative worth exploring. Local universities' undergraduate programmes in sociology, economics, or statistics can eventually take over responsibility for this type of training on a more permanent basis. Some of the advantages of conducting the training locally at the junior and intermediate levels are that a larger group of students benefit from it and that the courses can be addressed more directly to the local-population situation using the available demographic data as examples. On the other hand, the teaching staff of regional centres is, presumably, apt to be better qualified and have more experience with the analysis of different types of basic data. Furthermore, the interaction with students from other countries of the region may serve not only to open broader perspectives but also to establish links that could contribute to professional interchange in the future. Whatever the arrangements adopted might be, courses such as those mentioned above could probably be successfully delivered in rather short periods, certainly not exceeding 8 to 9 months.

In the past, the bulk of the funding for this sort of training has been provided by the UN. Considering that a large portion of candidates are likely to be attached to government agencies, continued UN support seems appropriate and necessary.

Social Science and Demography

Skills in demographic analysis plus considerable exposure to the theory, methodology, and applications of one or more of the social sciences are basic prerequisites for undertaking research on most of the topics identified in Part II. The training associated with the acquisition of these skills has usually consisted of participation in formal programmes of study leading to the M.A. degree. Whereas 10 or 15 years ago graduate programmes of this sort were by and large available only in the developed countries, as noted in the preceding chapter, such programmes are now to be found at a number of universities in Latin America, Asia, and Africa, and at several of the UN-supported regional centres. Since a large proportion of the people who will eventually work on population and development in the different regions will almost inevitably pass through these programmes, it is important that they be strengthened and that there exist funding mechanisms (utilizing national and, when necessary, international resources) to ensure an adequate flow of able students to them. Competitions for fellowships to attend such programmes could be administered by the institution itself or by national research councils. Fellowships for foreign students are likely to pose the greatest problem and it is here that international donor agencies may be able to play an important role. Two additional steps worth considering to strengthen such programmes consist of providing opportunities for faculty members to go abroad for further training and establishing arrangements with developed-country academic institutions that would permit the interchange of visiting professors. The possibilities of unilaterally seconding young developed-country scholars with experience in research topics related to the country or region where the programme operates should also be investigated.

Social Science, Demography, and Supervised Research

Virtually all developing countries seem to be in short supply of scholars with a solid background in one or more of the various social sciences who have a thorough grounding in population and a proven ability to carry out research. Top-level researchers with these qualifications are clearly required for many of the research projects recommended in this Report. For individuals of exceptional ability, the most direct way of obtaining these skills is to follow a programme of formal training leading to the Ph.D. or an equivalent degree that includes the opportunity to do a major piece of research under the supervision of accomplished experts in the field. For the moment, nearly all the institutions offering population-related training at this level are located in developed countries.

Perhaps the major question with regard to Ph.D. level training concerns the stage at which candidates should be identified and funded. While it is often practicable to lure doctoral students into the field at an advanced stage of their course work with support for population-related theses, in the case of students from developing countries, such a strategy implies a much-reduced pool of applicants in comparison with that which might be forthcoming to a competition for fellowships to finance a full course of study. Increasingly, candidates for Ph.D. level training from developing countries will already have done some graduate work, often an M.A., within their own region. In their case it is important for them to find programmes that recognize their previous training and that permit them to advance to the thesis stage with a minimum of unnecessary impediments.

As recently as 6 or 7 years ago, the majority of the fellowships held by students from developing countries for population orientated graduate study in the social sciences were made available by the private foundations, largely by way of open competitions run on an annual basis for candidates from all over the world. In recent years this source of funding has all but dried up. In some measure it has been replaced by increased allocations for fellowships by the UN and also by some of the better-off developing countries, but the flexibility and prominence of the earlier competitions are notably absent.

While it is easy to associate top-level research skills with successful completion of doctoral studies, for individuals with, say, an M.A. degree and prior research experience, there may be other ways to acquire virtually the same skills without re-enrolling in a formal degree programme. In particular, the missing elements of supervised research and socialization into a competitive and productive research group are, in principle, available wherever research of the necessary calibre is going on. In the future, it would seem well worth exploring and developing this sort of opportunity both inside and outside of the regions.

Interesting Social Scientists of Proven Capacity in
Population and Development

Clearly, the field has much to gain when it can entice either well-known or very promising social scientists to take an interest in population. This may be a particularly apt strategy to rely on when it is recognized — as it has been in this Report — that certain issues have been neglected and that there is a need for new sorts of skills to deal with them.

Providing opportunities to do population orientated post-doctoral study and research to recent Ph.D.s with little or no previous exposure to population has proved to be a viable way to lure some accomplished younger scholars into the field. Similar, but even more flexible, programmes of study at prestigious institutions have often served to attract quite well-known and senior economists, sociologists, political scientists, anthropologists, and so on to population-related research.

Policy Analysis

For some time schools of public policy and of public and international affairs in the developed countries have been attempting to train people to apply social-scientific methods and insights to the analysis of policy issues, without at the same time loading the students down with the thorough grounding in the theoretical issues of a single discipline that is expected of academic researchers. To the extent that such programmes are successful at producing people who are capable of tackling policy issues in general, with some modifications they should also be able to produce population-policy analysts. Such professionals would be capable of translating the results of both descriptive and theoretical research into meaningful information for use in the policy-making and policy-evaluation processes. They would be able to fill many of the needs that government departments and, particularly, national population councils have for staff members that are able to produce diagnoses of a variety of population-related issues and to make use of research findings to inform policy-makers as to how much is known about the nature of the relations between demographic variables and government policies. Candidates for this sort of training would in most cases already be employed in the public sector, in either junior- or middle-level positions.

Opportunities for interdisciplinary policy orientated training in population have only recently begun to emerge, mostly in the developed countries. There seems to be every reason to develop these opportunities with grants for curriculum development as well as with fellowships. It seems clear, however, that such training could, eventually, reach many more candidates and be of greater relevance if it were conducted within the regions. Ideally, programmes such as that now being set up at the University of Michigan with the collaboration of the Population Council will provide useful experience that can be assimilated by those regional centres with a sizeable staff of social scientists when they attempt to launch similar programmes some time in the not too distant future. The development of these programmes at regional centres would also have the benefit of strengthening their capacity to provide *ad hoc* seminars and other on-site training that is urgently needed by many government units with responsibilities for population policy.

In the IRG's view, high priority should be attached both to providing training that will meet the more immediate staffing needs of universities, research centres, and government; and also to the goal of attracting people into the field who by virtue of their ability, preparation, and experience will provide leadership in research and analysis in the years to come. In terms of the availability of financial support, the latter objective seems to have been relatively neglected in recent years. But perhaps the most essential point is that to meet either objective more than money will be required. Also critical are mechanisms — both national and international — that will serve to identify needs and opportunities, and respond to them with expedience and imagination.

The Role of Local versus Foreign Resources

The extent to which research should be financed by local as against foreign resources is clearly one of the most controversial and bothersome questions facing both donors and recipients of external population assistance. In individual countries the amount of local resources that are made available for social-science research on population is clearly positively related to the quantity of public money spent on research in general, but the share of the total research budget allocated to population is apt to be related to the government's interest in the area — that is, to the scope and seriousness of its population policy. Thus there is enormous variation between countries and regions in the amount of local resources that are available for this enterprise. Foreign or international donors in the field are usually wary, however, of carrying 'too large' a share of the burden or, particularly, of undertaking commitments that will not in a 'reasonable' period be taken over by domestic agencies or institutions. This concern is, of course, justified, but it can easily be carried to extremes, especially in the case of institutional support. According to a report on institutional and human resources for population research in South-East and East Asia:

> The relatively strong research institutions in the region should not be penalized for their success by the premature cutoff of core support by donor agencies (as has unfortunately happened in a number of cases). Rather, the stronger institutions should be viewed as models of

what can be accomplished and as potential sources of assistance to weaker institutions in the particular country and in the region. This view implies institutional support over an extended period of time, to permit continued growth and flexibility of operations even after an institution has become theoretically 'self-sustaining' from local support and from the ability to attract project grants. There is not yet a single institution in East or South-East Asia that is optimally equipped to conduct research of high quality on population and development, and none is likely to attain that capacity in the absence of sustained and generous institutional support from the international donor community. (East–West Population Institute, 1978, p. 32.)

Increasing the Policy Relevance of Research

Prescriptions as to how to increase the relevance for policy of social-science research and analysis are becoming increasingly abundant in the context of both more- and less-developed countries.[4] The recommendations range widely, touching on issues such as the nature of the product and the way it is presented, as well as the sorts of people who should be involved in the selection of topics for research. One notable feature of the discussion is the confusion that seems to exist as to whether 'policy-relevant' research is somehow different from other or 'academic' research in the way it is done, or whether the distinction of relevance derives principally from the question of what is being researched. The view of the IRG by and large coincides with the latter, and thus a large part of this Report is dedicated to sorting out which topics are most relevant for policy formulation and on which additional research could yield meaningful results in the next decade. There are, however, a number of issues related to process rather than substance that appear to be well worth taking into account. For instance, one of the main conclusions of this Report is that evaluative research with respect to the impact of public programmes on demographic variables deserves more attention than it has received heretofore. This conclusion is in large part based on what the Group detected as one of the principal 'felt needs' of policy-makers as these were expressed in the series of the IRG workshops. It is almost self-evident that one way to accomplish the recommended redirection of efforts would be to involve policy-makers more closely in discussions regarding what topics ought to be researched.

Clearly, the most direct way to give policy-makers a greater say in what directions research is to take is to locate an appreciable research capacity within the government agencies responsible for population policy. Another means of increasing communication between policy-makers

[4] See, for example, Ilchman, 1975; Ilchman and Smith, 1978; Morgan, 1978; Schmandt, 1978; and Torres, 1977.

and scholars that might lead to the same result would be for both to attend periodic workshops on research priorities. A third and perhaps even less direct means of achieving the same end would be to promote a regular interchange of personnel between public and academic institutions. In most countries such interchange takes place anyway due to swings in the balance of political power, but it could be augmented by the creation of possibilities for individuals to take 'sabbaticals' in the other sector.

In discussions of these issues, stress is often placed on the need to present research results and findings in a form accessible to policy-makers. There is, of course, considerable merit to this suggestion, but it may be the case that efforts along these lines undertaken by the researcher will not draw out from the research in question the implications for policy that government officials are most interested in. It is here that the 'policy analyst' described above in the subsection on training may be able to have a considerable impact. What is more, the very fact that research becomes subject to this sort of critical scrutiny is likely to exert a healthy influence on the directions that are taken by researchers and to promote dialogue between the two sectors.

Another theme that surfaces from time to time is the idea that it is possible to take policy relevance too far. This is no doubt a possibility if efforts to 'enforce' policy relevance end up placing a myriad of restrictions on what kinds of investigations can or cannot be undertaken. But more often than not the issue arises over the time frame within which research is undertaken. The IRG has taken the position that in addition to descriptive and evaluative research that should yield results within a year or so, there is also a need to undertake research that is only likely to yield concrete results that will be of tangible use to policy-makers if it is pursued with diligence and perseverance over a period of time that may exceed, say 5 years. The Group is of the opinion that there is no automatic equivalence between the time horizon under which research is undertaken and its true relevance to policy. Given the current state of knowledge, there is an obvious need to undertake research with quite different time horizons, and if in the name of policy relevance a government seeks to direct all resources to short-term investigations with direct implications for immediately forthcoming policy decisions, this may indeed constitute an impediment to progress in answering some of the major questions that policy-makers will face over the longer run.[5]

---

[5] For an example of this sort of situation, see the description of the Philippines in East–West Population Institute, 1978.

Increasing Productivity

One of the problems facing population research institutions in many parts of the world, but perhaps most acutely in the developing countries, is that of increasing the productivity of the personnel attached to them. This problem is magnified in a situation of scarce resources. Institutions and individuals engaged in research can only be evaluated in terms of the relevance, quantity, and quality of the final products of their research efforts. Not infrequently, these products either are not forthcoming or take a long time to be produced, deal with subjects of secondary importance, or fall short of professional standards. In the developing countries the cause of some of these limitations is often related to conditions of work and the general environment in which research is conducted. Because salaries are frequently inadequate, professionals attached to these institutions are forced to commit themselves to additional remunerative tasks. Often, in part due to shortage of staff, they are assigned excessive teaching loads. All this diminishes considerably the time actually devoted to research activities. In addition, because demand frequently exceeds the supply of qualified personnel, the climate within academic institutions is generally not very competitive, and there are few incentives to publish at the rate which in other circumstances would be necessary for achieving professional recognition and other rewards from the system. To the extent that low productivity in research is the result of a shortage of resources, there may be steps that national research councils and international donors can take to improve the situation. In the event that the problem lies elsewhere, there is often little that outsiders can do to improve the situation. One alternative worth exploring might consist of including in grant agreements certain types of incentives and rewards for performance at high standards, such as tours abroad to visit academic institutions or to participate in technical meetings of particular interest, outlets for publication of meritorious work, and free access to necessary bibliographic materials.

Local professional associations can also play an important role in improving the productivity of research by helping to identify researchable topics of true relevance to the country concerned. By offering seminars and lecture series they can serve to increase the level of knowledge and professionalism of their members and also create incentives for the presentation and discussion of research findings, thus providing an environment for criticism and feedback from peers.

The Dissemination of Research Findings

Developing-country scholars in many cases appear to have inadequate access to information on population and development research issues being discussed, explored, or elucidated by their colleagues in other Third World countries. The reviews and workshops undertaken by the IRG have revealed how very little is known by researchers actively working in the field about what is being done in regions other than their own. Although several specialized reviews are published within the different regions and sub-regions distinguished by the IRG, by and large these do not reach audiences beyond the region where they are issued. The interregional information flows that do take place are for the most part transmitted through developed-country journals. But these journals appear to be in-adequate instruments for the task in that relatively little work done by developing-country scholars finds its way into their pages. The reasons for this phenomenon seem to extend beyond the scientific quality of the work. For one thing, papers that are written in a language other than English or French and sent to a journal before translation can usually only be reviewed by a limited number of individuals; and if the paper is translated by the journal, the translation may be less than fully satis-factory. The result is almost certainly a bias in favour of those papers reaching the journal in the language of publication. Providing Third World authors with greater access to qualified editorial assistance and/or translation services before they submit their papers to journals would help to redress the current imbalance.

But the issue of disseminating research results between regions is perhaps too important to be left to the vagaries of the review process of journals (editorial boards) that do not accept this mission as one of their foremost objectives. Certainly one alternative would be to establish a Third World population and development review for this purpose. A more immediately feasible proposition that could serve both as the fore-runner of such an enterprise and as a stimulus to the publication of more Third World material in developed-country journals would be to create an international clearing house run by a committee of developing country scholars that would actively seek out promising work being undertaken around the world and disseminate it in a series of working papers to be issued in English, French, Spanish, and Portuguese.

So far this discussion has focused entirely on interregional information flows, but intraregional flows are also extremely important and cannot be taken for granted. Journals published within the regions and regional population associations can play crucial roles not only as a means of transmitting information, but also as means of fostering criticism, debate, and an efficient interchange between the producers and also the users of research.[6] Parenthetically, regional journals can serve as natural outlets for translations of relevant papers published in other languages.

[6] Some developing countries are large enough that there may be a need to create mechanisms to ensure adequate communication between researchers within the country. The Indian and Brazilian population associations both seem to be playing a useful role in this regard.

Role of Regional Institutions

A persistent concern among donors in the population field has been the role and importance that should be attached to regional institutions. While there is definite recognition of the contributions to research and training that they have made in the past, there are questions as to what they should be doing in the future. How should they relate to national research and training efforts? As these become stronger does there cease to be a need for regional institutions? Or, at the other extreme, where national institutions are weak, is the development of regional institutions a viable substitute for national efforts?

The regional institutions that have the longest history and have had the greatest impact are those of the UN. In addition to five UN-supported regional demographic centres, there are population divisions in three of the regional economic commissions, and some population-related activities have been undertaken by the regional offices of the ILO, FAO, and UNESCO.

Within the UN responsibility for the over-all substantive co-ordination of the regional demographic centres falls, at least formally, on the Population Division. Unfortunately, for lack of sufficient personnel with adequate knowledge both of the field and of the region concerned, co-ordination has been minimal and has failed to establish the links and communication between centres that would help them to learn from each others experience. As for financial support from the UN, responsibility lies with the Fund for Population Activities (UNFPA). Because continued support from the Fund requires periodic evaluations of performance, the contributions of the centres to the development of training and research in population in their respective regions have been subjected to scrutiny. In general, the evaluations have been favourable, and there is wide recognition that, for the most part, the centres have acted as important catalysts for raising awareness of the need to study population phenomena and to train personnel with the required qualifications to help develop technical analysis of demographic variables and studies on the interaction of these variables with other socioeconomic factors. To different degrees and following different approaches, the centres have been instrumental in training significant numbers of professionals in the demographic field. Some of them have been developing at their headquarters and promoting at the country level, research programmes to address population issues identified by governments of the region as important for population-policy implementation or for specific socioeconomic programmes or plans. The centres differ in the extent and nature of their publication programmes, but it is felt that in most cases they have contributed, together with publications issued by some of the regional economic commissions and regional development institutes, to the enrichment of the bibliography on population and development.

There seem to be two aspects in which the UN-supported centres differ the most. One is the amount of direct technical assistance they can and actually do provide to governments and national institutions in the region. The other is the links they maintain with the regional economic commissions and other organizations of the UN system working in the area of population and/or development in the region. ESCAP, ECWA, and ECA each have population divisions that operate independently of the regional centres and which conduct research and provide technical assistance to governments. In Latin America, on the other hand, ECLA has no population division but relies on CELADE for research and technical assistance.

In judging the potential future contributions of the regional centres the following considerations seem relevant:

1. In no case should the existence of a regional or a subregional centre constitute a reason for not developing national academic institutions for teaching and research in population and development. On the contrary, the centres should have as one of their functions the provision of technical assistance for the establishment and/or strengthening of national institutions. In some cases they should also establish collaborative research endeavours of a comparative nature.

2. The centres should maintain close links with the pertinent UN regional economic commission and, when necessary and advisable, undertake some of the technical assistance in population required by governments and national institutions in the region. In like manner, they should keep abreast of other international organizations working in the population field in the region, and when possible, collaborate with them.

3. Above all, the centres should develop the capacity to evolve their teaching and research programmes in accordance with the changing demands posed by emerging population issues.

Integrating population policy within the over-all context of development planning requires considering the reciprocal interaction of population policy and policies dealing, for example, with employment, agrarian structure and agricultural development, and education, as well as with the broad development strategy. There would seem to be a natural role that could be played by the UN regional organizations working in these fields (ILO, FAO, UNESCO, regional planning institutes, and regional economic commissions) in assisting governments to analyse the nature of these interactions.

The UN regional organizations are statutorily limited to working with governments. While this feature is advantageous under certain circumstances, it can be a strong limitation in others. They cannot relate easily with academic institutions, particularly private ones. Regional offices operated by private organizations such as the Population Council are, however, in a good position to develop close links with academic and private research institutions. While most of the international organizations of the UN system are staffed primarily by professionals from the region, the reverse is often true of the regional offices of private agencies. There are, again, advantages to both situations, but what is more important than nationality is that the personnel be knowledgeable about the population problems of the region and be responsive to them.

In contrast to the typically large staff of the UN regional organizations, the regional offices of private organizations often operate with a very small staff, which severely limits their chances to make a significant impact on the population field in the region. In many instances, for lack of secure core funding, the few professionals attached to these offices have to devote considerable portions of their time to securing funding for specific projects, which limits even more the time they have available to make constructive research contributions. UN regional bodies are also encumbered by the 'project syndrome' imposed on them by donors who prefer not to commit themselves to providing core support for extended periods of time.

There are at least two other important types of regional institutions. First, there are those research and training centres that are located on the fringe of a region but whose programmes are either aimed at, or are, closely related to, the problems and institutions of the region. The East–West Population Institute and the Department of Demography at the Australian National University are two important examples with reference to East, South-East, and to a lesser extent, South Asia. CEDOR plays a similar but smaller role with reference to Africa. Another type of regional organization is the specialized international research institute. The primary business of such institutes is research rather than training, but they usually provide technical assistance to, and conduct comparative studies of, the countries in the region or subregion where they are located. To date, most of the institutes of this type with an interest in population, such as the Institute for Nutrition of Central America and Panama (INCAP) in Guatemala and the former Cholera Research Laboratory in Bangladesh, have had health and nutrition as their primary interest.

Taking all of the different sorts of regional institutions together they are considerable in number. Clearly, not all of them have been equally successful, nor are they equally capable of playing a major role in accomplishing and promoting social-science research on population and development in the years to come. It does, however, seem critical that those regional centres with the potential capacity for leadership be provided with the opportunity to develop and exercise that capacity. The research and technical assistance activities of regional organizations are a necessary complement to those activities suggested for development at the national level. But unless the former are provided with adequate and longer-term financial support, the latter could be seriously jeopardized.

Data Collection

Early on in the process of defining its task, the IRG decided that it would not address questions regarding the adequacy of the data base and ways of improving it directly, but rather that the Group would take up such issues only in so far as they were pertinent to the individual research activities it recommended as deserving high priority. In part, this decision was dictated by a sense that a concentrated evaluation of this area would constitute a rather major diversion from the task of recommending research priorities. Also of some influence was the fact that a number of other organizations — notably the UN and the US National Academy of Sciences Committee on Population and Demography — are active in this area. Nevertheless, as is apparent from the relevant parts of Chapters 1–10, the Group became aware that in several regions and in several areas of research problems with the existing data base do seem to constitute an impediment to further progress in research. The two subregions that seem to be most disadvantaged in this respect are West Asia and Sub-Saharan Africa. The most disadvantaged field, on the other hand, is probably international migration. Also with regard to data collection, it is perhaps worth referring again to the general emphasis that is placed on the Group's recommendations on producing geographically and socially disaggregated estimates of levels and trends in demographic variables.

But from the point of view of capacity building and institutional development, the one main finding that should be stressed here is that in many developing countries there is a notable under-utilization of existing data. This phenomenon is due mainly to a reluctance by institutions, both governmental and academic, to release data sets that they have collected so that they may be analysed by researchers outside the institution. There are a variety of rationales behind the restrictions that presently exist, but one of them is clearly to protect against 'data robbing' by foreign analysts. In most cases there are extremely valid reasons for giving the researcher who designed and implemented a survey first shot at its analysis. But his privilege should not be extended to the point where data is kept out of the public domain until it is so old that it is of no interest. Needless to say, any arrangements that could be made to share data sets among research centres within the same country could do a great deal to eliminate their under-utilization.

In the case of census and vital registration data, part of the problem is that the tabulations made available in published form are not sufficiently detailed. With regard to censuses, when politically feasible, the optimum solution is to provide researchers with direct access to 'public-use' samples so that they may manipulate the data in the manner of their choosing. The large-scale effort made by CELADE to collect and distribute samples from recent Latin American censuses is deserving of special mention in this respect.

Country Priorities

Perhaps the final question that international donors have to ask themselves is which countries deserve highest priority for the allocation of assistance. Needless to say, there are a number of different criteria that might be brought to bear. Among the different types of countries that could arguably be selected as ones in which it would be especially worthwhile to promote further development of social-science research on population and development are the following:

1. Those at a very low level of development and that have severe population problems as indicated by high rates of fertility and mortality.

2. Those where the demand by policy-makers for research results is greatest.

3. Those where the institutional base is currently weakest.

4. Those where the opportunities for important research breakthroughs are most promising.

5. Those with the largest populations.

In the IRG's view these are all sensible criteria, but it is quite clear that any one of them taken alone would yield a set of priority countries that would exclude some nations that scored high on one or more of the other competing grounds for selection. For this reason the Group believes that an attempt to come up with a well-defined list of priority countries on the basis of statistical indices, such as that recently made by the UNFPA, is likely to be counterproductive.

Some Guidelines

After examining the present situation regarding capacities for population training and research in the various regions with which the IRG has concerned itself and offering some specific suggestions as to future actions worth pursuing in each of them, a brief analysis has been made of some of the major questions concerning the amount and direction of future support for these activities facing persons and institutions interested in strengthening and expanding them.

From the preceding exercise some general guidelines seem to have emerged. They are summarized below.

1. *Redress the balance between institutional and project support.* The insistence in recent years of granting funds for the support of single projects has resulted in population assistance having made less of an impact on the development of research capacity than would have been the case had more of these funds been transmitted in the form of institutional support. While support for the development and/or strengthening of institutions may at first sight appear to be a more expensive enterprise than project grants, and require involvement over a longer period of time,

experience has shown that such support often contributes effectively to establishing an environment for researchers that is conducive to a more permanent and productive commitment to the population field.

Premature withdrawal of core support to recently launched institutions is an all too common occurrence. Donors should give serious consideration to extending the period during which this support is provided well beyond the point when an institution gives the first appearances of having become self sufficient. Similar treatment should be considered for regional organizations involved in population training and research that have achieved a recognized level of scholarship, and whose services and support are in demand from countries of that region.

2. *A renewed emphasis on training.* Although in several of the regions there is now a considerable number of qualified individuals engaged in social-science research on population and development, considering the size and complexity of the research agenda being recommended by the IRG in this Report, almost nowhere is there room for complacency. An expansion of the funds available for fellowships, especially for training at the highest levels, is almost certainly justified. So, too, is a renewed effort on the part of both national and international donors to identify opportunities where training of whatever kind, could make an important difference. In this regard perhaps special mention should be made of the sizeable new demand for persons capable of designing and evaluating governmental interventions that has resulted from the creation of government units to manage population policies. To respond effectively to this demand, new sorts of policy-orientated training programmes are needed. Over the next few years a considerable effort should be made to develop such programmes, especially on a regional basis.

3. *Special efforts to bridge the communications gap.* One of the IRG's more surprising findings is how little is known in the respective regions of the developing world about the research that is going on in the others. A similar problem exists with respect to communication between the regions and the developed countries. These impediments to rapid progress in research are certainly among the most easily surmountable that have been identified in the Report. With a relatively modest investment the international donor community could facilitate major improvements in the dissemination of research findings.

4. *Foster a pluralistic, multi-level system.* To ensure that progress in research proceeds on several fronts and to protect it, to the extent possible, against conjunctural crises, a wide variety of institutions — university departments at both the national and provincial levels; university-based and non-governmental research centres; population analysis units within government departments; and regional centres — should all be candidates for the longer-term support suggested above. Each type of institution is apt to have a comparative advantage at conducting a particular kind of research but what overlap may exist is likely to be beneficial. Social-science research

on population is, more often than not, involved with issues that are at once difficult and sensitive, and about which there are fundamental disagreements between different sectors of a society. The greater the number of independent points of view that are able to participate in the debate and develop alternative policy conclusions, the less likely are serious mistakes to go unnoticed.

References

Demeny, Paul. 1972. 'Asian Universities and Population Policies.' *Studies in Family Planning*, 3 (10), 249–50.

East–West Centre. East–West Population Institute. 1978. 'Capacity for Social Science Research on Population and Development in South–East and East Asia: A Report on Institutional and Human Resources'. Appendix 5 to the Final Report. El Colegio de México: IRG.

Ilchman, Warren F. 1975. 'Population Knowledge and Population Policies.' In *Comparative Policy Analysis*, R. K. Godwin ed., Lexington, Massachussetts: D.C. Health.

— and Theodore M. Smith. 1978. 'The Search for the Hyphen in Policy Relevant Research: Some Notes on the Kinds and Uses of Knowledge.' Paper presented to the Bangkok PASS Meeting.

Morgan, M. Granger. 1978. 'Bad Science and Good Policy Analysis.' *Science*, 201 (4360).

Schmandt, Jurgen. 1978. 'Scientific Research and Policy Analysis.' Ibid. (4359).

Torres, Fleur de Lys O. 1977. 'Linking Research to the Policy Process.' Paper presented to the Seminar on the Utilization of Research Findings for Family Planning Programme Development, 5–7 October 1977. Manila: Population Centre Foundation.

CONCLUSION

The preceding chapters have covered a great deal of ground and a wide variety of recommendations have been put forward with respect to needed research on population and development and the kinds of support that an ambitious agenda of this sort will require. The main purpose of this closing chapter is to consider the procedural implications of the Report, but before doing so, we take advantage of this opportunity to make a few parting observations that may help to place the Report in its proper perspective and thus avoid a number of possible misinterpretations.

Throughout the Report, but perhaps especially in Part II, considerable scepticism has been expressed with regard to the notion that development related processes such as increases in per capita income, industrialization, urbanization, education, and so on, will produce similar demographic changes in all countries irrespective of their social and cultural characteristics. This gross simplification, which is not at odds with the premises underlying a considerable portion of prior research in the field, amounts to the application to population of a more general view of development as a uniform definable sequence to which all societies must conform under penalty of remaining poor and backward. It is the IRG's view, however, that the qualitative differences in the paths of development and social change that individual countries have followed, and are presently following, must be adequately taken into account before demographic change can be understood and successful policies be implemented. Hence the emphasis in the Report on the need to study the institutional and structural arrangements in each society and their changes through time. This is not to say, however, that knowledge and policy experience is in no way transferable across national boundaries. Clearly, there is much that is transferable and much that is not. What is especially needed are the insight and the capacity to draw the distinction.

Another broad and all too obvious conclusion underlying many of the recommendations in the Report is that demographic change lies at the heart of the development process as a whole. In the examination of the state of knowledge on the demographic variables, in each case the object was seen to be a part, albeit an important part, of socioeconomic change taking place at the national, regional, and sometimes world level. This being the case, it is the Group's opinion that population problems are most usefully analysed in terms of how they fit into the larger picture. In this sense, as one participant in a seminar on the demographic transition put it several years ago, demographic blinkers are clearly a hindrance. Since demographic change is usually a reflection of other basic changes occurring in the society, it is often counterproductive to focus too narrowly on the phenomenon itself. Demographic response is often only one of a variety of alternative ways that individuals or groups may react to changes in their economic, social, and political environments. Similarly, it may also be a mistake to concentrate too narrowly on 'population problems'. Although in some instances clear-cut differences may exist between the interests of individuals and those of society as a whole, in the demographic sphere as elsewhere it is more usually the case that what is beneficial for some is harmful for others. Demographic trends are apt to become problematic in the measure that they impinge, or are seen to impinge, on specific conflicts that take place over matters as diverse as the cost of urban services and the claims that one generation makes upon another.

The view has been expressed all along that better information and a more complete knowledge base will lead to better policies. The Report points confidently to research needs that if filled would lead to improvements and refinement of present policies. It also recommends other more fundamental kinds of research that could potentially provide the basis for policy options considerably different from those in current favour. But it is here that we should be careful not to promise too much. It would be naïve in the extreme to think that social-science research will eventually indicate easy solutions that, embodied in programmatic changes or institutional rearrangements, would do away with untoward demographic behaviour but not involve major changes in other aspects of economic and social activity. Rather, the choices that emerge are likely to be difficult ones, more often than not tied to far-reaching changes in the over-all style of development.

If this is an insufficiently attractive prospect on which to base a major commitment to social-science research on the determinants and consequences of demographic behaviour there is one additional thought that might serve to tip the balance. Many of today's population policies are based more on accepted beliefs than demonstrated realities. To the extent that many of these beliefs are wrong and might eventually be used to justify more forceful measures, an improved factual base with which to disprove them would almost certainly serve to prevent a considerable amount of injustice.

Procedural Implications

It is not without some presumption that the authors of a report such as this one can address the question of the uses to which it might be put. Yet the Group's views on this matter had a major influence on the actual work undertaken by the IRG as well as on the content and format of this volume. It should also be made clear that the nature of the final product was not clearly spelt out in the project's original mandate and that the IRG enjoyed a considerable amount of latitude regarding what sorts of findings and recommendations it should strive for. This is not to claim that the Group fully met the different goals that it set for itself — there are several important areas where it clearly fell short — but rather that there were very real questions about who the Report was to be written for and the purposes it might eventually serve.

In the first place it is worth repeating that the Report is not directed solely at the donor agencies that commissioned and financed the IRG. If it had been there would have been a premium on coming up with a manageable list of feasible projects, together with a precise specification of the funds, personnel, and administrative arrangements that the projects would require. Both the Report and the responsibility for executing the recommendations would have belonged to the donors; the policy-makers and scholars in the countries themselves, already consulted, would be left to respond to the donors' initiatives.

The 'follow-up' that the Group envisions is of a quite different nature. The IRG feels strongly that all three groups to which the Report is addressed, and which in various ways have all participated in the project, have a mutual interest in an improved knowledge base for population policy and a joint responsibility for analysing the Report and carrying out those recommendations that they find worthwhile.

Although the recommendations and guidelines contained in the Report are mostly of a quite general nature — typically more like broad approach lights than well-lit runways — it seems clear that the Report and its appendices contain material that should be of immediate use to each of the three audiences. For example, scholars in different parts of the world will in all likelihood be provoked by what the Group has identified as some of the flaws in current theorizing and, we hope, be stimulated by the recommendations for work on what up to now have been relatively neglected questions such as the relation between development style and population, and the role of political processes in the determination of population policy. In a somewhat different vein, it is also likely that one of the greatest services that the Report and especially its appendices can serve is to familiarize researchers in the different regions of the developing world with the work that is being done in other regions.

With respect to the usefulness of the Report to policy-makers, if the Group has correctly interpreted their needs and the major policy issues in the developing countries, then this document should provide them with a summary view of the amount of knowledge on the fundamental demographic variables that is available to support the decisions with which they are confronted. But, more important, policy-makers should be able to find in the Report guidance for determining the research activities that promise to be of the greatest relevance to the issues that arise in their national context, and which they, in turn, should play an active role in promoting.

As indicated above, the Report may be somewhat more general in its recommendations and less specific with regard to needed external resources than some donor agencies might have wished. But, on the other hand, by outlining a set of directions that it feels social-science research on population and development should take in the future, the Group has provided the donors with an alternative, although not totally different, path from the routes that they have followed in the past. What seems an especially important conclusion of the Group's work is that the job of building the capacity to do social-science research on population in the different regions is far from over. The donor community has a very definite role to play not only in fostering the development of new research institutions, but also in continuing to support those that already exist. In addition to pointing to specific needs at the regional level, the Report suggests guidelines as to what an appropriate strategy for supporting both research and institutions in the 1980s might consist of.

In closing, it is worth repeating that the IRG's activities received the support and collaboration of many people from around the world. To the extent that the project has been successful in coming to terms with the question of what social-science research can and should contribute to population policy, it provides evidence that donors, scholars, and policy-makers can communicate effectively with each other about what it is that needs to be done and how the task should be accomplished. Further communication of this sort at both the country and regional levels would seem to be essential to the successful execution of this or any alternative research agenda.

SELECTED DOCUMENTS PREPARED FOR THE IRG

Atria, Raúl. 'Population and Development Planning: Some Notes on the Policy-Making Capacity of the State in Latin America.'

Behm, Hugo. 'Sobre Investigaciones de Interés para las Políticas Relativas a la Mortalidad en la América Latina.'

Berelson, Bernard. 'Social Science Research on Population, or Where are we, Where are we going, Where should we be going, How do we get there, and other thoughts: A Personal Appraisal.'

— 'Research Priorities: Family Planning Programmes.'

Erder, Leila T. 'City Population Analysis in West Asia and North Africa with Particular Reference to Egypt, Syria and Turkey.'

Friedlander, Dove, and Goldscheider, Calvin. 'Population Growth and Policy in Israel: An Overview.'

Harewood, Jack. Population Policies in the Caribbean.

Jones, Gavin W., and Potter, Joseph E. 'The Economic Consequences of Population Change.'

Mabogunje, Akin L. 'Research Priorities for Population Re-Distribution Policies in Africa South of the Sahara.'

McNicoll, Geoffrey. 'Fertility Policy: Research Issues and Strategies.'

Preston, Samuel H. 'Research Developments Needed for Improvements in Policy Formulation on Mortality.'

Tabah, Léon. 'Quelques Problèmes a L'intersection de la Population et du Developpement.'

Tabbarah, Riad B. 'Some Thoughts on International Migration: Questions and Research.'

Urzúa, Raúl. 'Internal Migration in Developing Countries: A Discussion from a Population Policy Viewpoint.'

INTERNATIONAL REVIEW GROUP OF SOCIAL-SCIENCE RESEARCH ON POPULATION AND DEVELOPMENT (IRG)

Acknowledges the Assistance of:

Wannaku Abayasekera
Ladipo Adamolekun
Aderanti Adepoju
Jalal Uddin Ahmed
Francisco Alba
Joop Alberts
Laubel Aldana Martínez
Alex Alens
José Arias Huerta
Raúl Atria
Ahmed Bahri
Barnett Baron
Carlos Barros
Hugo Behm
Raúl Benítez
Eva Bernhardt
Assiz Bindary
J. S. Birks
W. R. Bohning
José Luis Boncompagni
W. D. Borrie
Bryan Boulier
Germán Bravo
James Brackett
Enrique Brito
George Brown
Rodolfo Bulatao
P. J. Burton
Gustavo Cabrera
Pierre Cantrelle
José Otamar de Carvalho
Lee-Jay Cho
Julien Condé
K. E. De Graft-Johnson

Alan Lavell
Malsiri Dias
V. Diejomaoh
José Donayre
Leila Erder
Dov Friedlander
Angel Fucaraccio
Saad Gadalla
Brígida García
Halvor Gille
Elías Gómez Ascárate
Miguel Gómez Barrantes
Gerardo González Cortés
Jorge González Durán
Fernando González Quiñones
Calvin Goldscheider
James Greig
Jack Harewood
Oscar Harkavy
Nigel Harris
Roushdi Henin
Rodolfo Heredia
Misael Hernández
Allan Hill
Monowar Hossain
T. O. Ilugbuhi
Charles Keely
Alan Keller
J. Kidenda
Timothy King
John Knodel
Raj Krishna
Mary Kritz
Aprodicio Laquian

Paul Demeny
Fernando Mangual
Mario Margulis
George Martine
Parker Mauldin
William McGreevey
Geoffrey McNicoll
Anthony Measham
Ananda Meegama
Walter Mertens
Wilfred Mlay
José Morelos
Zibeon Muganzi
Mark Mujwahuzi
Axel Mundigo
John Naranjo
Orlandina de Oliveira
Chukuka Okonjo
Simeon Ominde
Manuel Ortega
Filologo Pante
Soma Perera
Victor Piché
Agustín Porras
Samuel Preston
Valeria Ramírez
Ronald Ridker

Crescencio Ruiz
Norman Ryder
Landing Savane
Patrice Sawadogo
Sheldon Segal
Frederic Shorter
Alan Simmons
Ozzie Simmons
C. A. Sinclair
Masri Singarimbun
Paul Singer
Parmeet Singh
David Smock
George Stolnitz
Léon Tabah
Conrad Taeuber
George Tapinos
Erica Taucher
Susana Torrado
Mario Torres
Luis Unikel
Stephen Viederman
Pravin Visaria
Carl Wharen
Juan Wicht
Edward Wijemanne
João Yunes